MW01534865

Editorial Director USA
Pierantonio Giacoppo

Graphic Design
Paola Polastri

Editing
Martyn Anderson

Colour-separation
Litofilms Italia, Bergamo

Printing
Poligrafiche Bolis, Bergamo

First published November 1995

Library of Congress Catalog Card
Number: 95-081451

ISBN 88-7838-011-3

Copyright 1995
by l'Arca Edizioni
Via Mosé Bianchi 101
20149 Milano
All rights reserved
Printed in Italy

Curtis Worth Fentress

Curtis Worth Fentress

Preface by
Paul Goldberger

Introduction by
Maurizio Vitta

CURTIS WORTH FENTRESS   JAMES HENRY BRADBURN

Contents

Foreword

by Curtis Worth Fentress

The character of architectural firms may sometimes appear monolithic. They rarely are, regardless of whose name is on the marquee. C.W. Fentress J.H. Bradburn and Associates is no exception. Architectural design of large-scale projects is a team effort. It is a craft that embodies the work of many, not only the extrapolated skill of constructors, masons, carpenters, laborers, etc., but also the expertise of renderers, model makers, draftspersons, and conceptual thinkers. As such, the product of their labor is an integral part of the creation of architectural visions. The spirit and effort of this group is embodied in the work presented here.

The first of this group is my partner, James Henry Bradburn. His intellect and ability to tackle and solve complex tasks, and his tenacious affection for architecture and the process of building, have lead to the creation of heretofore impossible technological solutions: the first monolithic structurally glazed building in the Rocky Mountain region and perhaps the world; post-tensioned limestone spandral beams; and, the largest structurally-integrated tensile fabric roof ever built are all attributable to his desire to explore architectural technology in new ways. To him goes my heartfelt gratitude.

To the rest of my colleagues, who have worked at the firm between 1980 and the present, your contributions have been immeasurable and I applaud you. It is with your diligence and your expertise that we have led this once small, Denver-based, firm to the forefront of American architecture. It is with your persevering efforts that we will continue to define what architecture needs to be, indeed what it has the potential to become on an international level and into the 21st century. We have sought to redefine thinking about both regionalism and context. We have created buildings with a humanizing focus. And, we have inspired the public to rethink the need for the application of sound aesthetic design to public projects not just functionalist engineering. With our latest work at Clark County Government Center, National Wildlife Art Museum, Seoul International Airport, and the Denver International Airport we have sought new visions and put our principles and theories into tangible form. But, however desirable the moment, now is not the time for pause or reflection. We have only begun. Contemporary architectural historian and critic, Roger A. Chandler once said that to be a good architect one had to first be a good architect. This means that no amount of positive discourse about bad architecture will make it good. It also implies an intuitive manner of creating wherein the process is innate and the quality is naturally high. As principal-in-charge of design I salute each of my team for being good architects.

Preface

by Paul Goldberger

Curtis Worth Fentress emerges out of a long tradition of American pragmatism. His architecture is bound by neither ideology nor theory; its forms spring from a conscientious reading of program and context. This is architecture shaped by circumstances. What it reflects is not the heroic position of the form-giving architect but the accommodating position of the listening one, determined to find solutions that reflect the specifics of the situations at hand. And yet. If that were all that was going on here, this architecture would be of no interest. Accommodation is admirable as a social goal, but questionable as an esthetic one.

The real achievement of Fentress and his firm, C.W. Fentress ——J.H.Bradburn and Associates, is to have forged a point of intersection between the pragmatism of their design process and more serious esthetic intent. Fentress has wrestled out of this non-ideological, client-driven way of making architecture a consistent level of quality, as if to prove that pragmatism and esthetics need not be mutually exclusive, as if to say by following a client's needs he does not believe he must therefore abandon his own. Indeed, this notion is probably as good a summary of his career as any: it has been a quest to find means to deliver serious buildings to clients who seek quality but may not speak an architectural language, and yet stand waiting for a knowledgeable architect who speaks theirs.

It is no small accomplishment to have been able to bring a level of architectural seriousness to developers, government agencies, public authorities and institutions that had heretofore avoided, even feared, it: this is a form of breaking new ground in architecture that ultimately can affect the larger culture as much if not more than innovations in pure form. By bringing to fruition the Jefferson County buildings in Colorado, the Denver International Airport, the Colorado Convention Center, the Clark County Government Center at Las Vegas, the Natural Resources Building for the State of Washington and the National Museum of Wildlife Art at Jackson Hole - not to mention numerous buildings for private developers - Fentress has thrust architecture into the public consciousness across the western United States, and done so in a way that has made it an accessible, comfortable part of the wider public culture.

This is not an achievement to take casually, particularly in an age in which the culture of architecture has tended often to speak to itself more than to a broader public. If Fentress's architecture is not at the cutting edge - though, to be fair, such projects as the Denver Airport and the Jackson Hole museum surely extend the parameters of their typologies in significant ways - it is in virtually every case free of the hermetic, self-referential quality of so much contemporary architecture. It seeks to establish a bridge between the concerns of the architectural culture and the more practical, but often also esthetically-driven concerns of the general public. Fentress buildings are visually strong, often possessing clear, geometrically derived symbols that give them some degree of iconographic presence in the public eye. They are also generally quite responsive to program; they are invariably connected in some way to their physical contexts, and more often than not they are designed with an acknowledgement of the latest technological advances in materials and construction systems.

The Denver International Airport, completed in 1994 but not opened until 1995 owing to serious problems in the (not Fentress-designed) baggage-handling system, is a good case in point. Indeed, it represents the firm's conceptual and political strengths as successfully as any project yet designed, given how powerful are the forces massed against architectural quality in public works in the United States. Fentress Bradburn joined the project after the airport's basic layout, by Perez Associates, had been set; their job was to work within a limited budget to bring some degree of architectural presence to a design that, if not revised, threatened to look nearly as banal as the Atlanta Airport. The solution proposed by Fentress Bradburn was both technologically and esthetically striking: a huge fabric structure, its

multiplicity of peaks providing monumental space within the airport's main terminal building and a striking profile without.

That the form of the fabric structure loosely echoed the snow-capped Rockies was a pleasing piece of symbolism, and may well have helped city officials, not known for their support of ambitious works of architecture, to accept it. But for all the neatness with which the building's abstract form can be brought to suggest the mountains (and for all the appeal this association has for users of the building) the truly important thing here is the way in which monumental interior space has been created in a fresh way at reasonable cost. The main terminal at Denver is one of the few airports in the United States that confers a sense of lift, where natural light and appealing form combine to create a civic monumentality. Fentress here joins Eero Saarinen, Helmut Jahn and Norman Foster on the short list of architects who have managed to wrest out of the nearly impossible functional demands of the airport program a genuine piece of architecture.

Jackson Hole is altogether different: where Denver is light and soaring, the wildlife art museum is low to the ground and heavy. It is a kind of abstract version of a pueblo, sheathed in Arizona red rock and set tightly into a cliff beside the National Elk Refuge north of Jackson. The lines are crisp, as a pueblo's lines are not,

but the building hugs the earth in the same way, and like the best architecture of the Native Americans, it is at once powerful and quiet. The design process here is worth thinking about. Fentress knew at the outset that neither the program nor the context would permit a conventional building of glass or metal, but there was some local pressure to go in what might be called a conventional post-modern direction, toward a building of wood that followed the vernacular style of Jackson and the Grand Tetons. No doubt such a building would have been easy to sell to a community skeptical of both private and institutional development. But the belief that the prominent site and the museum's program required a new kind of solution ultimately prevailed, and what resulted seems, in the end, to be both fresher and more sensitive to the particular nature of this site than a historicizing structure of wood would have been.

Because Fentress thinks relatively little of style per se, he tends not to think of contexts in terms of style, either. From the first project he worked on in Denver, the Amoco Building of 1980, designed when he was with Kohn Pedersen Fox of New York, he has thought of context in a larger, more conceptual sense. It can be the symbolic context of the mountains to create an iconic image for the airport, or the urban context of the confluence of streets and grids, emerging out of a consciousness of how a tall urban building is perceived from various vantage points against different backgrounds. Amoco, at the point of intersection between two different street grids, is a kind of punctuation mark at the end of a visual axis - a role in the cityscape far more important than its specific architectural style, which is more or less a sort of sleek, late-modernism of the late 1970's. Similarly, Fentress's 1999 Broadway of 1985, a few blocks away in downtown Denver, acknowledges both the presence of a landmark church at its base and the different roles each side of its complex form play in the larger pattern of the downtown cityscape.

If the price to be paid for this is a building that is not always coherent as a form, 1999 Broadway nonetheless makes an essential polemical point, which is to assert the importance of the tower as a multi-faceted, multi-functional organism in the full context of the city. Indeed, its relative lack of unity can be said in this case to be a conscious act, a kind of deliberate anti-narcissism.

This is a strong building that does not seek, like so many buildings of the 1980's, to flaunt its own formal agenda in the face of larger urban concerns; it seeks, instead, to do the opposite, to demonstrate how its forms have in fact been generated by the complexity of the urban context around it.

There are other noteworthy buildings in this oeuvre as well: the Jefferson County Judicial and Administration Building, which gracefully interprets the time-honored civic symbol of the rotunda in modernist garb: the Clark County Government Center in Las Vegas, a more abstract attempt to symbolize the notion of an open and accessible government without reverting to traditional classical form; the Colorado Convention Center in Denver, where a stepped-back entry pavilion of glass and metal serves both as a spectacular symbol of entrance and as a sly means of deflecting the eye from the scaleless mass of the convention center itself.

In each case, a problem has clearly been thought through from the beginning, with no predetermined sense of what sort of formal results this quest will yield.

It is no accident that the architect who Fentress cites most often as an influence - aside from his former employer, I.M.Pei - is Eero Saarinen, whose body of work plays a significant, and often underappreciated, role in the architectural history of postwar America. Saarinen broke the stranglehold Mies and orthodox modernism had on American architecture in the 1950's with his refusal to hold to any formal or stylistic direction, and his insistence that every architectural problem yielded a different kind of architectural solution. Saarinen's work, if viewed unsympathetically by some of the most theoretically-minded critics, is nonetheless generally considered to have represented a rare moment in American architecture in which the commercial mainstream and the notion of an architecture of serious social and esthetic purpose managed some degree of confluence. It is that confluence, that merging of wide acceptability and deeper esthetic value, that Curt Fentress seeks to re-establish.

The Architect and Architecture

by Maurizio Vitta

The collocating of an architect in the history of architecture excludes the notion of centrality that distinguishes this process in other fields like the history of art. An artist can only be placed in his appropriate context through a process of centralization (chronological history revolves around the history of artistic production as a whole, which, in turn, orbits around the margins of individual works, for their part centered on the artist's biographical background etc.); in architecture the relations between the general and specific follow much more complex patterns calling into question a wide range of subjects, even society as a whole. The architect is reflected in architecture through a maze-like interplay of mirrors fragmenting each's own image and guaranteeing the logical consistency of the whole thanks to the precarious balance between its separate parts. Hence the geometric figure of the circle, whose irresistible projective tension towards the centre defines an artist's historical background, is opposed, in architecture, by the figure of the eclipse: the Baroque form par excellence that relentlessly contrasts opposing focal points and draws the meaning of things not from the things themselves, but from their endlessly shifting relationships.

Curtis Worth Fentress is no exception to this rule. And why should he be? In his relatively brief (considering his age) but eventful career - already rich in projects and constructions - Fentress has condensed all the essential features of the history of architecture in the latter half of the XXth century: an emphasis on technology as it progresses at a breathtaking rate; the problem of inserting individual buildings into the bewildering maze of the contemporary city; the anxieties surrounding urban development; the clash between innovation and conservation; the emergence of a new form of topology; a redefining of the relations between ethics and aesthetics, architectural form and social form or, more generally speaking, culture and purpose, and so forth.

Like all contemporary architects Fentress has tackled the intricate variables of a disciple compelled to follow its own course without the aid of mediation or shrewd aloofness from the harsh reality of a world undergoing chaotic change; this means that each of his separate works is grounded in the major issues of contemporary architecture, providing a key to their interpretation and referring on, in each separate case, to other issues and other problems.

The Questioning Powers of Design

Fentress belongs to the latest generation of designers whose legacy from the history of philosophy lies in the concept of "nihilism" (in the Nietzschean perspective of the "complete nihilist", conscious of the disintegration of being in an indiscriminate procession of values or, to borrow an expression from Gianni Vattimo, "in the indeterminate transformations of universal equivalence") and whose inheritance from the history of architecture is "pluralism" (an indefinite notion which, in any case, confirms the crisis in major design systems and, in its most extreme offshoots, even branches into neo-eclecticism).This is not, however, a totally negative inheritance. The end of modernity, taken as a culture based on an obsession with the new, passion for denial and exasperated projective tension towards the future, has unleashed latent energies that had long been locked away and which, for the time being, have been transformed into the concepts of "memory", "continuity" and "subjectivity". In architecture this has resulted in the re-emergence of notions such as "place", "context", "alteration", "expressiveness", relations between "project" and "location" and so forth. Apart from occasional manifestations, which over the last twenty years have been grouped together under the rather ambiguous, and now outmoded and useless, label of "postmodernism", the waving of these ideas in the midst of western culture has led to a change in climate which, although rather unclear and incomplete, now calls for an acceptance of new responsibilities.

Philosophical projects, and architectural projects in particular, have begun to "question" the very meaning of "design". Each new construction carries with it the elements of a radical stance that constantly calls into question the underlying tenets of architecture. The collapse in hierarchies of meanings leaves us all free to assign our own peculiar values.

The reluctant confession of one of Dostoyevsky's characters - if God does not exist anything is possible - is now taking on its full paradigmatic force: the decline in major systems opens up infinite possibilities for the designer; but since each available option has only itself to answer to, the ensuing project will be both a solution to the needs at that particular moment and a questioning of the very meaning of its own existence.

Architecture and Complexity

Of course, nostalgia for the architect in his role as a social demiurge (an image powerfully projected by the exponents of the Bauhaus Movement) still runs silently through our culture. This is quite understandable. As recently as 1955, in "Scope of Total Architecture", Walter Gropius wrote that the modern architect's "vocation" was as "an organiser-coordinator, whose task it is to solve all formal, technical, sociological and commercial problems and combine them into a general unit". According to this vision, architecture represented the unity of rational thought capable of controlling every aspect of mass society.

In relation to this, Fentress loves to quote, not without a certain irony, the hero of Ayn Rand's novel, Fountainhead, and William Blake's "divine architect". Nevertheless, as he actually points out: "Although we may gaze backward in time, a return to the Ayn Rand or William Blake image of the architect is impossible even if such a thing were desired." This quote is, nonetheless, full of implications: Howard Roark, the hero in Ayn Rand's novel, was a firm believer in rationalist architecture and fought, with the individualism of an artist, against the triumph and overpowering conformism of the urban scenario of the day; as for William Blake, he placed Urizen, the "creator of men", at the centre of his criticism of enlightened ideas based on science and technology, transforming this god into the source of repressive morality and non-visionary philosophy. Fentress's scepticism is quite justified. Western mass society of the Thirties and Forties has been transformed, on the threshold of the XXIst century, into a complex social system, further complicated by the mass of variables it itself creates. In such a complex situation, technology, on the one hand, produces a balancing effect and, on the other, turns out to be yet another variable contributing to the instability of a system by which it is directly affected. Conversely, the innovative thrust generated by economic structures, whose solidity is largely guaranteed by an accelerated consumption of values, clashes more and more frequently with the collective desire for certainty and assurance. The architect is therefore obliged to find social solutions to a wide range of contradictory requirements, meaning that not only forms but even functions need to be constantly updated.

Unity through Design

Like all architects belonging to his generation, Curtis Worth Fentress is acutely aware of this complexity and its repercussions on architecture. He is, above all, confronted with American reality, in some respects a paradigm of its western counterpart; and, more specifically, he has chosen to locate his firm in a definite area of the USA, the inland States, grounded in their own highly peculiar physical, cultural and geographical traditions.

Fentress's reaction to the architectural problems with which he was faced breaks with the mainstream tendencies that have gradually gained ground over the last twenty years. Not that he has ignored or underestimated the guidelines arising from the experiments marking the much heralded decline of modernity: on the contrary, he has taken due note and, in a certain sense, assimilated them. It is just that his actual architectural work has upturned the institutionalised procedures of the contemporary architectural scene. His constructions do not draw on any generic notion of architecture, rejecting the schemes of theoretical models. His constructions, taken either singularly or as a whole, are themselves responsible for defining the conceptual terms of his design work.

It has only taken Fentress fifteen years to sketch a clear map of his architecture. But in order to analyse the constants, structural lines and key issues on which he has focused his work - projecting his projects to the forefront of contemporary American architecture - each of his projects needs to be viewed as a self-contained unit, placed in its actual context and considered as a means of "questioning" the future of modern-day architecture. Bearing in mind that, as Fentress himself points out, "to the joy of most and the anxiety of few, architecture like its progenitor, humankind, is in a constant state of redefinition," each individual project reveals the underlying meaning of architectural work as an open-ended system in which each separate construction is not longer the "product" of an all-encompassing concept, but rather the "sign" of an all-encompassing process in progress.

Intuition and Technology

Two constants characterising Fentress's philosophical approach are architecture's relation to modern technology and an endeavour to design through "intuition". These mark the boundaries of his work's conceptual space; beyond them he sees nothing but a lot of babble about "isms".

Accelerated technological progress has, in his opinion, become a central issue for "large franchise firms, the ones which have virtually taken to the "nth" degree the techno-modern ideal in which futuristic technologies are obviously paramount to other architectural considerations."

Alternatively, Fentress goes on to say, "the most important thing to have happened in recent years is a real recognition that we are living in a world in which mass production has begun to produce mass information and that assimilation (context) is the key, not regurgitation". In this situation in which "the architectural process for a purely high-technology world has become postrationalized-technology for technology's sake applied by canon, we must no longer dismiss intuition off hand. It is that which we must explore and define."

Fentress has reached these conclusions in a relatively short space of time. He began with a group of projects in which his interest in building technology seems in some way to be expressed through the buildings' clear-cut geometric configurations. Having gained valuable experience working with I.M. Pei and Partners and Kohn Pedersen Fox Associates, he was already looking ahead. "The last few decades," he remarked commenting on his first major project, One Mile High Plaza, built in Denver in 1981, "have seen a loss of a sense of purpose and understanding of the elements that create urban fabric, as well as an incorrect response to the elements of nature and the use of energy." The tower's triangulated form is, in fact, the result of a careful study of local wind patterns; and its structure has been specially designed to reduce energy consumption by twenty percent.

This concept is further elaborated upon in ensuing projects. 116 Inverness, dating back to 1982, even alludes to the famous catalogue accompanying the 1932 International Style exhibition (in which Henry-Russell Hitchcock and Philip Johnson pointed out that the "effect of volume" had now replaced the "effect of mass"), immediately followed by a further comment on the fact that this is not determined by aesthetic requirements but by "a marriage of a structural sealant butt-jointed to each edge of the glass panels", enabling the construction of a totally uninterrupted surface of glass. The fundamental principles of modernism are interpreted rather than applied in these early projects. Even 1999 Broadway Tower, built in Denver in 1985, owes its arrow-tip profile to technical requirements: "It does cost more to make more corners," Fentress admitted, "but the benefits are that offices are more impressive with better views. Most people who advance in a company end up in a corner office, so it has that ring of prestige to it."

The Question of Context

Fentress is rightly concerned about the work conditions inside his buildings. In his eyes, architectural space must be transformed into a place: a "historical" rather than "geometric" space. He has moved beyond old-fashioned functionalism to focus not so much on how architecture is actually used - ergonomics, organisation of work, mechanics of flows and permanences - as its social connotations. Architectural space must be warm, welcoming and expressive; its origins lie in social history, models of social interaction and socio-economic theory. 1999 Broadway tackles contextual issues in these specific terms. The fact that the huge tower stands so close to the tiny Holy Ghost Catholic Church is dictated by programme requirements (unthinkable in Europe with its densely packed historical settlements, even for a construction built in 1943): here, history is recounted in the present tense. The real issue is adapting architecture to generate an immediate sense of place. If a building's function is to accommodate working environments, then efficiency and comfort must be interpreted in relation to business tradition. The hierarchical staff "pecking order" transforms space into a "sign" to be converted into an architectural idiom, for example through the construction of "corners".

Just as the modernist concept of "functionality" is interpreted in social terms, so "technology" is viewed in symbiosis with nature (light, energy). The aesthetic force of Hitchcock and Johnson's manifesto of 1932 is given a powerful social flavour, just as the moral force of Gropus's vision of the architect as supreme coordinator is replaced by the image of a designer tracing out the places of community life. In this respect the question of "context" is viewed in new terms: rather than just adapting a building to its "surroundings", even greater emphasis is placed on the shaping of interior space along cultural lines.

Interior and Exterior

There are always extremely tense relations between the interior and exterior in all of Fentress's architecture. The horizontal surfaces of his building plans create a clever interplay of collective relations. The layout of space is, in itself, imbued with considerable symbolic force: it creates orders, paths, priorities, behavioural models and social functions. Yet, the physical appearance of this space is apparently transformed when viewed in the form of elevations. The dialogue shifts onto a different plane: architectural form is brought into dialectical relation with the surrounding environment, and the interior composition claims its own autonomy without losing any of its force.

This is clearly the case with 116 Inverness, whose interlocking double "V" design immediately establishes a hierarchical ordering of space and function in a much more complex layout than in the exterior volumes; but the whole question is much clearer in those buildings where there has been a much more open attempt to express architecture in a "regional" idiom.The United Bank of Arizona is perhaps the first attempt to consider "context" in continuity with the past. Here in Tucson the site plans mirror the architectural style of Spanish mission courtyards, while the vertical structure is reminiscent of St. Augustine and San Xavier del Bac cathedrals. Nevertheless, we might rightly suspect that Fentress is not so much concerned with imitating Spanish colonial architecture as exploring the roots of American culture in this region. The formal echo of the bell towers of San Xavier is not an architectural revival, as can be seen by examining the building plans whose layout actually reflects certain business rituals. The project is clearly designed to establish much more complex relations with the historical, urban environment than simple architectural "mimesis" could ever afford.

Architecture as Rhetoric

Awareness of the existing environment - either physical or artificial - made slower headway in the USA, where the peculiar features of the nation's history resulted in quite different experiments and experiences than in Europe.

"The recent cultural phenomenon of historic preservation in America," Fentress remarked, "refocused our attention from what we wished the modern environment would become to what it actually had become: from theory to reality." This is his response to the individualism of modern architecture: "The discourse of modernism as a reactionary mode of expression against the dominance of stylized architecture literally and philosophically produced the physical discord we now experience in many American cityscapes. Although it is debatable that preservation is itself an architectural movement, it is arguable that as a phenomenon it has become a significant paradigm, the primary manifestation of what the whole of our culture is really beginning to look like and that the more popularized idioms of "isms" are made from observation by those in "ivory towers."

There is once again a fleeting allusion to the idea of projects "questioning" the underlying meaning of architecture in that they act in rather than on history. "Conservation" tends, ironically, to promote "difference", in that it revives places and periods from the past, peripheral truths and "regional" realities, and transforms recollection into change by, as the Italian historian of architecture Manfredo Tafuri has written, tending to provide "expressions of pietas for what has been or for past conquests, transformations that avoid the hybris of novum in order to "let be". Planning means occupying a position and taking up a stance in relation to a world whose profound vitality must be broached on an even standing: architecture abandons its monologue with modernity and reverts back to dialogue. It must be persuasive rather than pervasive and, to be so, it must rediscover its old visual rhetoric, or rather the ability to project itself onto the environment through figures of thought and speech capable of expressing profound common truths.

The Rhythms of History

From the late Eighties onwards, Curtis Worth Fentress's architectural research is marked by a profound re-assessment of its own design paradigms. The Jefferson County Human Services Building (1989), Colorado Convention Center (1990), Clark County Government Center (1992), General Services Administration Federal Building, National Oceanic and Atmospheric Administration (1992), National Cowboy Hall of Fame (1992) and Natural Resources Building (1992) all refuse to conform with pre-conceived models, focusing on a form of architecture that opens up to the historical present while acting as a bridge between the past and present.

These major undertakings are designed to openly display the architectural idiom in which they have been constructed through spatial configurations capable of being spontaneously transformed into symbolic expressions.

The clear-cut "sign" projected towers (the most individualistic of all images) vanishes to be replaced by more intricately plastic volumetric building structures; the figure of the circle, with its connotations of warmth and equality, is pushed to the fore: relations with the physical environment are played on materials selected for their compatibility with the light, colours, forms and textures of the place in which they are inserted.

There is no underlying style to all these projects. Principally located in regions such as Colorado, Oklahoma or Nevada, they respond to a wide spectrum of stimuli: the history of these regions is grounded in the very roots of the American nation with its myths and rituals, and the rugged landscapes of these astounding open spaces are deeply entrenched in the collective psyche. This means that each building is a law unto itself, the only underlying link being constant experimentation on a form of architecture designed to actually be history rather than make history. All this research and experimentation is, of course,

underpinned by a re-reading of modernity in a contemporary key, from the "analogical approach" outlined by Aldo Rossi in L'architettura della città (1966), to the concept of historicism debated at great length in Europe, and the daring theories proposed by Robert Venturi in Learning from Las Vegas (1972). Fentress filters all this design input through a pragmatism that exploits them as tools rather than absorbing them as models. Referring to the Clark County Government Center in Las Vegas, he remarked: "The (design) result is an indigenous solution which embodies the essence of this region by emphasising the sculptural qualities of the physical environment".

Fentress is being far too modest: the design of this building is actually one of the crowning moments of Fentress's career thanks to its structural layout and complexity.

As in other works by this architect, it contains a common denominator found in many other contemporary American constructions: the "classical form" of its structures, featuring simple geometric figures, the use of stone and carefully balanced volumes, constitutes a landmark on the American architectural scene (much less rich in old buildings than its European counterpart) as an almost metaphysical image, suspended in space and time in what might be termed De Chirico fashion.

Architecture and Identity

There is of course a definite propensity for metaphysics on the contemporary architectural scene, but it is only a secondary consequence of Fentress's own personal research and experimentation. He focuses much of his attention on "context" and "regionalism", starting from the historical-physical environment to eventually arrive at architecture, and not vice-versa. As early as the National Cowboy Hall of Fame in Oklahoma City he began to work on the archetypal images of specific locations: the canopy covered wagons of pioneers, rolling prairies and rugged mountain ranges are transformed into authentic design paradigms, signs of "symbolic relation" as Roland Barthes described them. For Fentress architectural identity is inextricably bound to the identity of specific locations; it is this latter identity that must be probed and explored in determining forms, spaces and structures.

Fentress's two greatest achievements lie at opposite extremes of his design spectrum: on one hand, the National Museum of Wildlife Art in Jackson, Wyoming (1993), and on the other, the new International Airport in Denver, Colorado (1994).

In the first of these two projects architecture is totally integrated with nature. The colour of the cladding stone, the building's flat, squashed profile and its rugged, uneven surfaces (light, colour, shadow, contours) create a primeval almost telluric image, welling up from the very bowels of the earth. However, upon closer examination, the signs of an archaic age may be detected in its cumbersome volumes, tentative apertures and primitive features of habitation. The ancestral origins of history and nature discover in architecture their most authentic vehicle of consolidation and expression: memory does not hide the past, it projects it into the immediacy of the present.

The concept is turned on its head with Denver Airport. The aim was to create an "iconographic symbol of Denver - one with a futuristic expression coupled with imaginative building technologies." The roof in particular, inspired by the contours of the Rocky Mountains, clearly epitomises an architectural style that draws on the past to project itself forcibly into the future. In this case it is technology that bears the weight of architecture, whose most immediately iconographic features are designed not to represent itself (as in high-tech aesthetics), but to act as a bridge between the past and future, or in other words to embed itself in the identity of its locations.

Projections

Curtis Worth Fentress's architectural horizons are the same as the rest of American and, more generally speaking, Western architecture. He interprets it as a new romanticism ("It is in fact a new romanticism that the marriage of contextualism and regionalism can bring to the once despised downtown district"), expressed not so much in terms of nostalgia for the past as in an overthrowing of rational canons in favour of a strong sense of history and nature (Fentress is quite right in claiming that the National Wildlife Museum "created a situation paradox-building to appear as non-building").

Labels aside, world architecture is now concerned with the instrumental values of technology - that tends to set itself up as an autonomous value - and the philosophical values of the genius loci - that far too often dissolve into pure "style". It is worth quoting Fentress again: "As we reach the end of another millennium we find that we live in an ultra-technological society, one in which the idea (intuition) is frequently subsumed by the "facts" (science and technology)".

Re-examining the roots of architecture requires an awareness of its concrete possibilities and, at the same time, its limitations (which is what the modernists failed to comprehend in the naive optimism of the XXth century).

Fentress has shown he has a clear conscience in this respect. "The encyclopedia of experience and the response to growing population and dwindling resources", he has observed, "make us realize just how ultimately responsible we are for our world. In this lie all the histories of regions, the delicacies of context, and the very survival of the human species."

This is the situation towards which contemporary architecture and culture in general are now heading. Behind us we can still hear echoes of the Proverbs of Hell that William Blake included in The Marriage of Heaven and Hell: "Drive your cart and your plough over the bones of the dead". And also: "The road of excess leads to the palace of wisdom."

Works

One Mile High Plaza

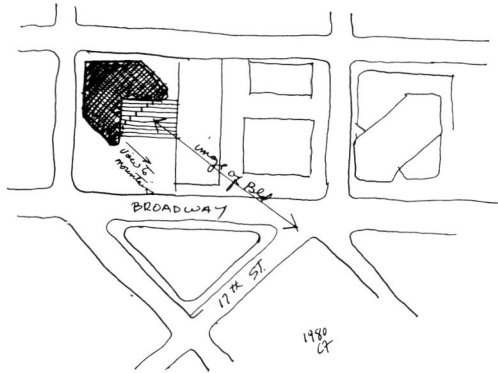

J.Roulier Interests commissioned Fentress and his design team to build a 37-storey corporate office block in Denver, Colorado.

The building, dubbed One Mile High Plaza, was designed for a choice site in lower downtown at a cost of approximately $70 million. This gracefully intriguing landmark on the Denver skyline has a steel frame and concrete core, a glass-granite skin, and granite, glass, gypsum board and carpet interiors. It occupies a gross volume of 947,000 square feet and has parking room for 1,000 vehicles.

The multi-angled building structure with its crystal-line-faceted face looks out westward towards the Front Range of the Rockies. At ground level there is an expansive plaza and glass-covered atrium that continues the cascading motif characterising the upper level of the building's crystalline facade.

Curtis Worth Fentress gave careful thought to the design philosophy underlying One Mile High Plaza. As he himself put it: "Every site has a set of contextual requirements that must be responded to. These fall into two categories: those of nature (sun, wind, topography) and those that are man-made or urban."

Bearing in mind the environmental conditions in Denver, more familiarly known as Mile High City, the building's shape is designed to reduce wind loads and decrease energy consumption by as much as 20% over compared to other office structures built during the same period. At a time when there was a general loss of sense of purpose and understanding of the elements that combine to form the urban fabric, One Mile High Plaza was a carefully studied attempt to reevaluate the design of urban buildings and the general approach to energy use by reverting back to some of the principles logically assumed during the early age of modern urban architecture.

Standard building plan
and, bottom of page,
plan of ground floor.

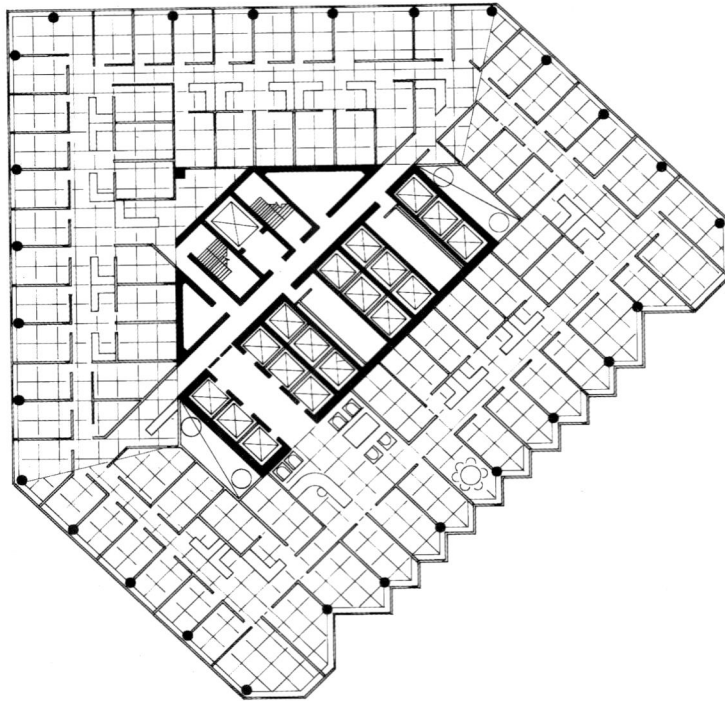

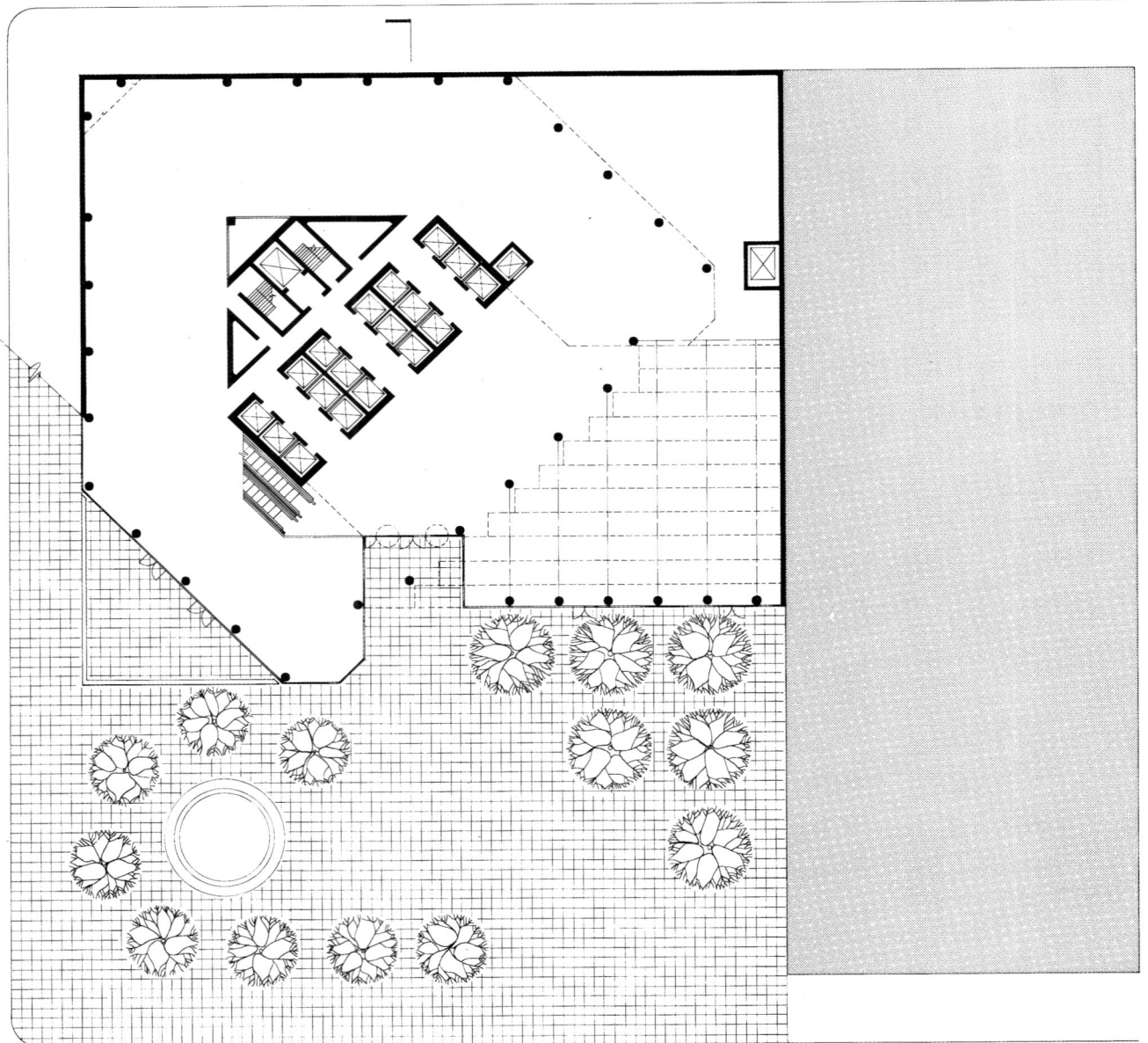

Two views of the model
showing the large glass
entrance in detail.

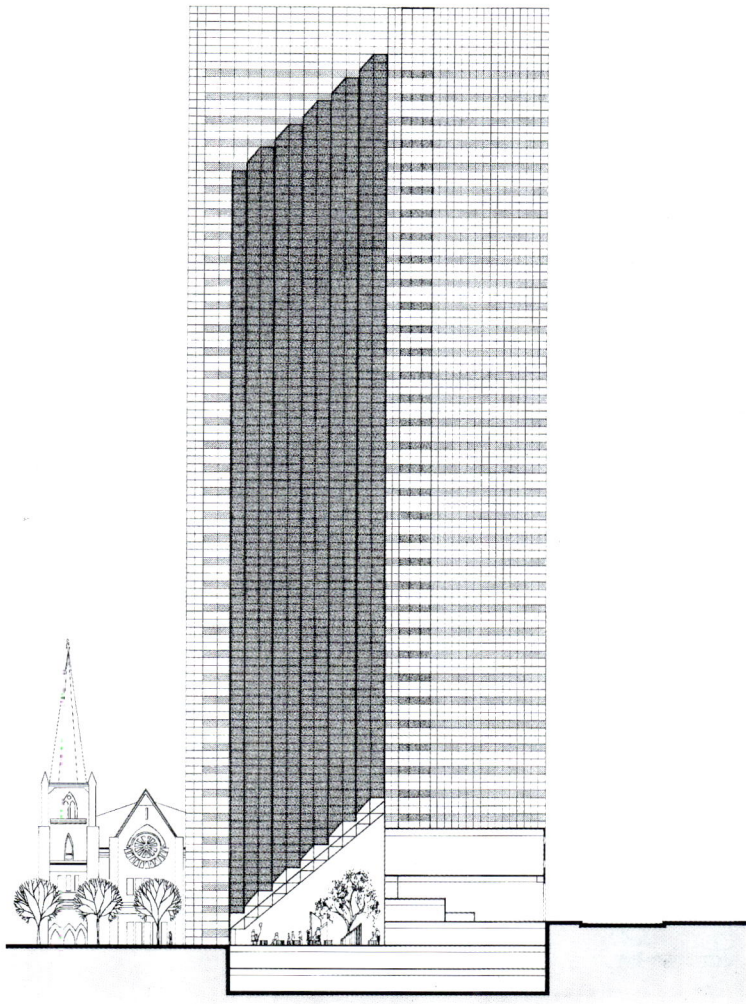

Top left, section
of the foyer; bottom
of page, section of
a wing of the building.
Right, another view
of the model.

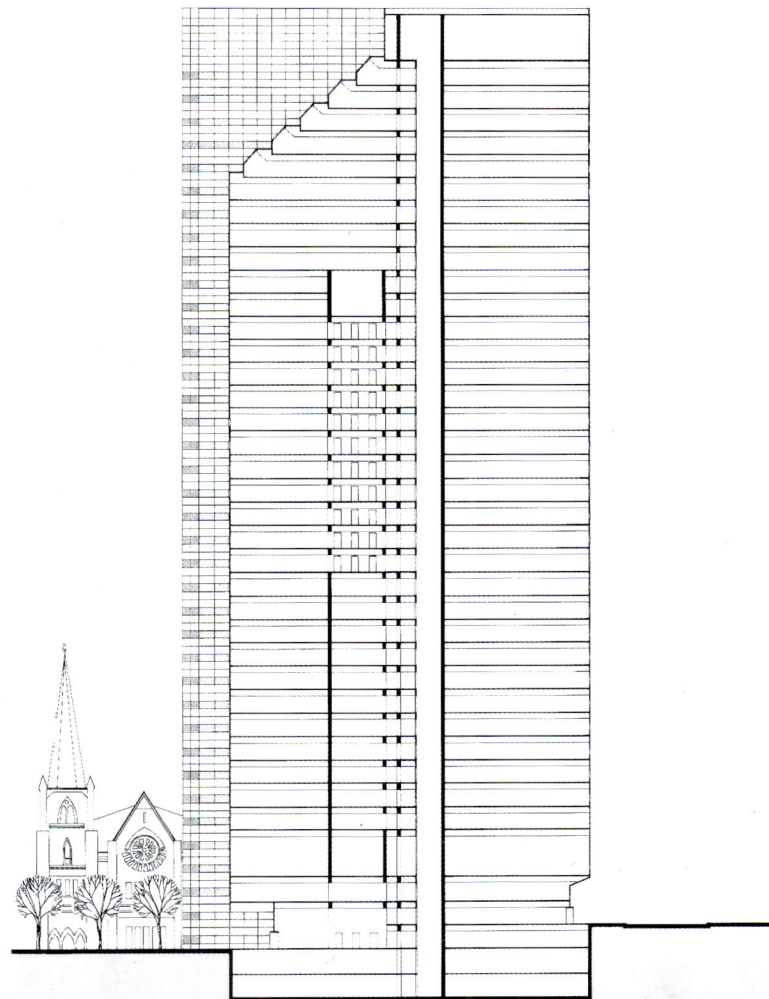

Two details of the model
showing the structure
of the foyer roof.

116 Inverness

116 Inverness Drive East is a 230,000-square-foot, low-rise corporate office building designed in a modified X-shaped configuration with four wings adjoining a central skylit diamond-shaped atrium.

The client was looking for a visually striking landmark to characterize the north entrance to an 840-acre business park in Englewood, Colorado. The building's interlocking configuration affords maximum use of perimeter and corner office spaces, allowing panoramic views of the rolling countryside in this superb suburban setting. This low-rise office building and low-profile parking structure were designed to blend in gracefully with the surrounding 18-hole championship golf course and the majestic front range of the Rocky Mountains.

The building is clad in alternating bands of green vision and silver spandrel glass, which, thanks to the use of new four-sided structural-silicone glazing, contribute to the project's aesthetically-pleasing appearance. The sleek grey and green glass building either sparkles in the sunlight or blends in perfectly with its natural surroundings in cloudy conditions. The glass and aluminium components of the glazing system were pre-assembled with structural silicone and delivered to the site ready to be attached to the curtain wall's structural system. The structural sealant was butt-jointed to each edge of the glass panels to eliminate the use of exterior mullions. This also prevented any danger of bite/overbite point loading on the glass, a familiar problem with traditional curtain wall glazing systems, and reduced the likelihood of glass breakage due to either thermal expansion/contraction or live-load deflection. Glass bound in a four-sided structural silicone system effectively floats on a highly durable, flexible adherent. The isolated aluminium structure behind the insulating glass also creates a thermal barrier, allowing the building to be heated by a perimeter hot water system and cooled by a variable air volume system. Since the structural silicone not only acts as a sealant between the framing system and the glass, but also as a gasket between each separate pane of glass, the exterior warms up more evenly all around the building. The silicone system is also used to support both inboard and outboard lights in the insulating glass section of the curtain wall.

The three-storey garage, accommodating parking space for 700 cars, is heavily landscaped and bermed on all sides. The entrance is integrated with the office building by a recessed angle matching that of the main structure. There are entrances/exits to all three levels - two of which, below grade, are reserved for tenants - on the north, south and east sides of the parking facility to keep traffic moving even at the busiest times of day. Exterior earth ramps provide access to the surrounding road network and a softly lit, fabric-covered "all-weather" tunnel leads through to the atrium entrance of the main building. Construction costs were minimised by the exterior use of poured-in-place concrete walls with sandblasted exposed surfaces.

Sculptures by the artist Karl Rosenberg have been carefully integrated to unify the entrance, lobby and atrium space. Rosenberg aimed at recreating inside the building the sense of motion created by reflections of the surrounding landscape in the silver and green spandrel glass panels. His hoop, masts and cable conjure up a crescendo of motion, progression and colour in a spectrum of natural hues and shades, integrating the sculpture into the surrounding environment and creating a pleasant feeling of warmth.

116 Inverness is the first monolithic four-sided structurally-glazed building in which a silicone sealant has been butt-jointed to the edges of glass panels to create a mullion-free exterior. It has rightly been described as the first complete expression of the International style as described in the 1932 "Modernist Manifesto" by Henry-Russell Hitchcock and Philip Johnson.

The building's site
plan underlines
the complexity of the
overall construction,
which, nevertheless,
can be seen, in the
picture above, to blend
in smoothly with the
surrounding landscape.

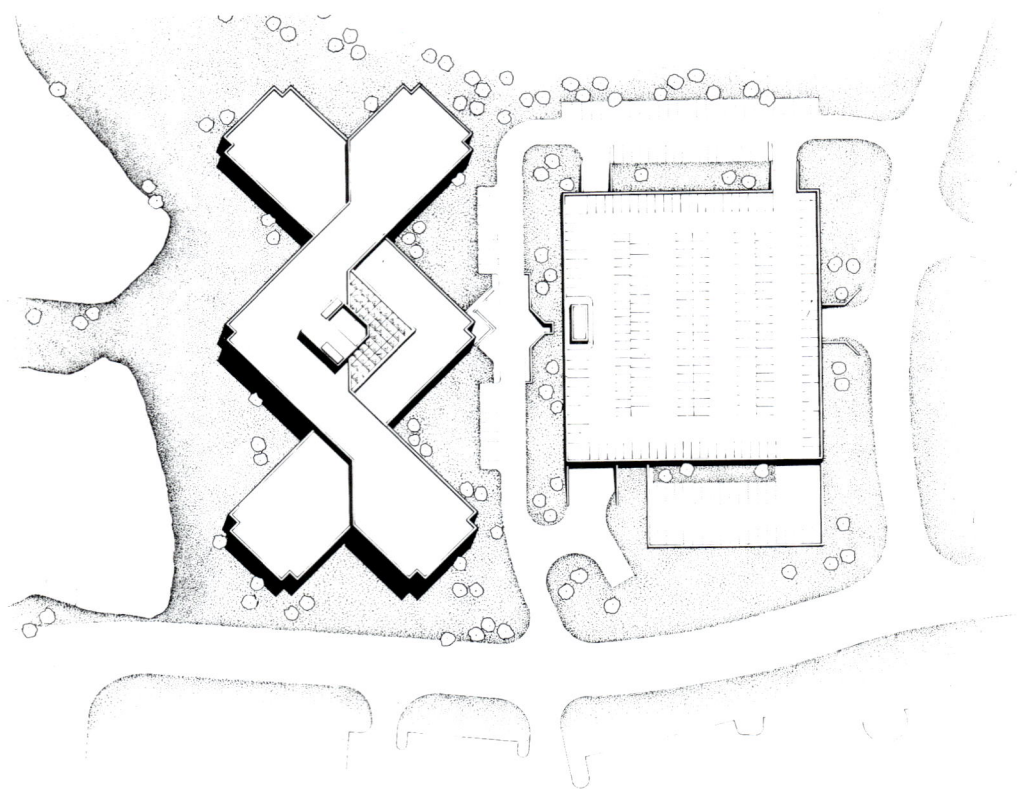

The alternating green
and silver bands create
a sense of lightness
and transparency.

Previous spread,
a picture of the building
entrance, whose interior
is shown on the
opposite page.
Below, a standard
building plan and, right,
another two pictures of
the lobby atrium
showing the sculptural
work.

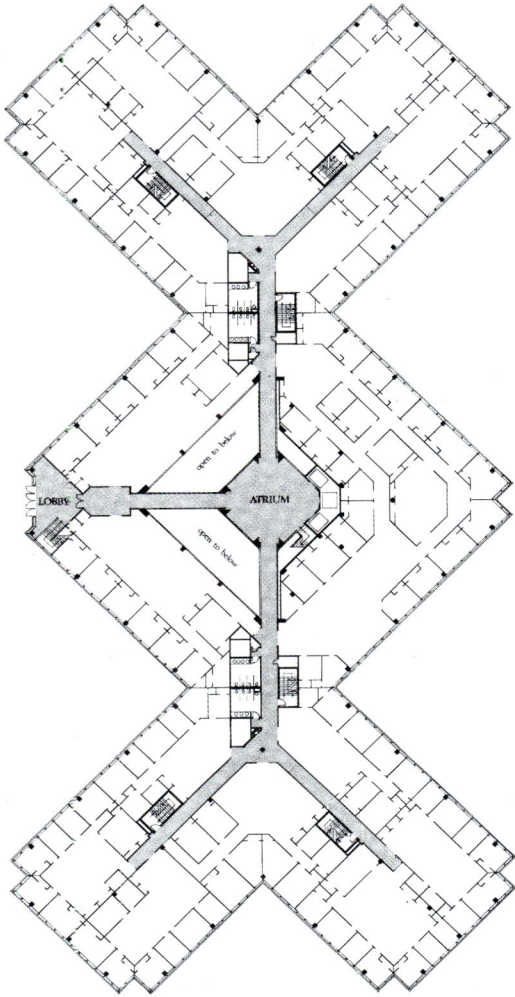

The building's flat
elongated profile
softens its visual impact
on the environment.

Another two views of
the construction, whose
crystal-clear transparency
is underlined by the
winter landscape.

Two pictures of the
building highlighting
its dynamic structural
layout.

Reliance Center

Architects constantly deal with scale, arguably the key issue as far as the American cityscape is concerned, and skyscrapers, as urban images of power and arbiters of vertical scale, have been subject to more critical design evaluation than any other type of building. Since H.H.Richardson first began testing the technological limits of what he called "proud and soaring things", many skyscrapers have been built just to demonstrate that such towering landmarks are in fact possible. Developers strain against regulatory limits as they compete to build the city's tallest structure, and although there is no real economic advantage to tallness in itself, there is a certain prestige factor in being able to boast this elusive honour.

Fentress Bradburn's project for the Reliance Tower was an attempt to reconcile the issue of human scale with the modernist aesthetic on which they were working at the time.

The 57-story Reliance Center, offering almost 1.5 million square feet of office and retail space, as well as parking for 2000 vehicles, is located on the 16th Street pedestrian mall in downtown Denver. The building actually breaks down into three major surfaces while maintaining an integrated three-dimensional fluidity. Abandoning the columnar rigidity of classical American skyscrapers, the base pulls out from the tower to create a welcoming plaza that resolves the proportional conflict of the monumental over the human: the tiered plaza greets users more gracefully than the blank fronts of traditional tower blocks.

The reverse side of the building is clad with monolithic mullionless glazing in a continuous glazed wall, an intriguing surface that cradles the center's activities while reflecting Denver's Rocky Mountain panorama.

The sweeping 270-foot-wide surface of reflective silver-grey glass facing the Rockies is held in place by a four-sided structural silicone glazing system, revealing an intricate interplay of architecture and engineering.

At the time of its design, the Reliance Center was the tallest building on the Denver skyline.

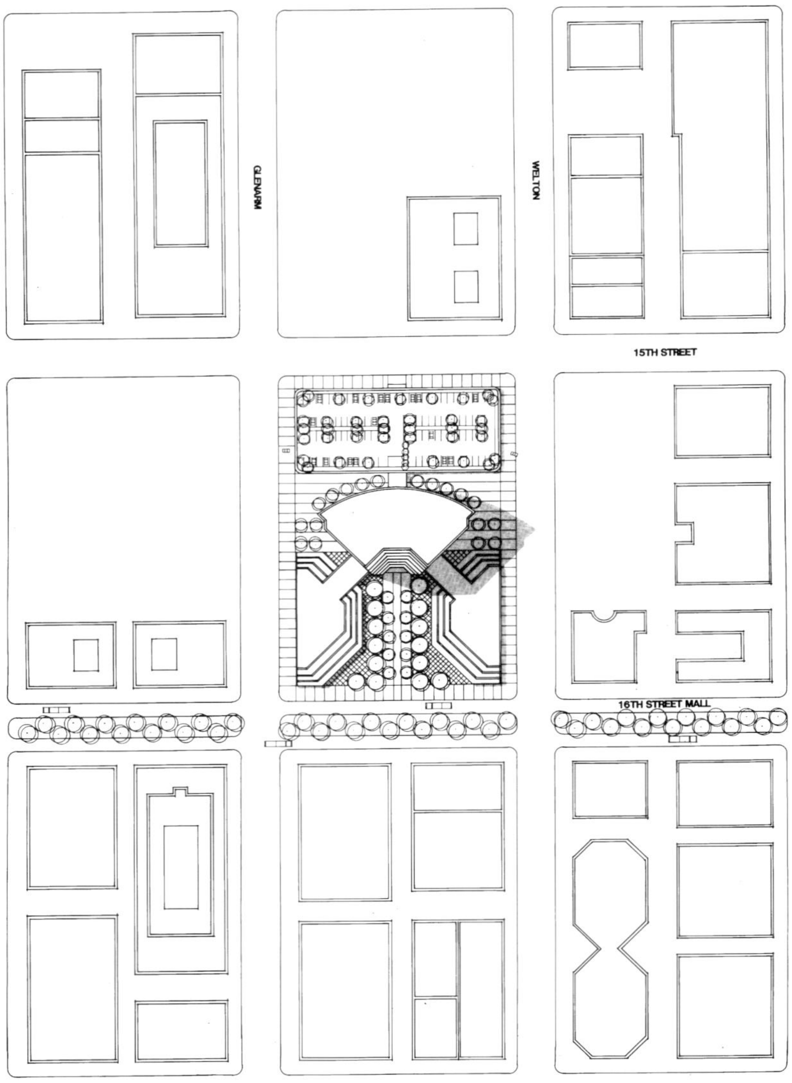
GLENARM
WELTON
15TH STREET
16TH STREET MALL

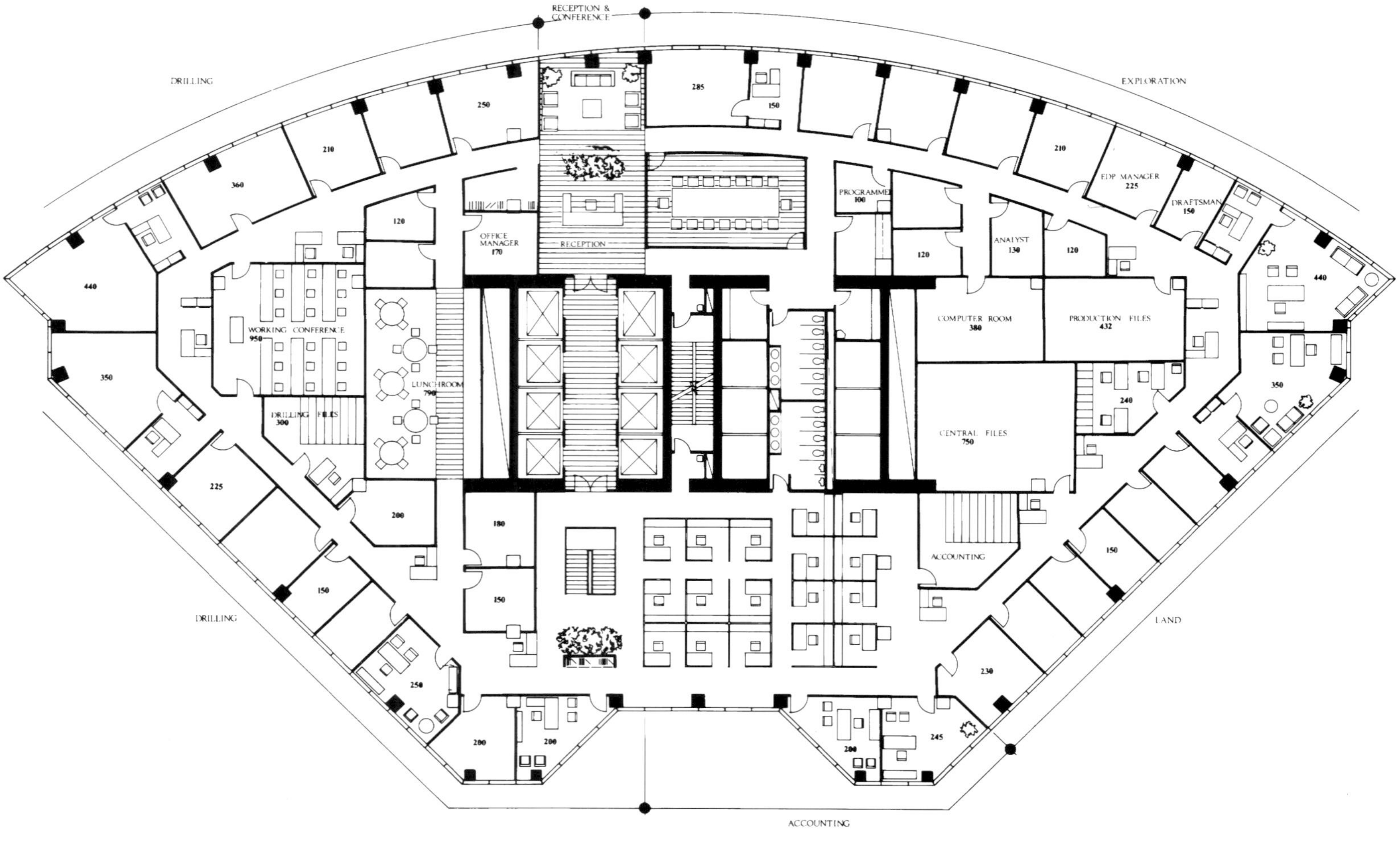
RECEPTION & CONFERENCE
DRILLING
EXPLORATION
250
285
150
210
360
120
OFFICE MANAGER 170
RECEPTION
PROGRAMMER 100
120
ANALYST 130
120
210
EDP MANAGER 225
DRAFTSMAN 150
440
WORKING CONFERENCE 950
LUNCHROOM 790
COMPUTER ROOM 380
PRODUCTION FILES 432
440
350
DRILLING FILES 300
CENTRAL FILES 750
240
350
225
200
180
ACCOUNTING
150
150
150
DRILLING
LAND
250
230
200
200
200
245
ACCOUNTING

Opposite page,
the overall site plan
and a standard plan
of the building.
Below, the two facades.

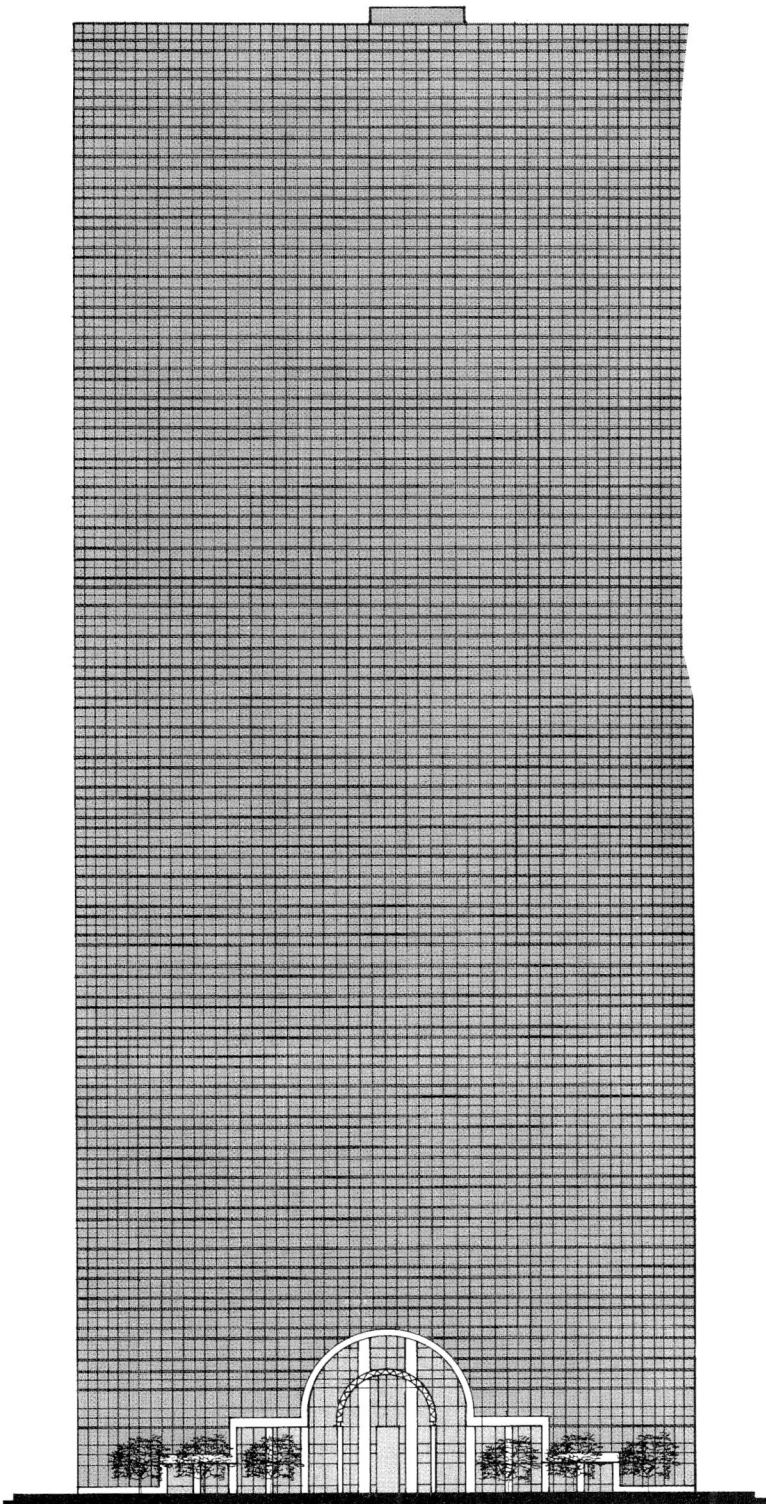

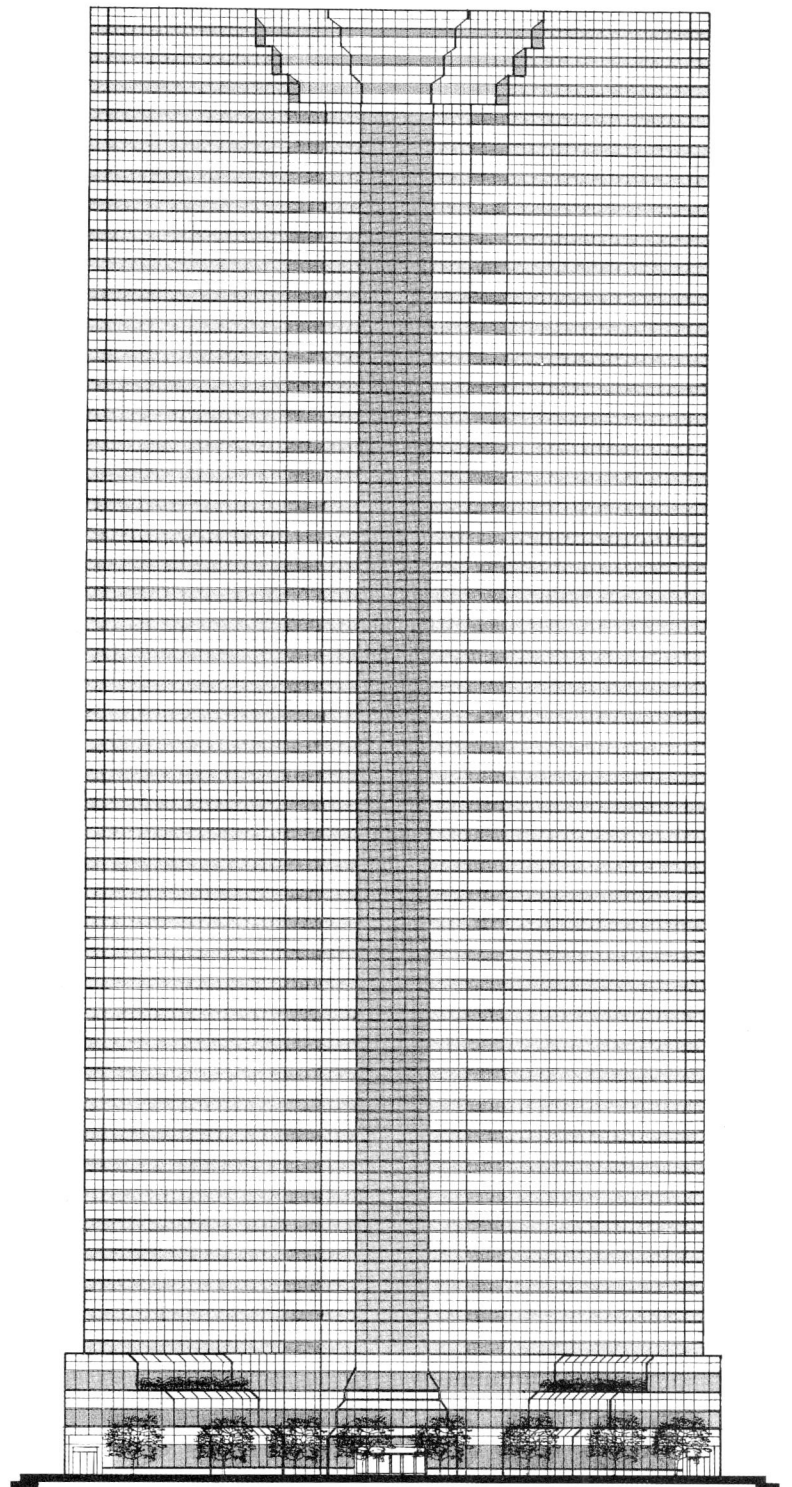

Two views of the model
showing how the
standard columnar
structure of a skyscraper
has been replaced
by a series of base
structures distributed
along the perimeter.

Balboa Company Corporate Headquarters

The project brief for the Balboa Company Corporate Headquarters refers to the creation of "a museum where you can house offices for serious thinking." The offices for a private investment company were to be located on the fifty-ninth floor penthouse of a downtown Denver skyscraper.

The company's corporate philosophy of quiet elegance, unpretentiousness and a low-key business approach were to be translated into concrete substance through an ingenious manipulation of materials, space and light. Unlike other similar designs, art in the form of the company's extensive contemporary and pre-Colombian collection was made an integral part of the scheme, rather than just an afterthought. The 10,000-square-foot penthouse offices are located on the south side of the building with a window wall running along the entire length of the office space. The design has been carefully conceived to extend and emphasise the sky's proximity and the breathtaking panoramic views, while maintaining an interrelated distinction between the sky, building and penthouse offices.

The offices are devised to reflect and blend in with the structure of the building. The interior design is stylistically related to the structure's main architectural motifs: the grid of the exterior skin is mirrored in the grid pattern of the woodwork, and the building's characteristic arc is reflected in the cornice work and bases of the bookcases. Fentress also designed a distinctive floor plan featuring sharply angled walls to foster a sense of greater distance and complexity in the limited floor space. The skewed planes lead visitors into spaces where works of art act as focal points, imparting a unique image on each private office and common area. The zigzag walls also create totally private, fully enclosed, sound insulated space, offering occupants their own personalised environment where even the furniture, chosen separately by each individual inhabitant, imbues the offices with their own characteristic style.

Black and white floors in a classic diagonal picket design, mahogany woodwork and cabinetry, and fine traditional furnishings are skillfully manipulated in a combination of elegance and humour, stateliness and comfort, modernity and tradition.

State-of-the-art energy conserving fixtures are incorporated throughout the work surfaces; low voltage incandescent art display fixtures combined with automatic window shades to reduce glare without causing any loss of vision. Sophisticated environmental controls are designed to maintain optimum temperature and humidity levels for both the occupants and artwork.

Fentress has succeeded in transforming a small, modest office space into an elegant executive suite by combining function and aesthetics in an unpretentious, straightforward, low-key design.

Two views of the
interior work.
Fentress has always
paid special attention
to the interior
arrangement of space,
creating architectural
structures that mirror
the organisation
of work activities.

Functionality
and elegant precision
characterise the design
of these interior
environments.

1999 Broadway

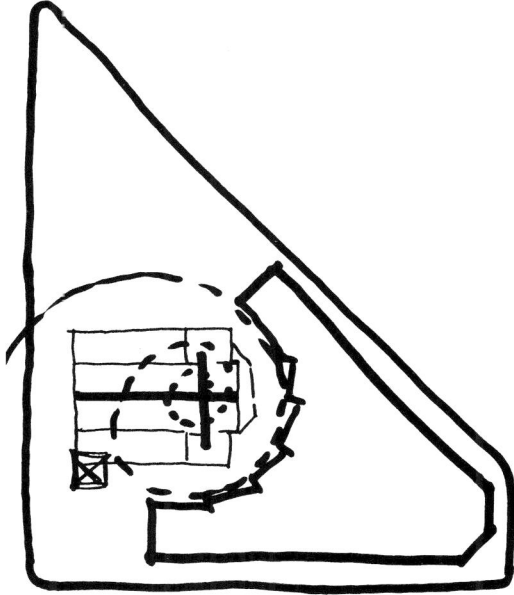

1999 Broadway stands on the same triangular single-block site in the central business district of Denver as the Renaissance-style Holy Ghost Catholic Church. Instead of overwhelming the diminutive stain-glass parish church, the new high-rise is designed to respect this historic religious landmark, endowed by a prominent city benefactor, while projecting an independent dynamic corporate image. Separated by forty years of architecture and widely divergent and conflicting purposes, the two buildings ultimately complement each other through a carefully integrated architectural design.

The tower structure is generated from an arithmetic spiral of reflective glass which cradles and dramatises the sculptural form of the old religious icon. The multi-faceted reflective-glass curtain wall literally wraps around the church. Resting on twenty-two 15.62 meter limestone columns, the tower interfaces with the church to form a tall- stepped arcade allowing the church to remain physically independent and visually open.

The office floors actually commence above the church roof, leaving a two-level expanse for public entry. Encased in glass, the 10,000-square-foot lobby area allows light to flood in without blocking the view of the church's rear facade. The tower's glass and limestone vocabulary reflect the pediment shapes, quoined corners and stonework of the old church. The sea-green reflective facade mirrors the green tile roof of the sanctuary, and limestone panels clearly allude to its brickwork. The textures and ornamental motifs of both the exterior skin and interior spaces are directly influenced by ecclesiastical imagery.

As part of the renovation plan, the church's green clay tile roof was replaced and its rear facade rebuilt in buff-colored brick and terra cotta to restore an exterior cruciform configuration.

The exterior materials chosen for the office tower were inspired by the colors and architectural themes of Gothic-style churches. Verde antique marble from Vermont, grey granite from northern Italy and bands of polished steel lend a sophisticated tone to the lobby and elevators.

There are also two exterior plazas which have been thoroughly landscaped with trees and lawns. One plaza, paved in green-grey granite, features an undulating wall with built-in seating to conceal the down-ramp to underground parking facilities. The other is landscaped with trees surrounded by granite boxes to provide extra seating.

The image of corporate power conjured up by the spine of the tower is set against the equally imposing symbol of strength represented by the church spire. Sanctuary and skyscraper peacefully co-exist in the form of two buildings whose historic symbiosis is unprecedented in modern times.

The project proves that architecture can be used to save existing historic landmarks while simultaneously fulfilling the requirements of modern commercial development.

Site plan of the new
construction built
alongside the old church.

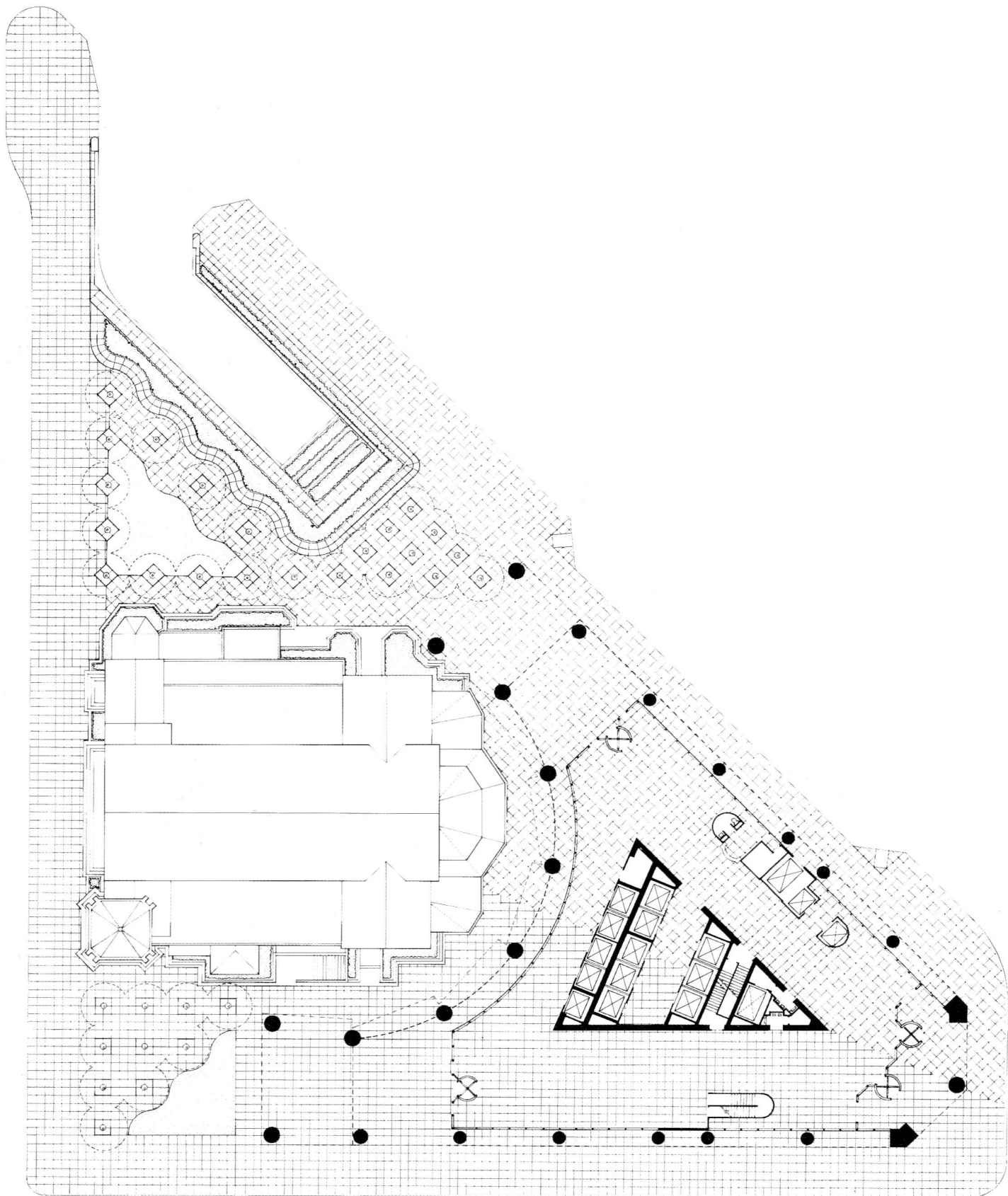

An evocative image
of the church alongside
the towering skyscraper.

A section of the
building showing a view
of the underlying
church and, opposite
page, a picture of the
finished construction.

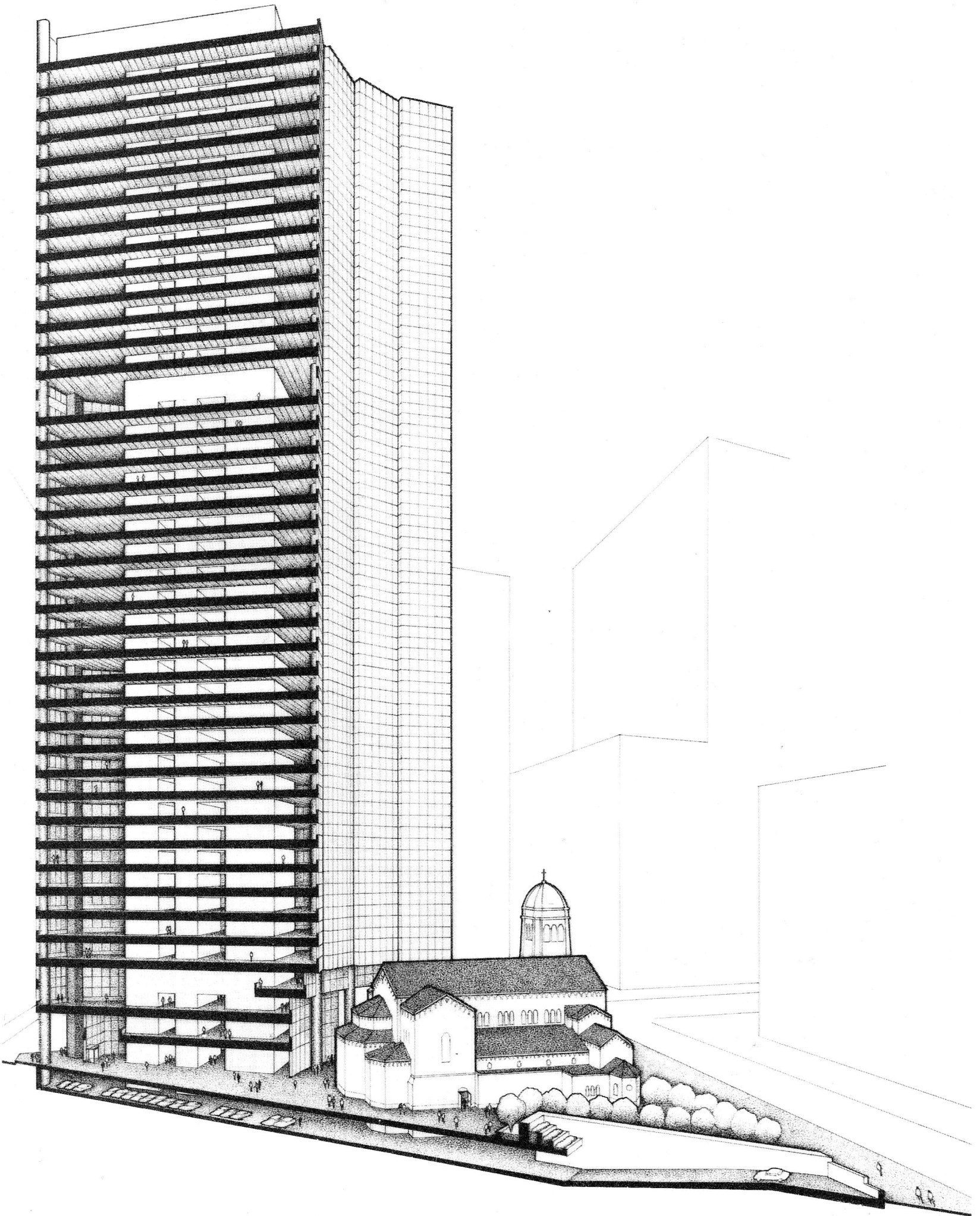

This page and opposite page, 1999 Broadway stands out sharply against the surrounding cityscape.

Opposite page and below, another two views of the skyscraper. Left, four plans of the building.

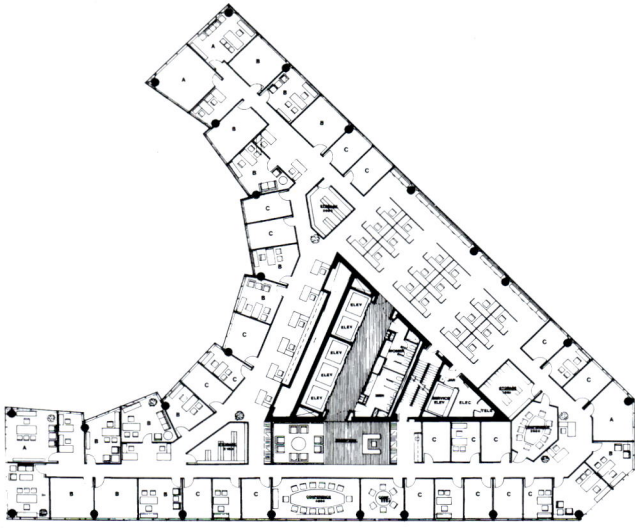

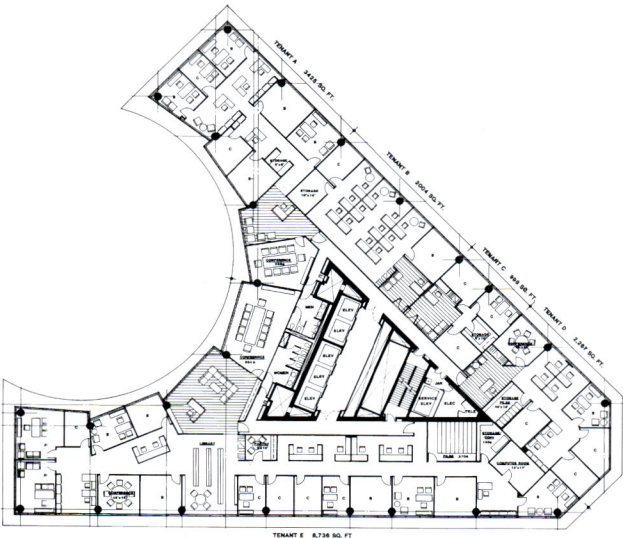

Two pictures of
the lobby interiors
of 1999 Broadway.

for Sale
572-3456
RREIT FUNDS

One DTC

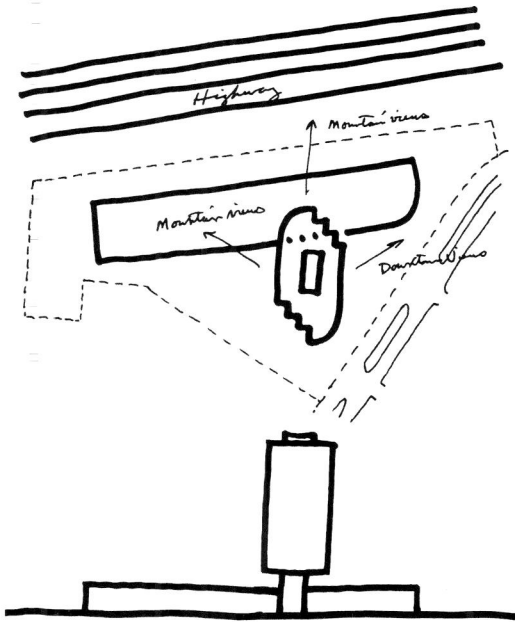

One DTC is a state-of-the-art "intelligent" office building located in the 900-acre Denver Technological Center overlooking the Rocky Mountains.

The architects were faced with the problem of designing a building and parking facilities on a small site adjacent to a noisy eight-lane highway, Interstate 25, while at the same time providing an open space for a park-like environment.

The rectangular site plan has quarter circle cutaways and serrated edges on two diagonally opposite sides, providing wide-angle views from eighty percent of the offices. The thirteen-storey building is elevated on 30 foot columns to create a grand entrance and port cochere under the elevated section and to link together the parking and building structures. The columns also open up the site and connect the plaza to the DTC pedestrian walkway system, allowing the building's mechanical systems to be economically located on the lower level of the parking garage, thereby maximising the amount of above grade rentable office space. One DTC's two entrances into a three-storey, glass-enclosed lobby are centered at street level beneath the cantilevered offices. There is also a four-level car park with space for 725 vehicles constructed around the office tower to provide tenants and visitors with a covered connection from the office building to their cars, and buffer noise from the nearby highway.

The high-rise office tower was erected using a standard slipform concrete core with a steel frame construction outside the core to bear gravity loads. An innovative curtain wall system allowed the use of high-quality polished and flame finished burgundy/grey Dakota mahogany granite, together with stainless steel and high-performance bronze reflective glass. Conventional thick slab granite with steel angles bolted onto a steel frame has been replaced by 22-mm granite, bonded with structural silicone to an aluminium frame, which is similar to, but even stronger than, ordinary glass curtain wall framing. All One DTC's major mechanical systems are computer controlled, including a digitally automated energy management system to monitor and correct temperature changes inside the building. The multi-tenant, shared telecommunications system is capable of providing voice, data and facsimile transmission, electronic and voice mailing, message centre services, and long-distance facilities. One DTC is notable for the way in which it incorporates materials and designs of timeless beauty and enduring quality in a "user-friendly" space. The orientation and elevation of the building, the layout of the parking facilities and their function as a noise buffer, the openness and sculptured beauty of the site and plaza, the grand yet personal scale of the lobby and the structure's harmonious symbiosis with the surrounding environment all combine to create a thoroughly efficient, yet totally humanized, business environment. Le Corbusier's piloti have been adapted to transform the "machine for living" into an American synthesis of the machine for working.

Bottom of page,
two standard plans
of the building.
Opposite, picture of a
facade showing its partly
curved and partly
staggered profile.

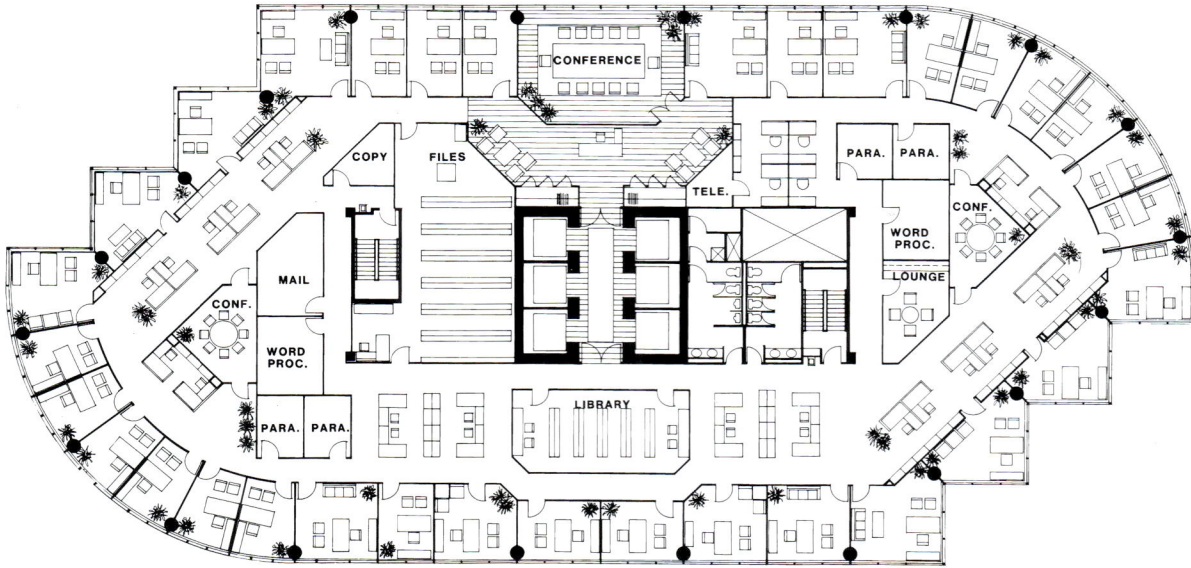

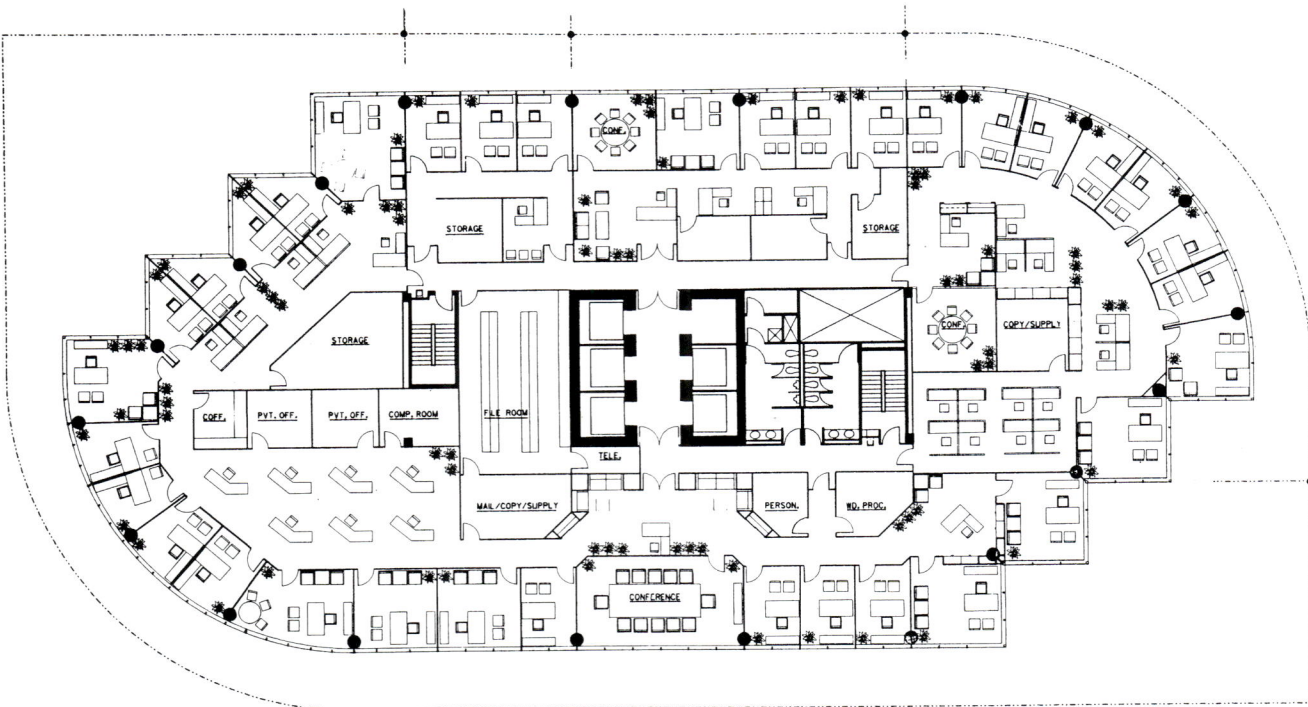

CONFERENCE

COPY FILES

PARA. PARA.

TELE.

CONF.

WORD
PROC.

MAIL

LOUNGE

CONF.

WORD
PROC.

PARA. PARA.

LIBRARY

CONF.

STORAGE

STORAGE

CONF.

COPY/SUPPLY

STORAGE

COFF. PVT. OFF. PVT. OFF. COMP. ROOM

FILE ROOM

TELE.

MAIL/COPY/SUPPLY

PERSON.

WD. PROC.

CONFERENCE

Planimetric view of the building and two views of its main facades.

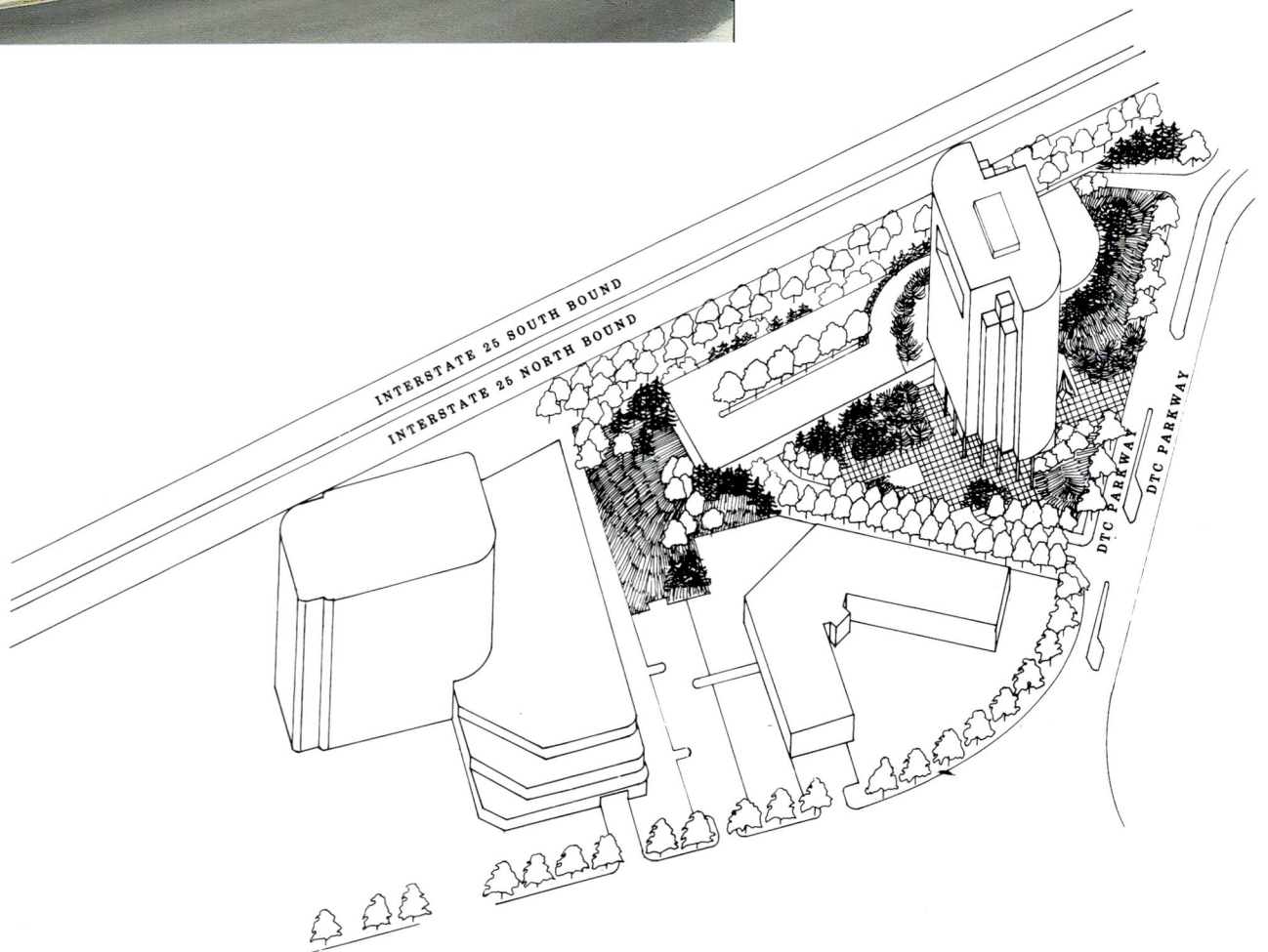

Despite its allusions
to XXth century
architecture, this
particular project
by Fentress highlights
some of the exciting
new developments
in contemporary
architecture.

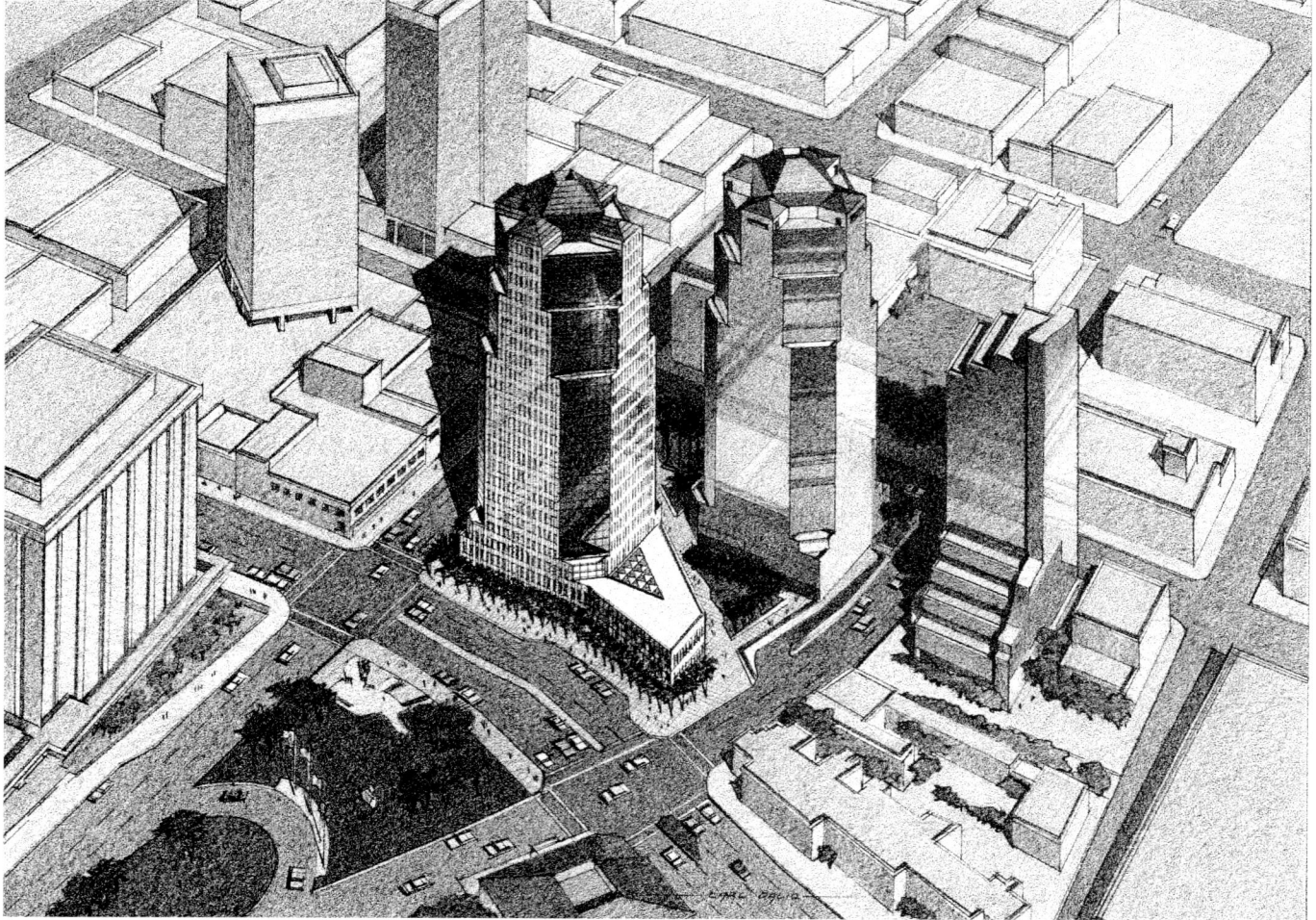

Norwest Tower

The 23-story Norwest Tower, the showpiece of downtown Tucson, is a majestic example of how a modern building should be integrated into its surroundings. It symbolically mirrors the neighbouring Spanish mission-style architecture with its tiered structure and domed top and also literally reflects the actual surrounding buildings in its mirrored walls. The irregularly-shaped tower is designed with two parallel lobbies, each leading into the bank. The lobbies' decorative scheme, full of contrast and vibrancy, is inspired by the blue night sky and orange desert sun characterising the local landscape. Stripes of deep red polished granite and light pink plain-cut granite conjure up the nuances of Tucson sand. A worldwide search was carried out to find just the right shade of pink granite and glass. The coated copper glass walls allude to the city's history as the copper mining capital of the United States. The lobbies' stucco ceilings are painted in the same slate blue colour as the sky.

Fentress has deliberately re-evoked as many clues as possible from the existing city and surrounding natural environment in the Tower's architectural structure. Its torso subtly echoes the bell towers of St.Augustine Cathedral and San Xavier del Bac, beginning as squares and gradually rotating by stages into octagons at the top. The multiple hipped roof is clearly based on the rooflines of Territorial and Victorian houses in nearby Armory Park and Barrio Libre.

Inside, the contextual allusions continue in the barrel-roofed public lobby that picks up the high, arched windows of the old Romanesque Valley National Bank building just across the road. The desert theme crops up again in the soft pink furniture and carpet on the ground floor, complemented by desert plants designed to form a miniature oasis. The high ceilings and abundance of windows create an open feeling.

Outside, a diagonal walkway bisecting the site connects the Tucson financial district to the downtown cultural centre. All the downtown walkways are paved in the same red brick, and covered pedestrian arcades formed by both the tower and palm trees create public spaces with their own seating facilities. The two plazas are landscaped with palm trees, soft earth berms and grass, and decorated with a central sculpture and bi-coloured flags hung in a regular pattern to enhance the sense of enclosure.

The Norwest Tower represented the first phase in a development programme for a site viewed as the gateway to downtown Tucson's financial, government legal and cultural district.

Planimetric view
of Norwest Tower and,
opposite page, a picture
of the finished building.

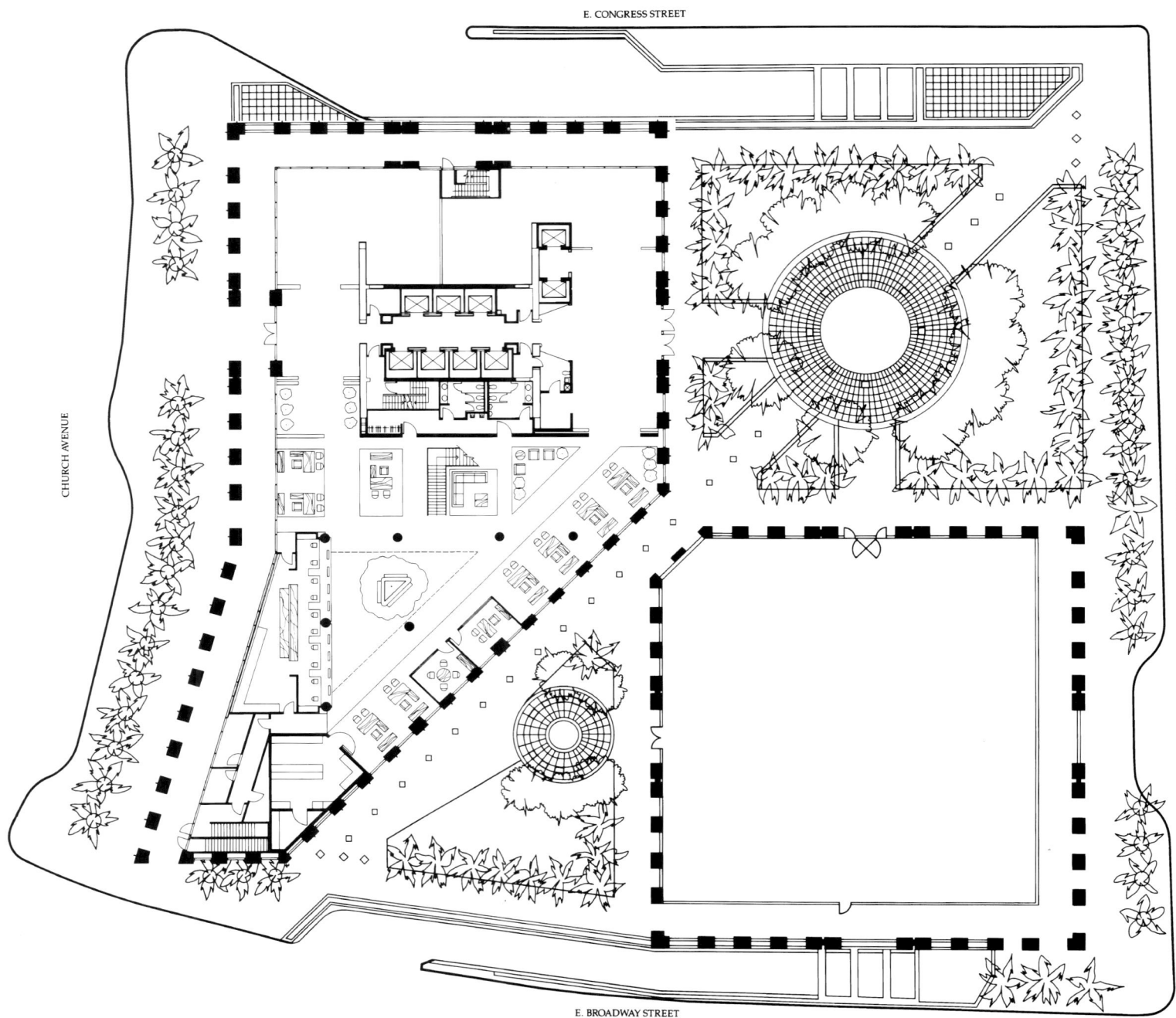

E. CONGRESS STREET

CHURCH AVENUE

STONE AVENUE

E. BROADWAY STREET

At this stage in his career Fentress's design experimentation took on much more intricate forms, as shown by the detail of the facade on the opposite page, the overall view of the building at the top of the page and, below, the site plan and volumetric layout.

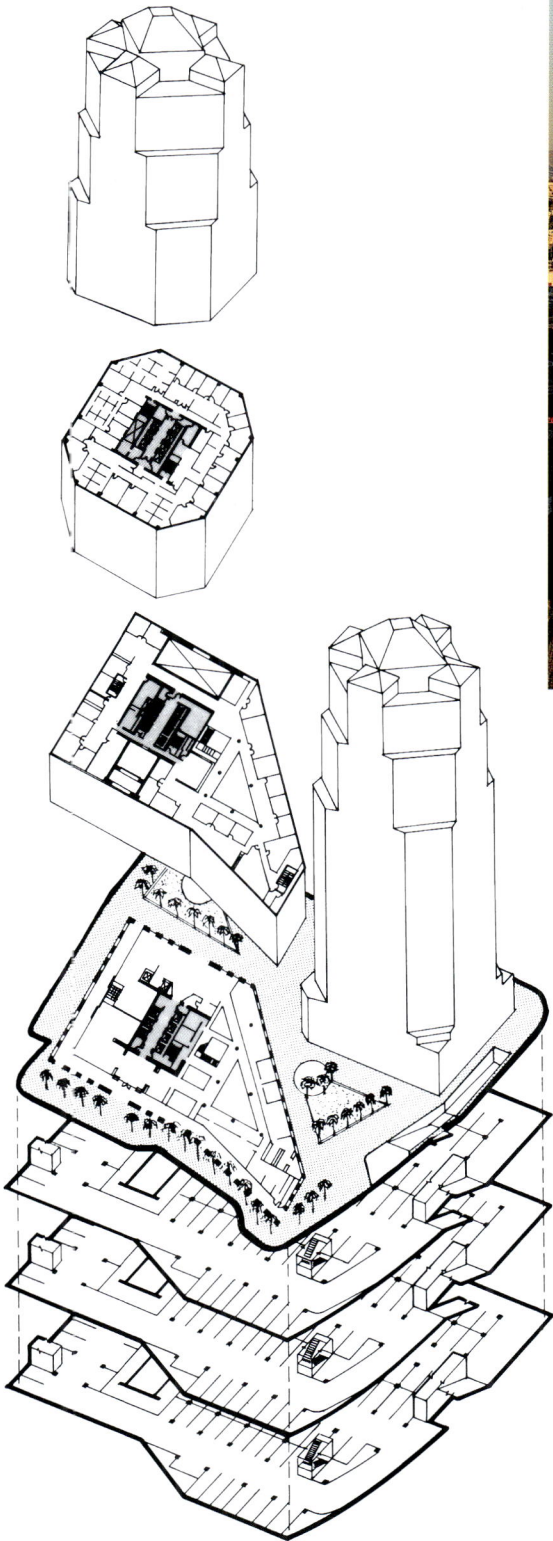

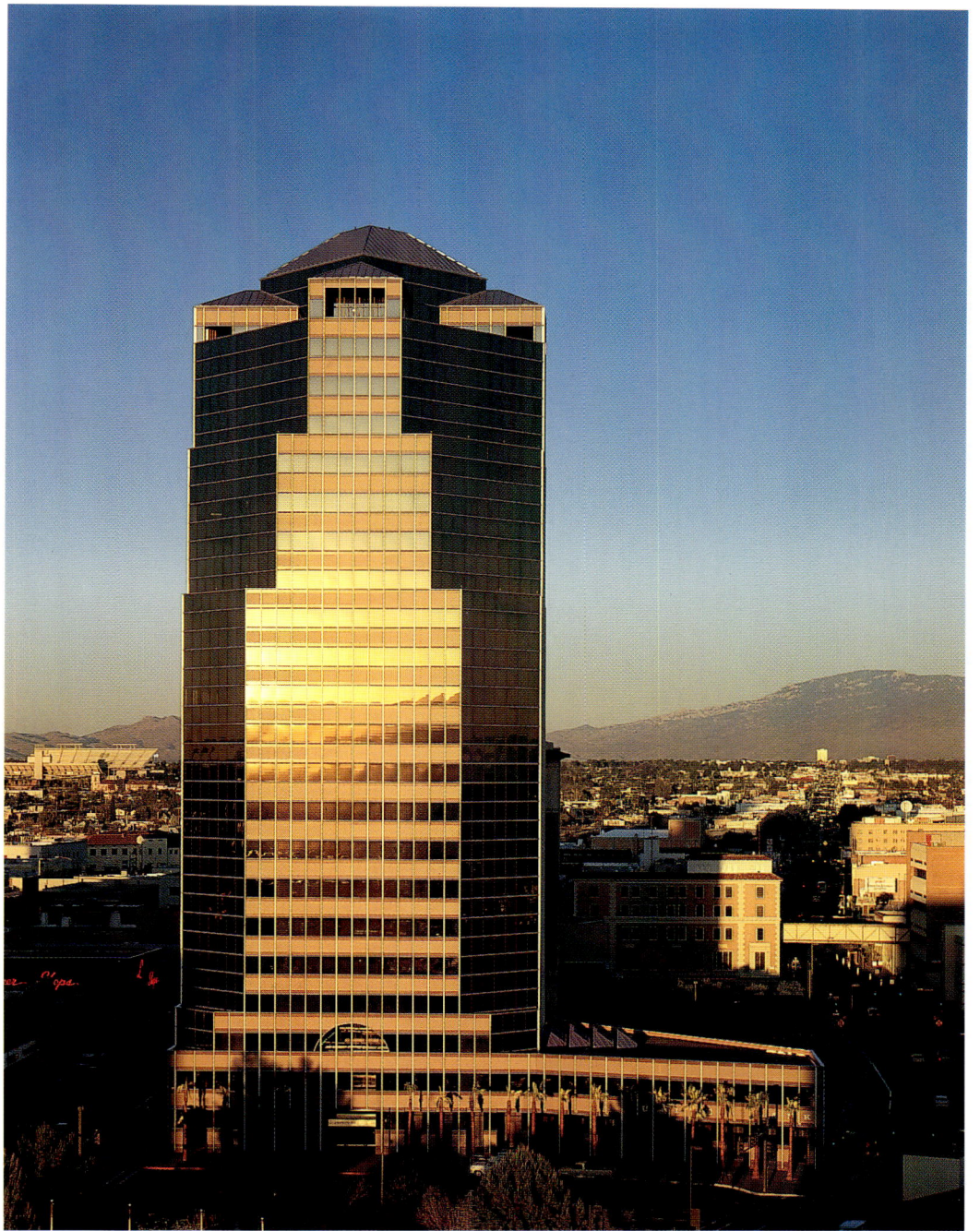

Two interior views of the building showing how its imposing forms are reflected in the spatial organisation and choice of materials/decorative features.

Oxbridge Towne Center

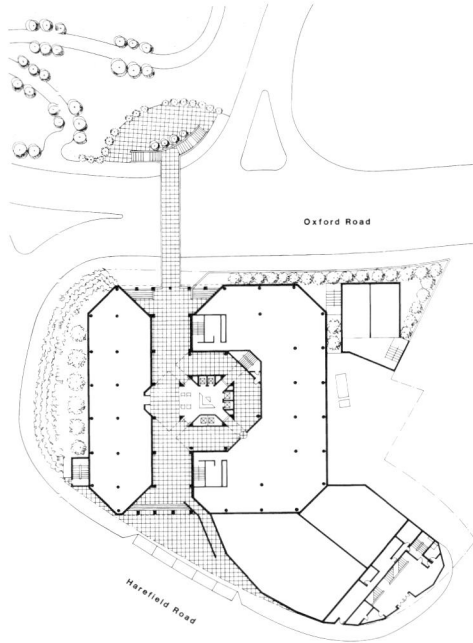

Following the example first set by Joseph Paxton's Crystal Palace, the design for the verdant-crystalline structure of what will eventually be Oxbridge Towne Center is intrinsically informed by the English garden belvedere. The Anglo-genesis of the belvedere garden springs from an Italianate idea. Having appropriated this distinctly Latin form, it was implanted into romantically landscaped English gardens. British landscaping over the past two centuries is renowned for its element of surprise.

Its primary features have traditionally been meandering pathways suddenly and unexpectedly opening up onto unusual architectural or scenographic contexts. Oxbridge, a town on the Ring Road just outside London, has a serendipitous urban plan which, in itself, provides these multiple meandering pathways. The metal-gridded and granite-based Towne Center creates a distinctive landmark, clearly visible and identifiable from the local motorway. Passing motorists cannot fail to notice the symbolic clock tower rising above the surrounding roofs. The site plan contains physical and psychological design elements that transcend the all-too-common office block.

The outside "garden" spaces are gradually incorporated in the inside office spaces creating a nine-storey synthesis of interior and exterior, rarely seen in office buildings in either Europe or America. A public pathway through the lobby/atrium connects the building to a nearby park, and four circulation bridges link the core of the complex to tenant space on each floor. A heavy stone base was used to create a horizontal bond with other facilities available on the site: a cinema, squash club and car park.

This skilful fusion of garden pathway and architectural landmark, interior space and external surroundings, neatly captures the historical flavour of an important English landscape concept in a sort of physical embodiment of that intangible experience of what it means to be English.

Oxford Road

Harefield Road

The center has
an extremely unusual
design conformation
for an office block.

Oxbridge Towne Center
is designed to provide
a powerful landmark
on the surrounding
cityscape.

Jefferson County Human Services Building

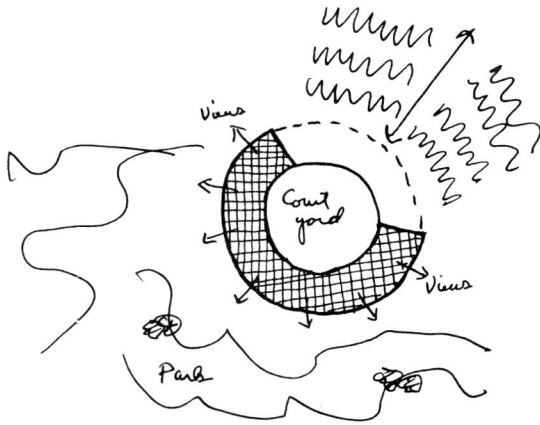

A lengthy analysis of facilities and population requirements in Jefferson County revealed a desperate need for new county programmes and services. Although efficiency was still an important factor in the design of the Jefferson County Human Services Building, the architects chose to focus on the building's psychological impact on its potential clients: troubled individuals who are likely to be intimidated by the impersonal architectural designs of government structures. The building is part of a 193-acre county government complex, whose master plan ties together human services, judicial services, county administration and law enforcement in a green-belt parkway. The building has been given an added, more human dimension by its welcoming, semi-circular shape clad in brick. The three/four-story structure fans out around a colonnaded plaza forming a landscaped courtyard that acts as a transition space between the building, parking area and surrounding countryside. The plaza is designed like a semi-formal, gardenesque sculptural court, providing a series of personal spaces and individual views of sculptural elements. The building sweeps upwards from a single-story pedestrian level to a two-story skylit atrium corridor, culminating in a curved, stepped backdrop of non-public offices. The architects opted for a custom gold-buckskin brick along the building's exterior and interior atrium corridor to reiterate the golden wheat, burnt sage and dramatic mineral-soil colourations found in the area. The brickwork wraps like a flush skin over the building's entire form. Tile-like insets of square granite punctuate its collonade and upper tier. Horizontal bands of dark maroon granite are similarly set between courses of rowlock to create a simple, eye-catching pattern that makes the entire structure "more accessible, more approachable," to quote Fentress. The building's structural skeleton is made of A572, Grade 50, rolled, high-strength steel sections, with lateral resistance provided by a combination of X-braced frames and core walls. Composite steel and concrete floors - lightweight concrete topping and steel decking over steel beams and girders - provide the necessary diaphragm action against lateral forces. The roof deck system is similarly constructed, except for the absence of concrete topping and the use of open web joists in place of beams. The circular building structure is designed in three segments, with two expansion joints placed between each segment to cope with both lateral and vertical soil movement and thermal expansion. A single column with slip joint haunches was specially devised to replace more conventional double columns. The building's colours and textures blend in perfectly with the Colorado landscape, reflecting great architectural sensitivity and careful attention to factors such as exposure, solar orientation and locational repercussions on parking, traffic patterns, site topography and drainage. The Jefferson County Human Services Building epitomises the firm's ideal of creating visual/physical communication links with the surrounding environment through an exceptional design, superb visual aesthetics and high-quality materials and workmanship.

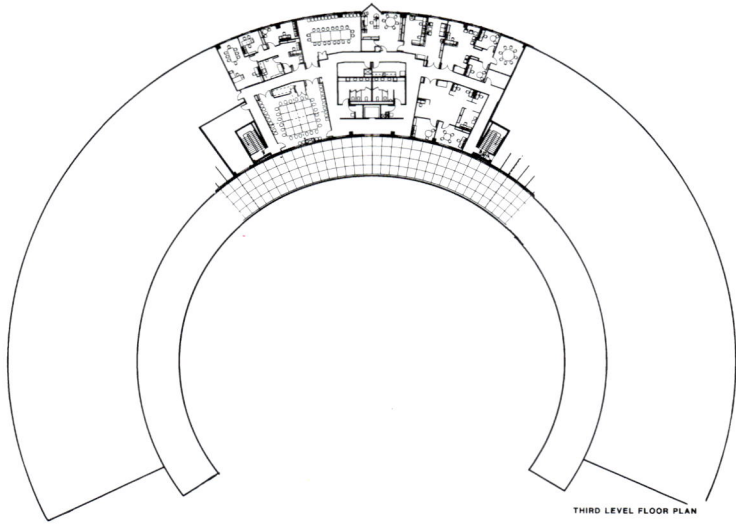

THIRD LEVEL FLOOR PLAN

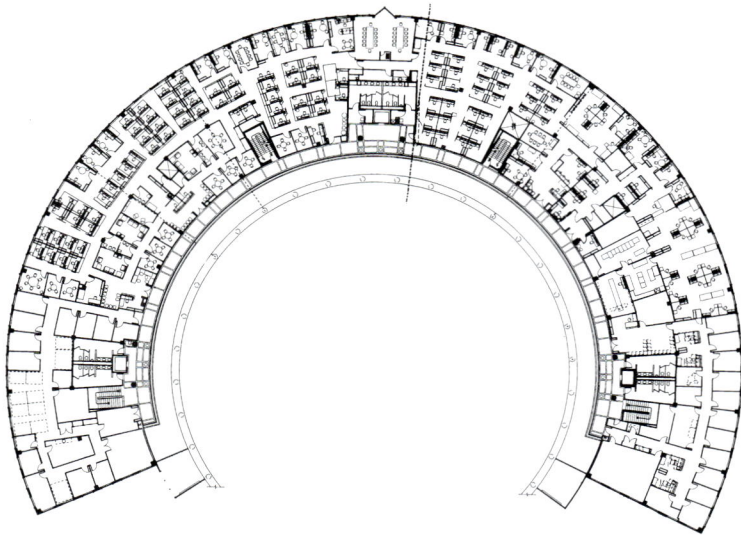

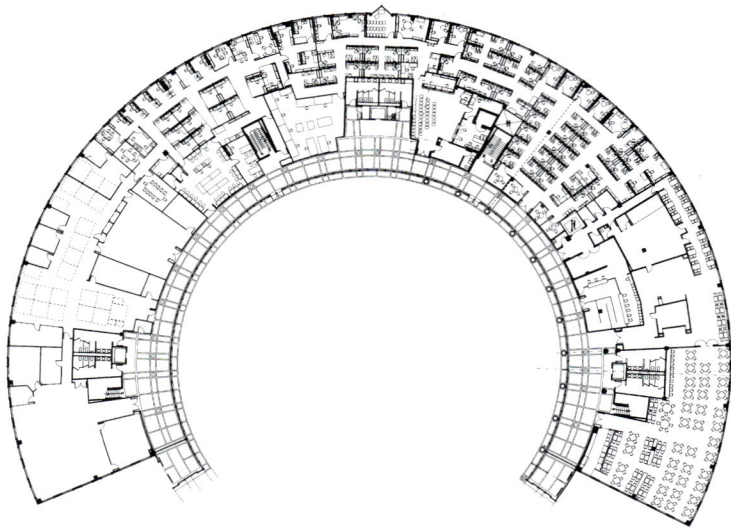

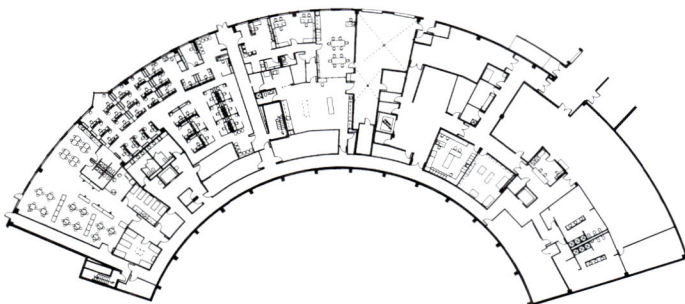

90

Opposite page,
four plans of the various
building levels.
Below, an overall view
of the building
immersed in the
surrounding landscape.

The circular design
creates a definite sense
of equality
and welcome.
Opposite page, detail
of the entrance.

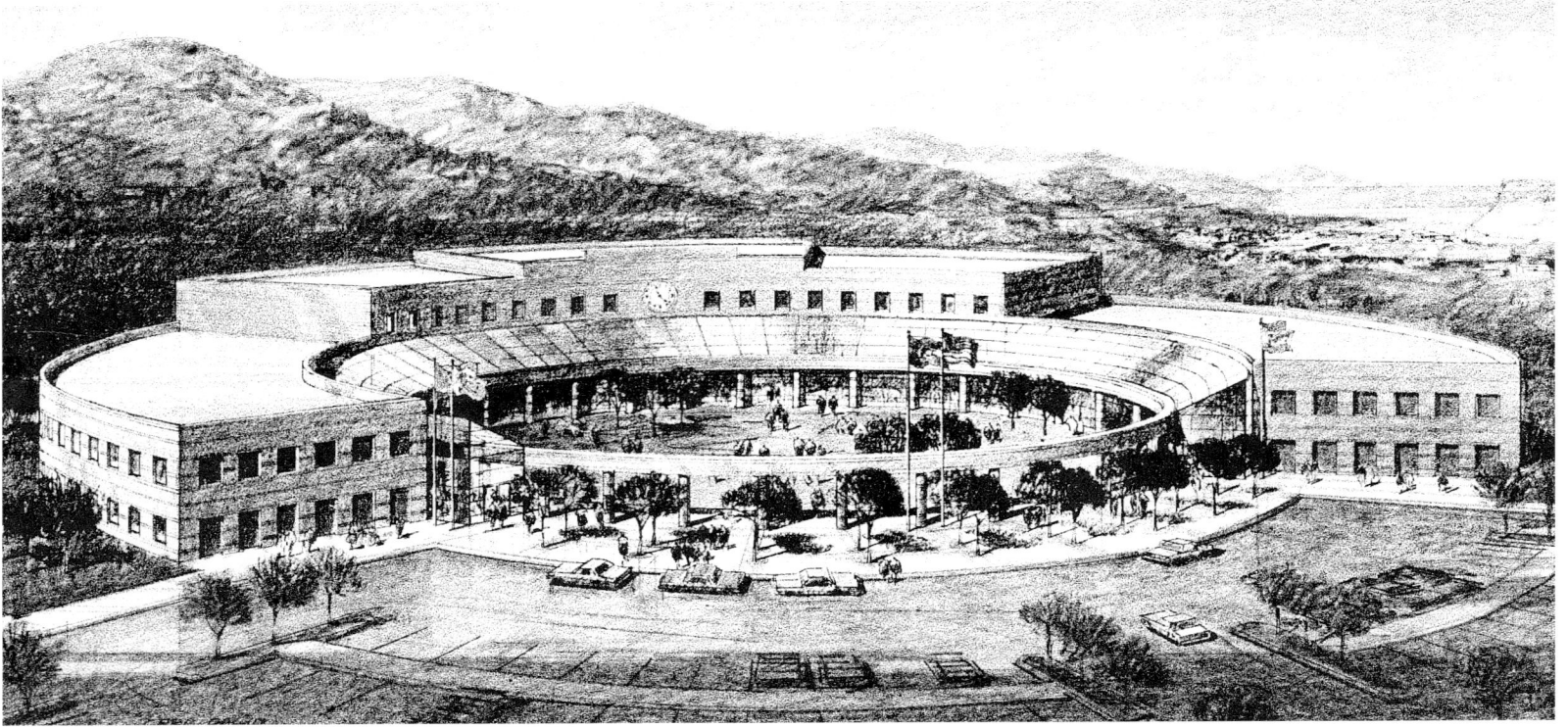

This and opposite page, two partial views of the large glazed interior corridor.

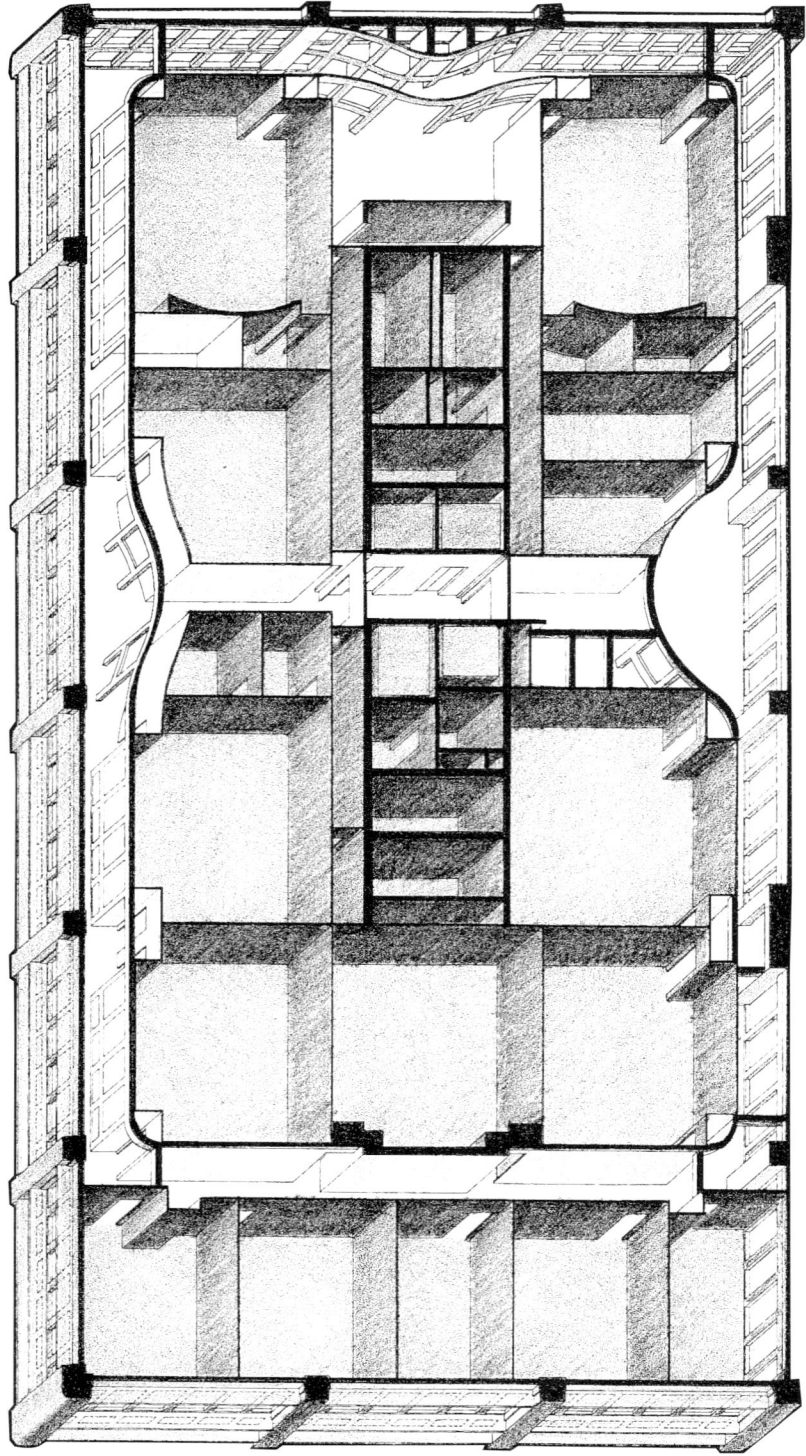

IBM Customer Services Center

The IBM Customer Services Center required a spatially functional interior office design sensitive to the client's image. The main functional requirements were ease of movement for large groups of people, clearly marked entries, durable materials, ease of maintenance, high-tech presentation rooms and darkened interior rooms for audio-visual presentations. The building's image had to express the stability, innovation, organisation and success of the IBM company in a high-tech environment.

The Denver IBM Customer Service Center and support functions occupy approximately 60,000 square feet over four floors. A perimeter corridor system, formed by a grid of deep window wells, was specially designed to create darkened presentation rooms. A wooden grid was fitted to the opposite wall of the corridor, using beams to tie the two together and define the entry areas to the various rooms.

At certain major intersections, the wood grid separates into an open drywall grid designed to define and open up the reception, waiting and break-out areas. The grid also deepens at columns to provide special niches for displaying products. The real focal point of the project is the third floor marketing facility open to the public for seminars and demonstrations of IBM products. There are two executive audio-visual presentation rooms and four environmental rooms equipped with audio-visual facilities for simulating various work situations.

The first and fourth floors share the same architectural detailing, materials and colours. The first floor is used primarily for large classroom presentations and houses a 10,000 — square-foot computer room. The fourth floor is occupied by the marketing support staff and also contains a cafeteria, vending service and guided learning center fitted with IBM equipment. Curvilinear furniture is provocatively juxtaposed against the grid layout, while the white and grey background color scheme is designed to physically embody IBM's corporate image. The seats in the demonstration rooms and reception, waiting and break-out areas, designed for personal interaction, are black, red and blue. The key to interpreting the overall interior design is the need to restrict the amount of natural light penetrating into the presentation rooms, which are located in the interior of the office allowing circulation to be organised along the exterior walls. Visitors can enjoy the natural light and views of the outside while following an interesting circulation of space.

The interior design is an inward extension of the building's exterior facade, carefully exploiting color to mirror the client's conservative, high-tech, sophisticated image.

Undulating vertical grids are freely incorporated to construct exhibition areas for new product displays.

The interior walls play off the curves and beams of the exterior grid to create a playful, yet sophisticated, notion of space that reflects the building's architecture and projects a unique business image.

A plan and interior view
of the IBM Customer
Services Center.
Work flow schemes
are crucial factors in
determining the design
of Fentress's
architectural projects.

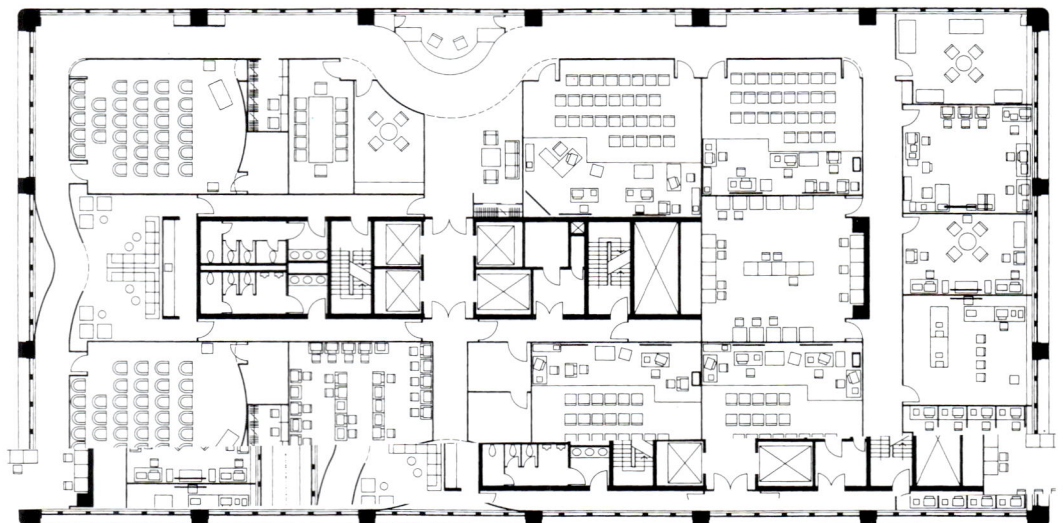

Another plan and view
of the Center's waiting
room.

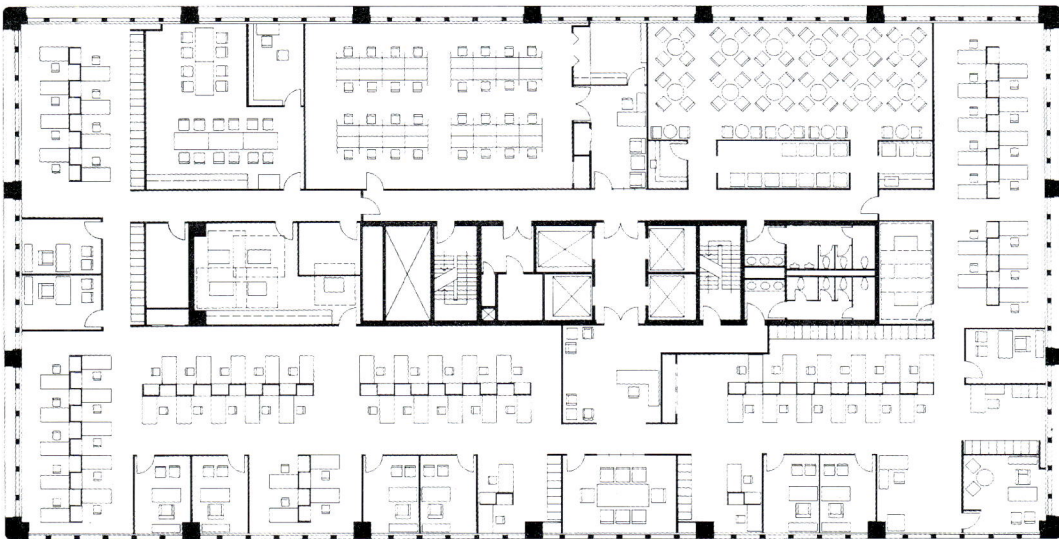

The curved central section of the building softens the geometrical precision of the spatial arrangement of interior space.

Every single detail
of Fentress's design work
is completed with great
attention and care.

Despite the highly
rigorous rationalization
of the Center's interior
spaces, all the rooms
are spacious and
comfortable.

Colorado Convention Center

The Colorado Convention Center is designed to provide a futuristic landmark for the convention, exhibition and meeting industry in the United States at a time of great economic development and opportunity.

City leaders appealed to the Urban Land Institute (ULI), one of the nation's most highly respected and widely quoted sources of information on urban planning, growth and expansion, for help in resolving the controversy and political wrangling that was hampering the design and construction of a convention center for Denver and the State of Colorado.

In a unanimous decision, the ULI committee selected Fentress Bradburn's "festive, friendly and exciting" project designed to establish a new positive image for the city.

The Colorado Convention Center comprises over one million square feet of structure, including 860,000 square feet of enclosed heated-ventilated space. Despite its lack of windows, the building has an open, airy, inviting environment in harmony with its surroundings. After extensive user group research, the massive volumes of space were organised into two public levels and four activity zones: 65,000 square feet of registration space; 100,000 square feet of meeting space; 300,000 square feet of exhibition space and a loading dock with twenty-seven bays.

Escalators, elevators and open stairways provide access to the second-floor exhibition hall which is split into three 100,000-square-foot halls and designed to support 350 pounds per square foot of live load.

Three sides of the building contain main entrances, while the fourth is camouflaged behind a park-garden.

The facade of the exhibition hall is clad in granite aggregate spandrels, creating a strong horizontal backdrop for all three main entrances. The contrasting vertical and horizontal elements breathe life into the building, whose mass is raised up by wing-like facades enclosing mechanical penthouses. The angle of the penthouses focuses attention. The relationship between the building's forms and geometry establishes a unifying theme throughout the interior.

Each design building side or edge has been designed to contextually fit into its surrounding landscape. For instance, as visitors approach from the east, they are welcomed into the building by concave shapes symbolising outstretched arms. On the other hand, the western entrance is curved in the opposite direction to guide visitors towards a magnificent panorama of the Rocky Mountains. The southern facade is decorated with an upwardly exploding structure of white columns, symbolic of the snowcapped peaks of the Rockies as they rise above the horizontal plains. This high-tech design provides a functional yet dramatic stage for convention activities in perfect harmony with the facility's exterior. The modern, contemporary materials and colours of the strong horizontal bands on the interior walls mirror those on the exterior, providing an atmosphere of excitement and festivity. Simple but bold geometric forms are a fitting backdrop for convention activities, providing stability for the entire complex. The building's style does not really fit any historical architectural category, such as modern, post-modern or even deco. It is a building of the twenty-first century, boldly projecting Colorado towards the future in the form of a unique and easily identifiable landmark. Its simple, honest and distinctive vision of the future provides the City of Denver with a positive new image.

Below, site plan of
the architectural project.
Opposite page
and previous page,
two exterior views of
the building entrys.

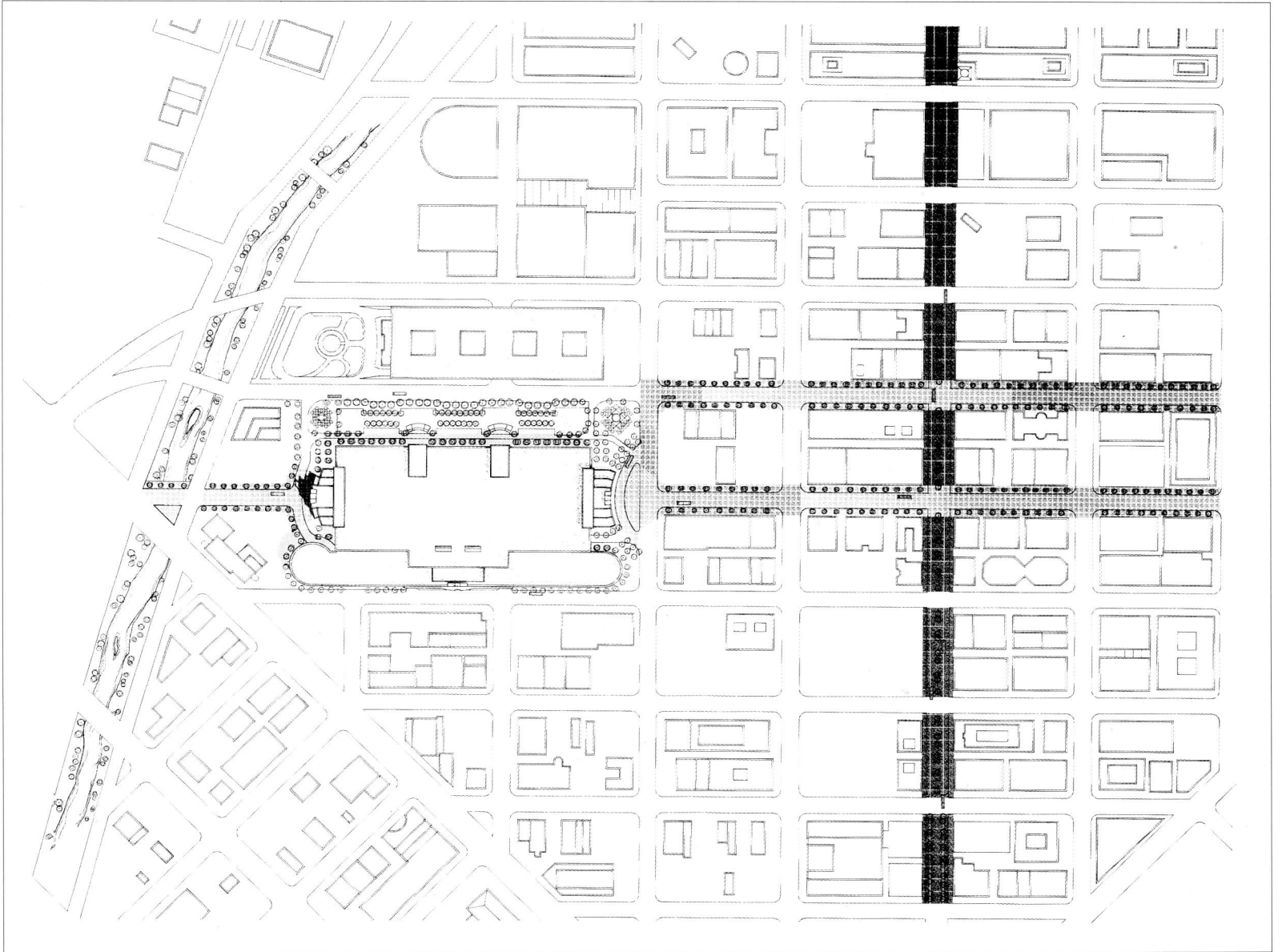

Plans of ground floor
and exhibit hall levels
of the building.

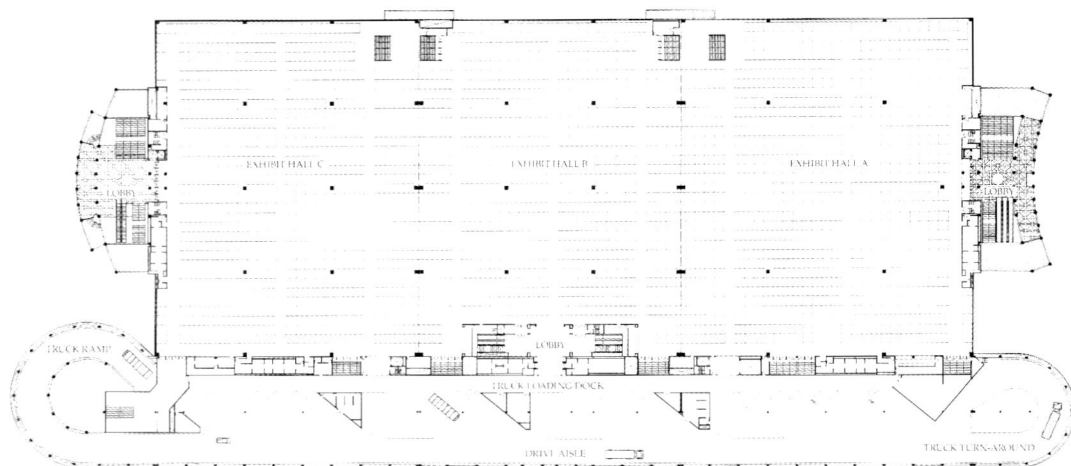

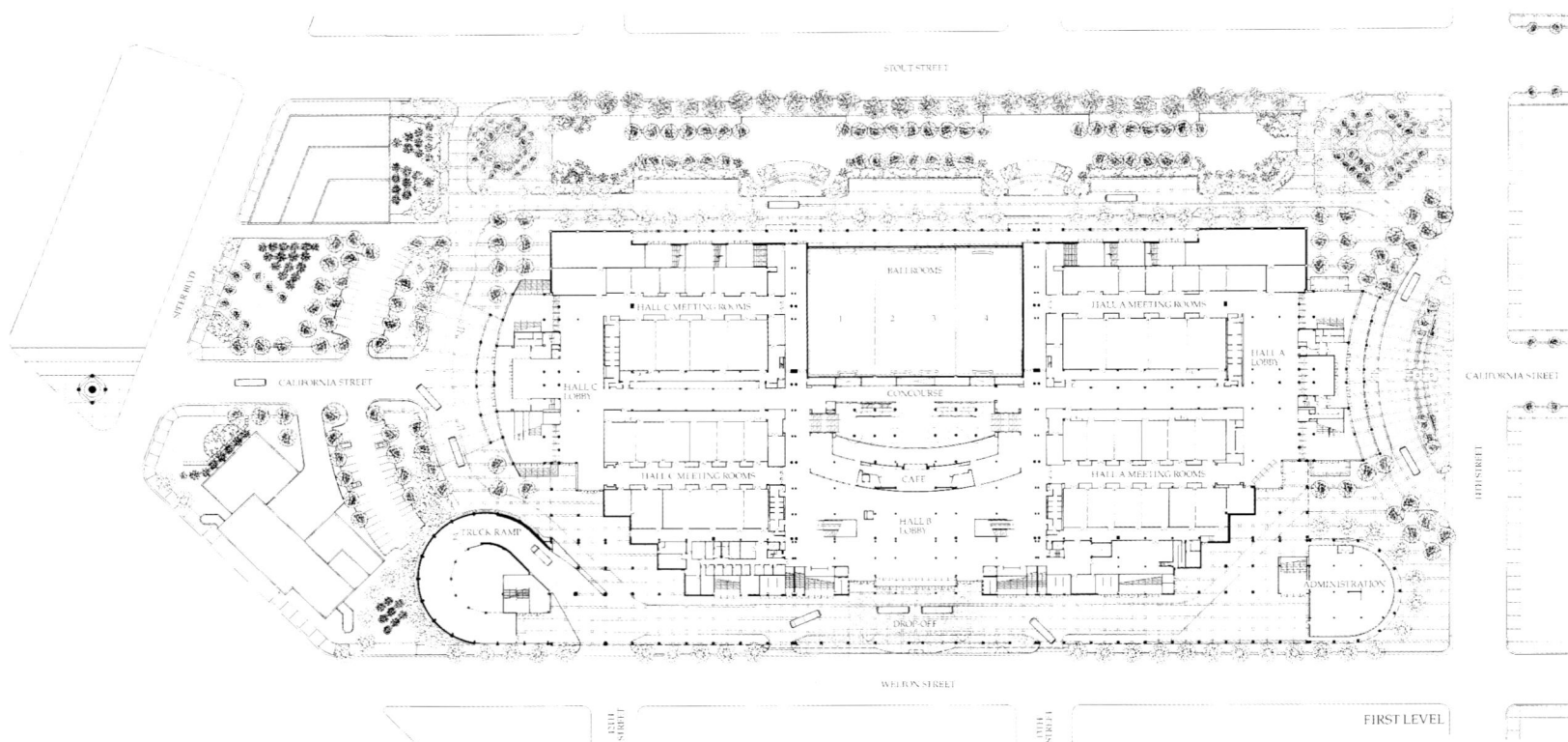

EXHIBIT HALL C   EXHIBIT HALL B   EXHIBIT HALL A

LOBBY   LOBBY

TRUCK RAMP

LOBBY

TRUCK LOADING DOCK

DRIVE AISLE   TRUCK TURN-AROUND

STOUT STREET

BALLROOMS

HALL C MEETING ROOMS   1   2   3   4   HALL A MEETING ROOMS

HALL A
LOBBY

SPEER BLVD

CALIFORNIA STREET   HALL C
LOBBY   CONCOURSE   CALIFORNIA STREET

HALL C MEETING ROOMS   CAFE   HALL A MEETING ROOMS

TRUCK RAMP   HALL B
LOBBY

ADMINISTRATION

DROP-OFF

WELTON STREET

FIRST LEVEL

The Center's interior
space mirrors
the building's intricate
architecture: a recurring
column pattern
and quadrangular
structural layout
reflected in the floors.

The building's public
function is reiterated in
the sober monumental
forms of its interiors.

Ballroom Two

Two details of the
lighting system inside
the Center.

Another picture
of the building interiors
showing the lighting
system in detail.

The decorative features
of the interiors mirror
the stylistic patterns of
the overall architectural
design.

Each detail of the
interior structure has
been carefully designed
to create a harmonious
stylistic whole.

Ronstadt Transit Center

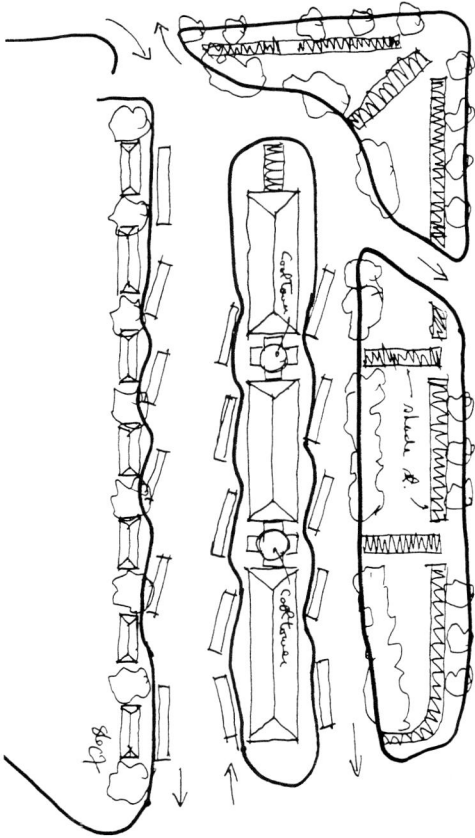

The great train stations of the late nineteenth and early twentieth century provide the inspiration behind this intriguing project that transforms the mundane business of travelling from A to B into a stage for social activity. The Ronstadt Transit Center, built on a two-block site in an historic arts district of Tucson, is the hub of the local bus system, capable of handling a full capacity hourly service. As incoming buses fill the eighteen available births, passengers can change buses or just simply embark or disembark. The 2.7-acre site blends into its downtown surroundings through an arbour structure that wraps around two sides of the bus depot. The arbour walls, fitted with seats where passengers can rest in comfort, and entrance archways are made of recycled turn-of-the-century brick salvaged from old buildings. Local artists crafted over 20,000 hand-hewn ceramic tiles to line the arbour's interior columns and beams, simultaneously capturing Tucson's "sense of place". Inside, the center is equipped with a variety of shelters, shade facilities and landscaping to ensure travellers can relax in peace and quiet. Other amenities such as restrooms, vending machines and an information kiosk are all conveniently housed inside the three central platform shelters.

With summer temperatures soaring as high as 110 degrees Fahrenheit, the architects had to devise special shade and cooling structures. The most unusual cooling devices are the two 50-foot cooling towers designed at the University of Arizona's Environmental Research Laboratory. The towers use a low-energy, natural cooling system to lower temperatures by as much as fifteen degrees Fahrenheit in a 20-foot radius. This innovative design is based on the kind of old-fashioned wind towers that were first used centuries ago throughout the Middle East. The center has as few paintable surfaces as possible to discourage vandalism. Similarly, the broad open views and brightly illuminated clearings provide no dark recesses, high walls or bushy landscaping in which to hide. The steel-wire benches and seating facilities are designed to ward off vagabonds and look about as inviting as a bed of nails, although this is actually misleading because they are surprisingly comfortable when sitting in an upright position.

The sensitive use of scale and local materials have allowed this ingeniously designed urban transit center to be smoothly incorporated in the local community and symbolically transformed into a multi-purpose park and arts facility, accommodating a whole range of events like the twice-monthly "Downtown Saturday Night Show." As an urban center of one of the nation's least romantic transport systems, the Ronstadt Transit Center could easily have been one of the dreariest and most forlorn landmarks in downtown Tucson. Instead, it has developed into one of the few likable, humanly scaled, user-friendly projects of its kind, perfectly blended into the surrounding cityscape.

This page, plan and
overall view of the plaza,
which can host up to
eighteen buses.
Opposite page, detail
of the top of one of the
two cooling towers,
which dominate the
Center.

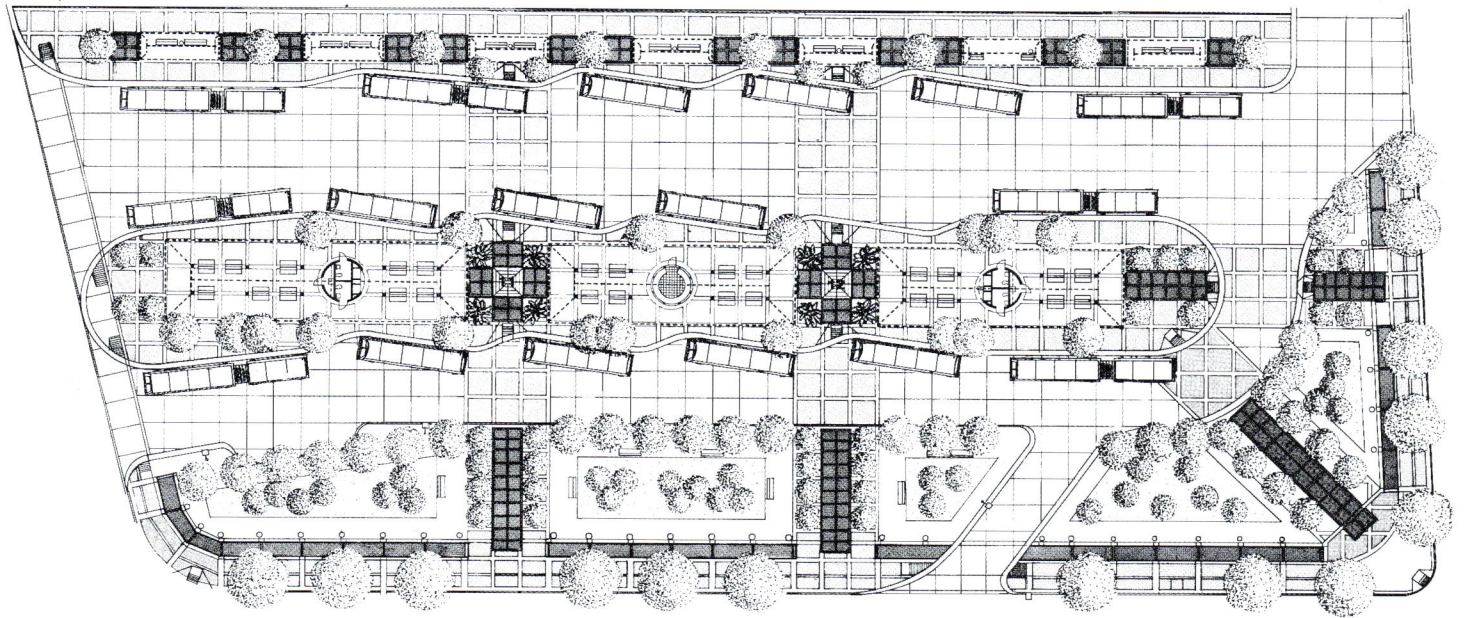

This page, a detail
of the decorative walls.
Opposite page and
previous two pages,
two views of the building
and its characteristic
setting epitomising the
site's cultural heritage.

National Oceanic and Atmospheric Administration

The General Service Administration Federal Building in Boulder, Colorado, is carefully designed to meet the specific needs of various divisions in the National Oceanic and Atmospheric Administration. The NOAA contains space environment laboratories, wave propagation laboratories, forecast systems laboratories, aeronomy laboratories, climate monitoring and diagnostic laboratories, and a national weather service facility.

The building had to meet a range of unique user requirements while interacting with the surrounding community and minimising impact on neighbourhoods to the south and east of the city of Boulder.

The facility is located on the eastern toe of a mesa extending from the base of a distinctive rock formation called the Flatirons. The nineteen-acre zone, inside a 217-acre federal campus, offers exceptional views of the Flatirons to the west and the city of Boulder and its surrounding plains to the east. A series of concept site plans, blocking and stacking studies, and three-dimensional building form studies were carried out to assess site access options, programme requirements, potential for future development, building form and character, and symbiosis with surrounding neighbourhoods.

A campus scheme, interior street scheme, stepped linear scheme and broken line scheme were each analysed in terms of building efficiency, site development, programme compatibility and building aesthetics. These preliminary schemes gradually evolved into one single, highly flexible, functional space.

The building was eventually located above Anderson Stream, that crosses the site from north to south, creating a natural foreground for an environmentally sensitive community image. The building's ultimate site orientation and location also catered for significant prevailing, downslope winds, which are often quite severe at certain times of the year.

The building's laboratories and ADP spaces are located internally with office spaces around the perimeter. Core areas allow modular distribution of building services and vertical stacking of mechanical-electrical systems. The core elements provide buffer spaces where temperature control is less critical than in-office, laboratory and ADP spaces.

The design also incorporates a major public space at the entry to the four level linear structure. This space acts as an internal lobby area, encouraging interaction between scientists and the general public. It may also be used as a public exhibition area for information displays, special events and other functions sponsored by the NOAA.

Planning work had to focus on special structural design requirements, such as above-average floor loads in laboratories, vibration sensitivity and environmental control specifications.

The building, which is stepped at the north and south ends, casts a silhouette of the surrounding mountains against the western sky. Building elevations are carefully gauged to create a pattern of punched openings with a sculptural wall interpreted in native flagstone and precast. These materials were chosen for their environmental suitability and compatibility with the building's fractured, sculptural form. The complex's faceted structure and the angularity of stone create a provocative interplay of light and shadow. These rhythms and repetitions of shadow and shade react to sunlight and clouds to set up a harmonious duet between the building and its surrounding landscape. Building entrances echo their agricultural setting with the front plaza paving reflecting the dual concept of geology and the erosive action of water.

The final building design is a stunningly unified architectural landmark, on a compatible scale with the adjacent research park and residential areas, that stands in the shadow, both literally and metaphorically, of I.M. Pei's NCAR on the hill above.

Overall view of the complex.

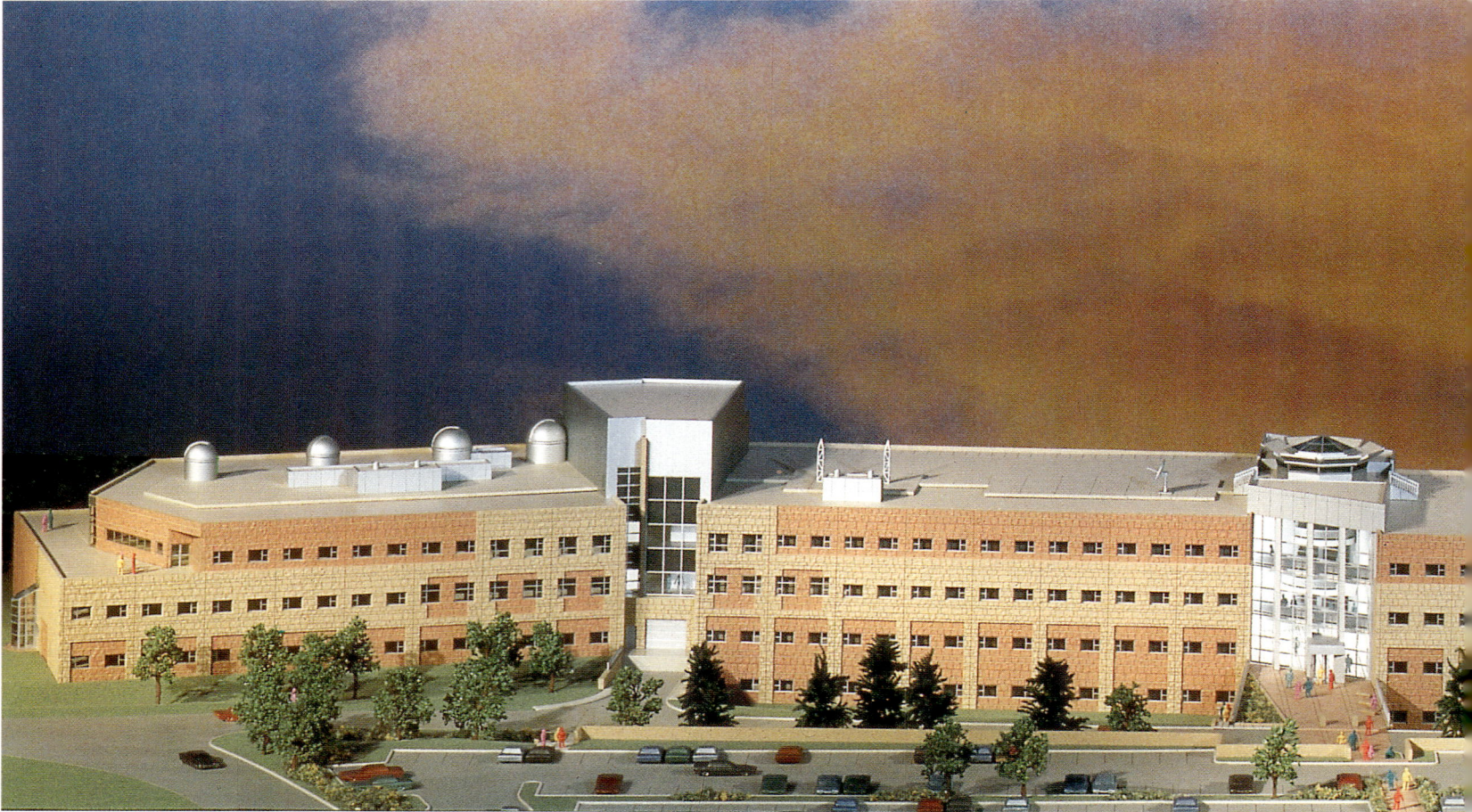

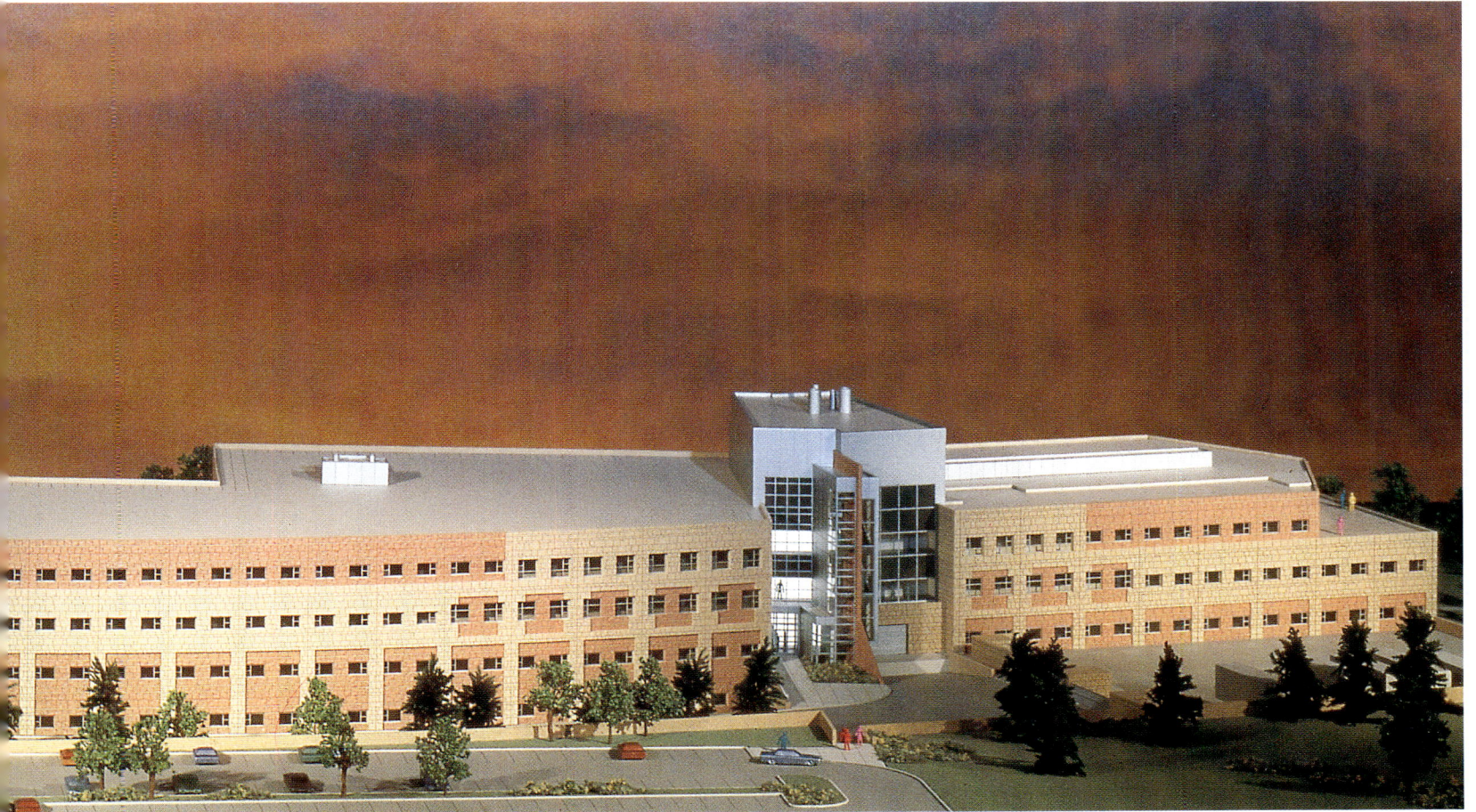

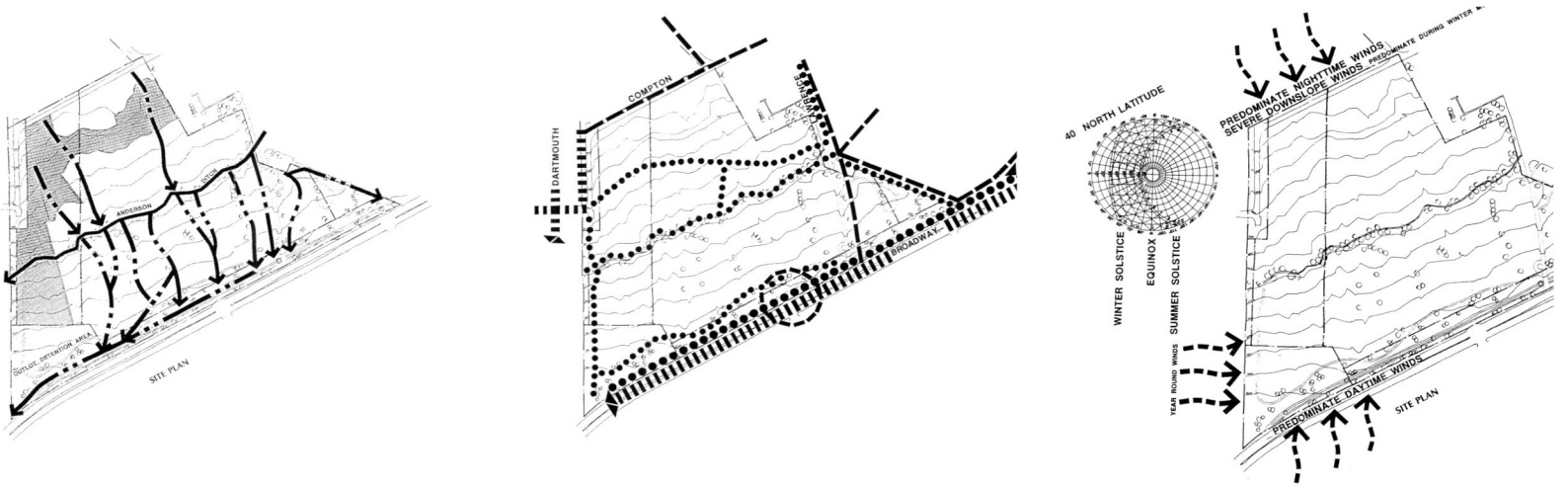

Master site plan and,
above, studies for the
site analysis.

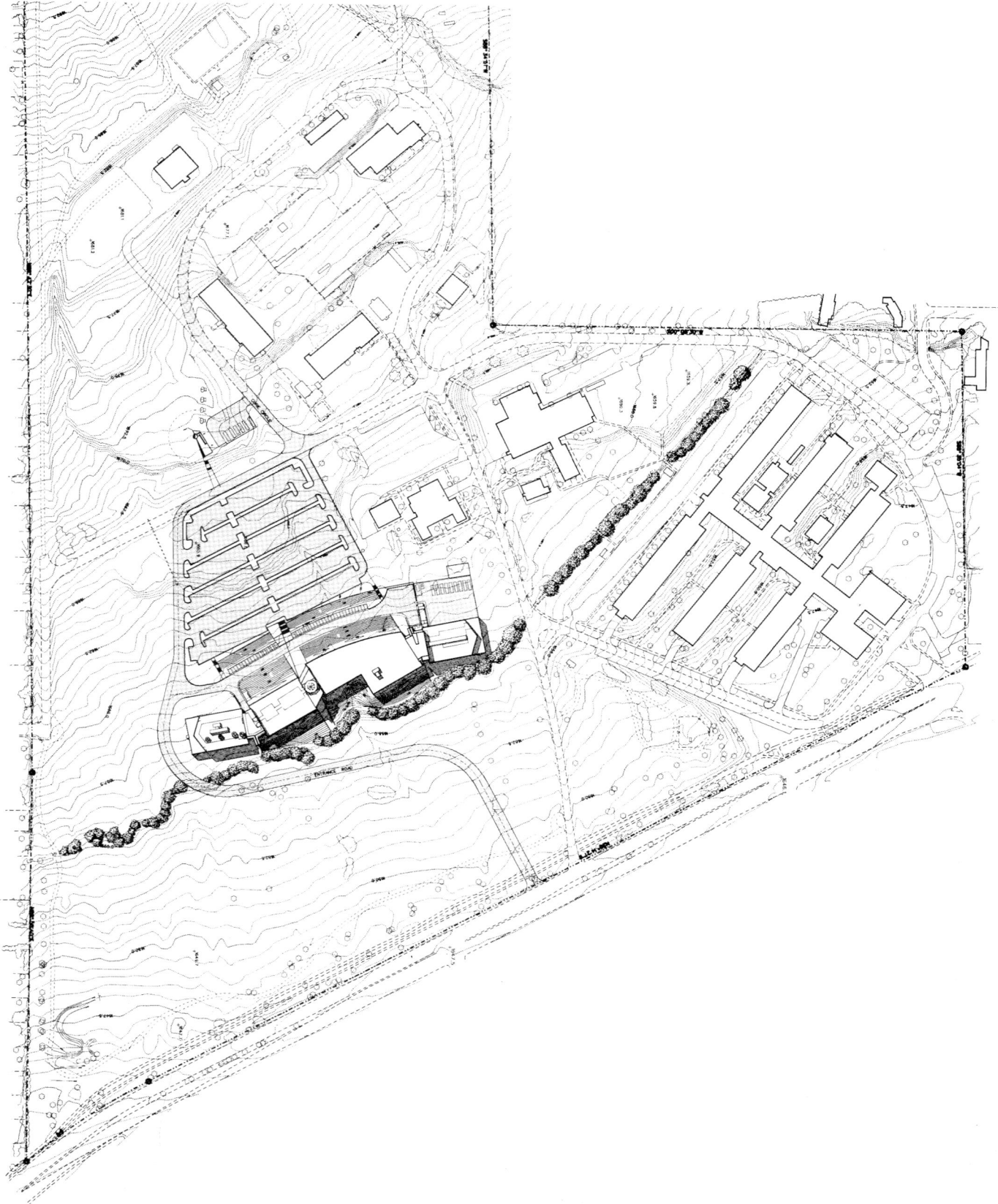

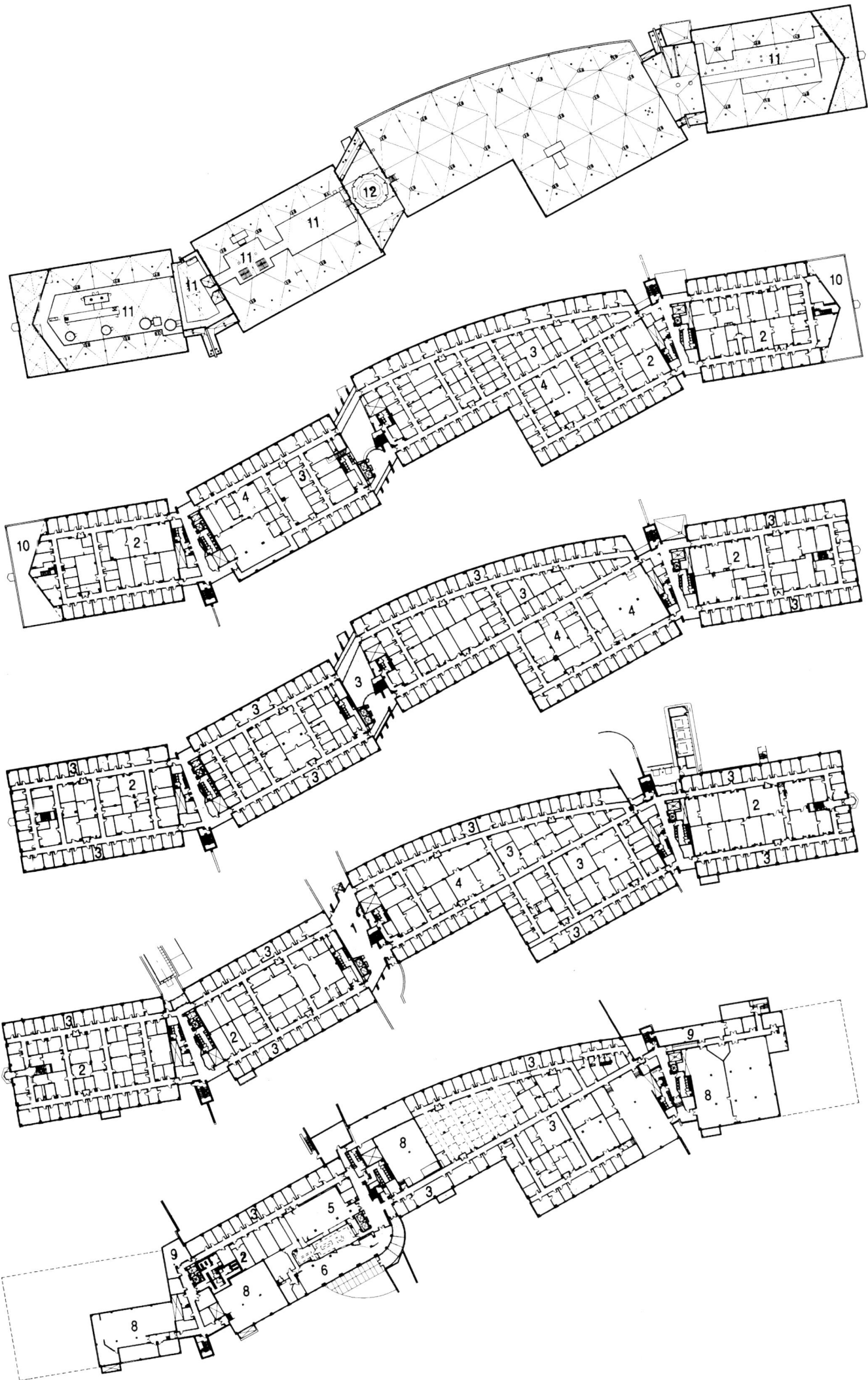

Plans of the various levels of the building.

1. Entrance gallery
2. Labs
3. Offices
4. Computer center
5. Presentation/Training
6. Cafeteria
7. Clinic
8. Mechanical
9. Electrical
10. Research terrace
11. Research pad
12. Weather Observatory

Two cross sections
of the building and
an overall view of the
model.

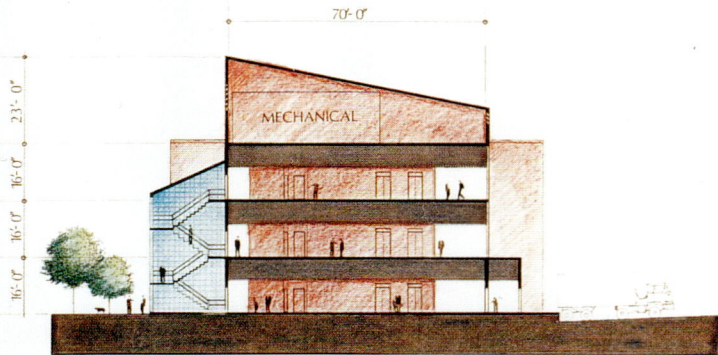

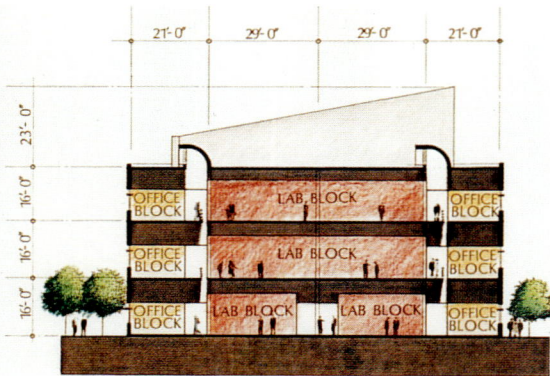

Jefferson County Judicial and Administrative Building

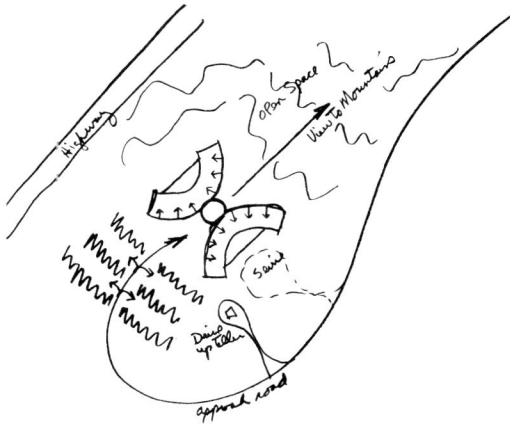

In order to keep pace with the intricacies of civic functions and rapid growth, Jefferson County needed a new, central, one-stop government complex to house its offices.

The new center groups together all governmental functions of administration, law enforcement and judicial services that used to be scattered all over the county. The master plan also establishes new street patterns, landscaping, hiking trails, leisure facilities, picnic areas, amphitheatres and locations for future expansion projects.

The building designed by Fentress Bradburn is surrounded by open space and offers commanding views across the 93-acre campus. Its user-friendly structure is divided into two curved wings joined together by a central atrium. The wings are designed to reach out into the landscape and physically embody the county's commitment to the ideal of "serving the people". The central glass rotunda symbolizes co-operation between different branches of government and, aesthetically, provides a focal point for the building's glowing lantern-like mass.

Inside, the public corridors are rich with allusions to the exterior architecture, hugging the building's windowed perimeter to afford majestic views of the front mountain range. Other important features include state-of-the-art energy management systems, an avant-garde audiovisual system for security purposes and a drive-up window facility for "express" payments.

In consideration of Colorado's beautiful climate and countryside, pedestrian trails were also constructed through both formal and native landscaped areas.

The design team went to great lengths to create a landmark project, projecting an image of quality, sensitivity to the environment, user-efficiency, and the timelessness associated with government as an institution.

A new image has been developed for the courthouse, restoring the county to its role as a predominate political force in state and local politics at a time when local control of issues is at the centre of political debate in American life.

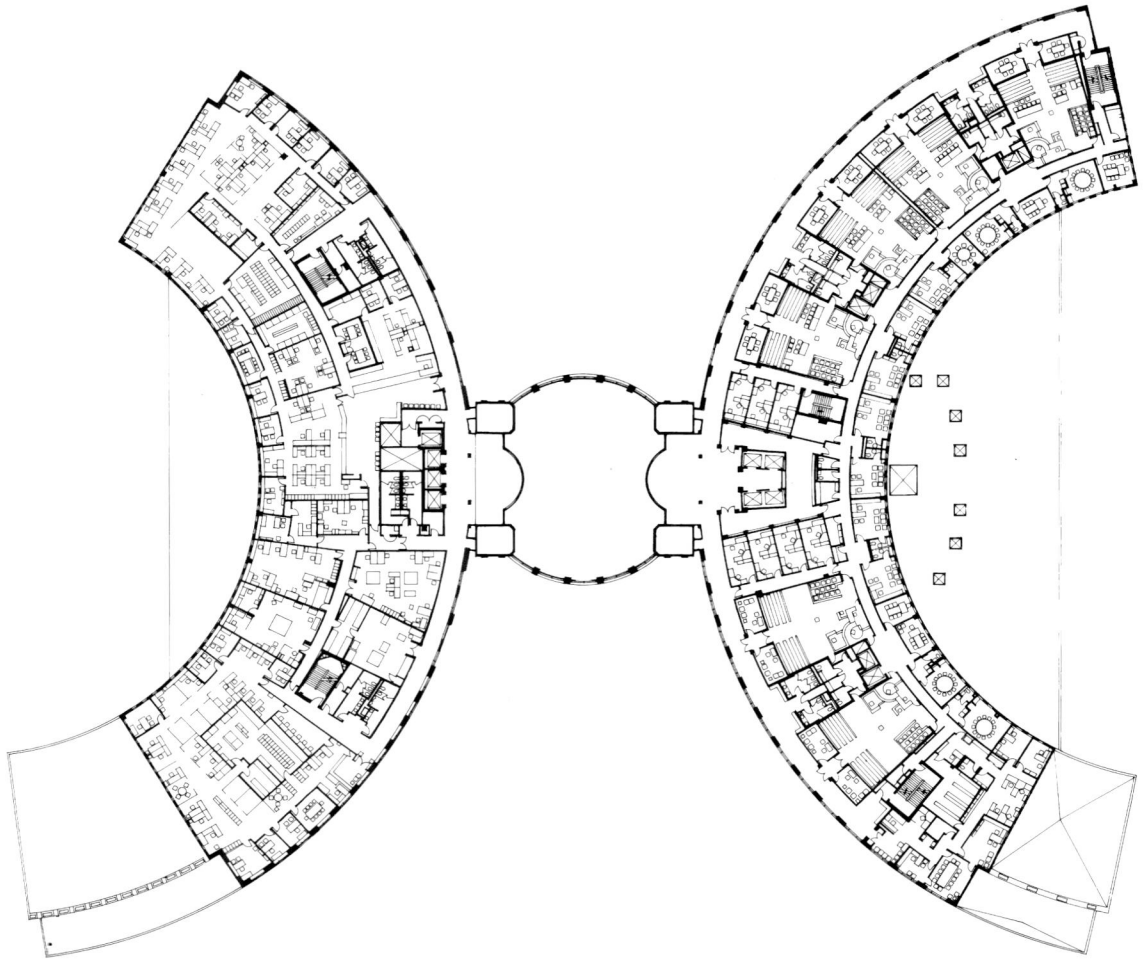

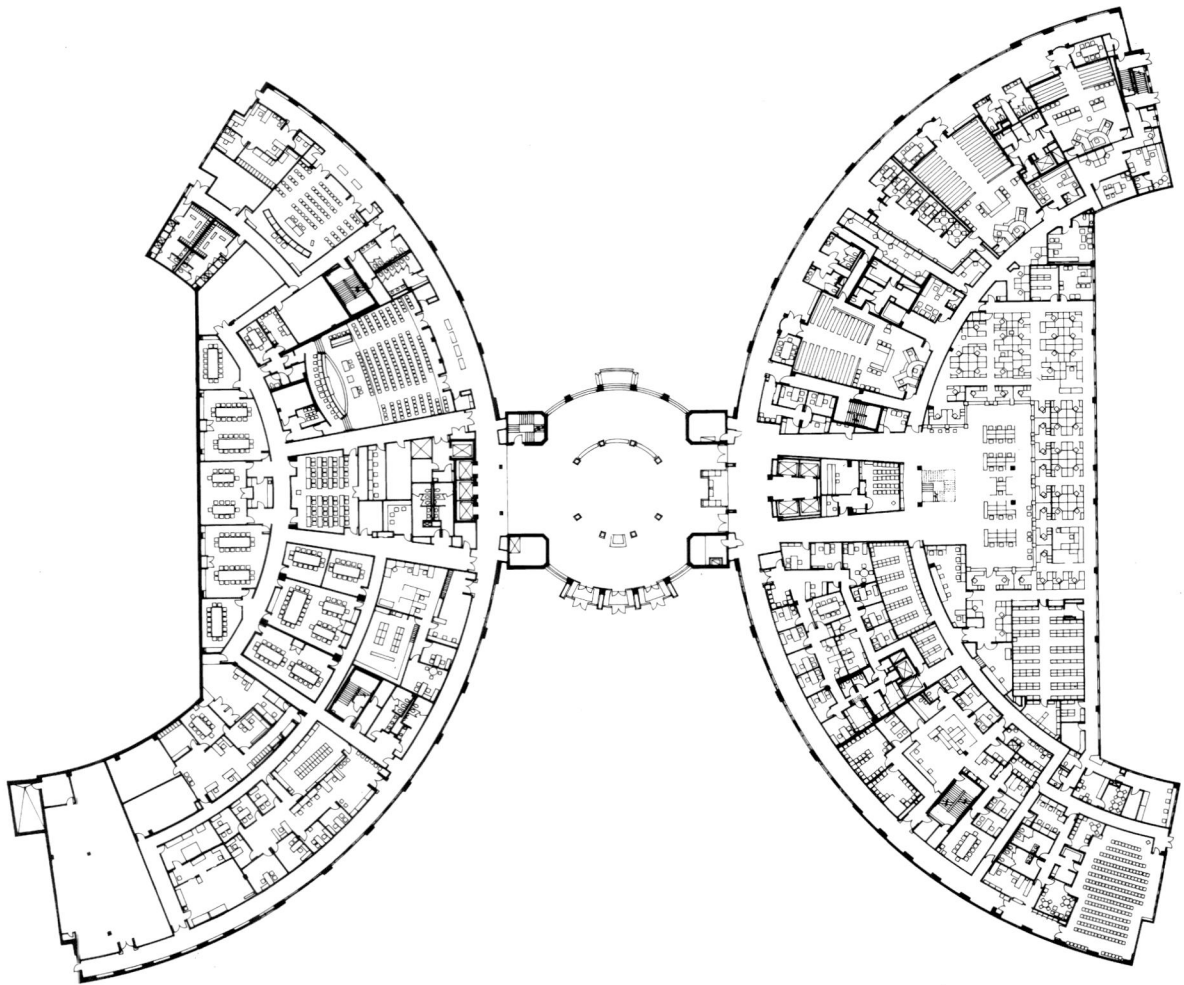

146

The two plans on the
opposite page, the
section at the top of the
page, and the overall
view shown below,
clearly highlight the
representational/symbolic
nature of the building.

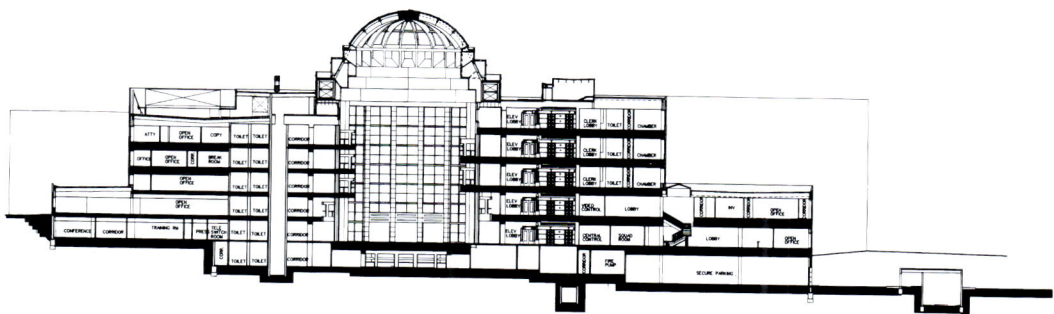

An overall view
and architectural detail
of the Jefferson County
Judicial and
Administrative Building.

N COUNTY

As always in Fentress's
projects, the interiors
are arranged to reflect
the main architectural
features of its exterior
image.

The interior design
is based on sober
rationalism and
comfortable elegance.

This overall view of the finished project shows its impact on the surrounding landscape.

National Cowboy Hall of Fame

The National Cowboy Hall of Fame realised that it needed to extend its existing 77,000-square-foot facility to create a new and unique identity as a nationally recognised western art museum. It was hoped that the 150,000-square-foot extension and renovation of the galleries and exhibition spaces would enhance its image and reputation.

The key to the National Cowboy Hall of Fame's new architectural design is the creation of an exciting new museum image, the devising of a functional, practical building plan and the construction of an ideal environment for the display of art. The underlying concept was to be a contemporary reinterpretation of the architectural metaphors exploited in the old building design, enhancing the character of the existing museum while creating a functionally flexible high-tech facility in perfect harmony with its natural surroundings.

The original two-level facility housed a gallery, exhibition area and administration offices. The architects redesigned the gallery and curatorial spaces so that the gallery could be relocated on the main level, leaving the lower level free for curatorial-storage functions. This allowed room for an additional 50,000 square feet of state-of-the-art gallery and exhibition space. In addition to new seminar rooms, an orientation theatre and extended museum store, a new banquet and exhibition facility were built to celebrate the five monumental triptychs of western landscapes by the artist Wilson Hurley.

The design team has also provided a new home for the startlingly impressive Buffalo Bill Memorial sculpture by the Oklahoma City artist Leonard McMurry. The sculpture's striking presence used to be virtually hidden in the surrounding vegetation, so a new backdrop setting was created to silhouette its profile against the surrounding tree line and land forms. Modern materials and twenty-first century construction technology were transformed into a highly dynamic form, approximately seventy feet high, floating behind the sculpture.

The overall architectural design draws on the old structures, surrounding landscape and spirit of the American west for which the community is renowned. Fentress has used his technical skill to create western images such as canopy covered wagons, camp tents and the native landscape of rolling prairie plains. An outstretched canopy acts as a funnel for the entrance, beckoning visitors into the Hall of Fame. The curved structures with their meticulously designed roofs blend in naturally with the existing buildings without having to resort to rather unlikely imitations. The interiors unfold along large and brightly lit exhibition spaces that gently guide visitors through the art works; the technically perfect structures provide highly effective facilities for all types of displays.

The architects have succeeded in creating an "international icon of the American Frontier and, by extrapolation, of America herself," in total architectural contrast to the "realistic impressionism" of the works on display inside the museum.

The sense of place and history are embodied in gestures, formal allusions, metonymies and gentle metaphors, all rendered in the simple language of modernity in perfect symbiosis with both the past and present. A new and unique institutional identity has been forged for the National Cowboy Hall of Fame, deeply rooted in the rich and vibrant traditions of the past, yet profoundly relevant to a sophisticated modern audience.

Once again, it may be said that Nature and History have found their justification in Art or, to be more precise, in Architecture.

Upper level plan and, below, lower level plan.

Right, the interior courtyard.

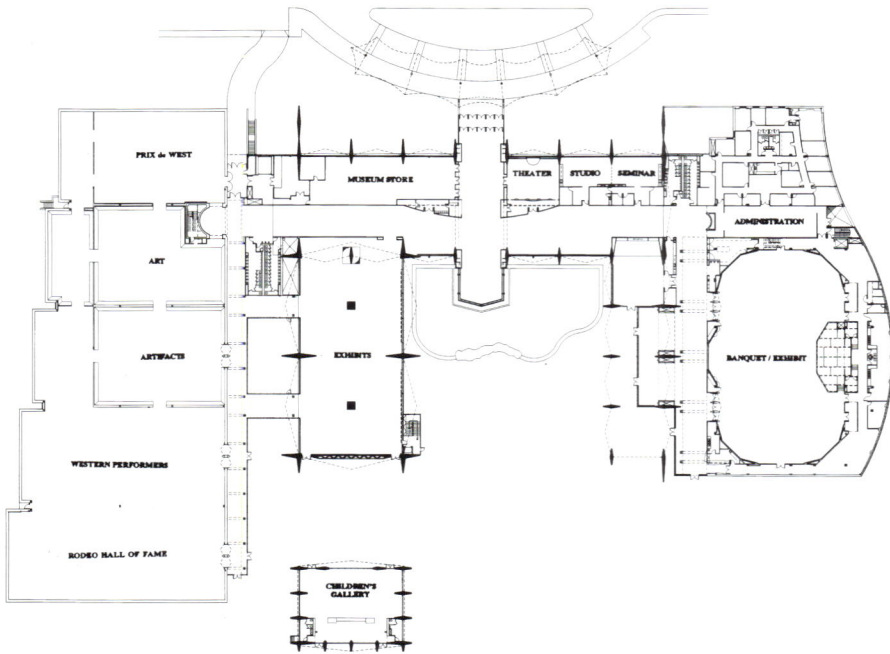

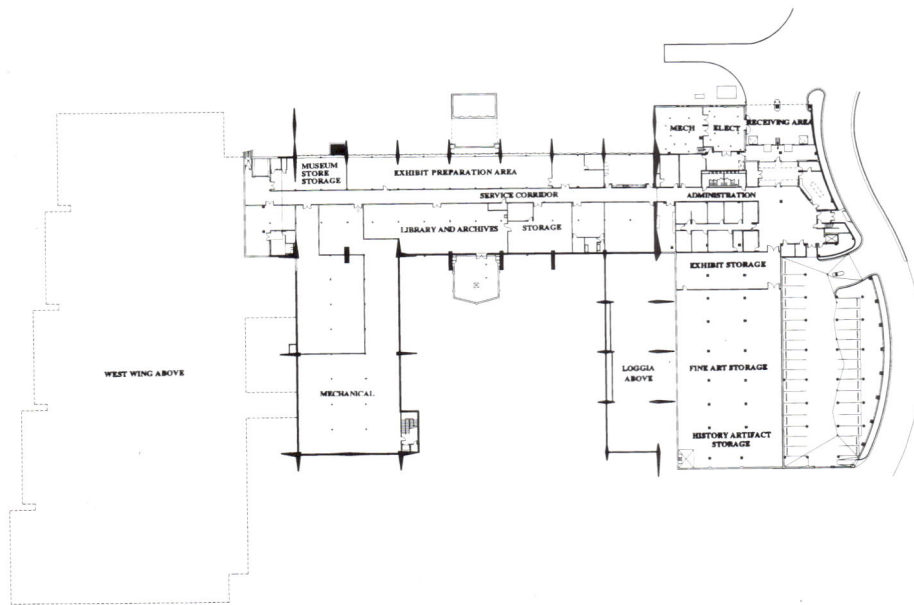

A view of the interior of the glazed gallery.

Right, the tensile-structure porch marking the museum entrance, symbolically reminiscent of the western canvases wagon.

Below and opposite
page, the large glass
lobby enclosing
the gallery and acting
as its focal point.

Natural Resources Building

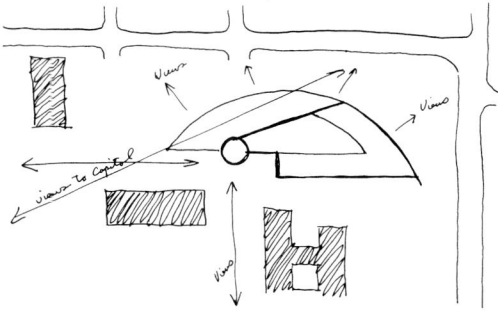

This complex architectural creation is skillfully designed to blend in with the capitol campus master plan, overlooking the city and harbour of Olympia, through a harmonious combination of technology, aesthetics, space and function of the very highest standard. The building's sweeping curves and elegant rotunda conform with the architectural style of the surrounding buildings and enhance the urban landscape through the use of natural shapes and textures typical of the Washington environment.

The final design successfully weds together two architecturally distinct sections of the campus while honouring the capitol and its symbolic dome. The 675-foot, curved facade draws on the geometry of the entire civic centre campus, while the off-centre rotunda anchors the building to the existing urban grid.

Like all eco-friendly structures, the building is inspired by nature.

The green truss work, supported on long, slender columns, conjures up the idea of a temperate rain forest canopy. The cantilever forms a sunscreen designed to minimise solar impact. Inside, the rotunda's hardwood columns allude to a forest environment and its terrazzo floor pattern, depicting the winding Columbia river and the farmlands and forests of eastern Washington, are clearly inspired by the natural landscape. The State of Washington, whose Departments of Fisheries, Agriculture and Natural Resources are all housed inside the complex, was looking for a design that would maximise energy conservation and tackle such environmental concerns as indoor air quality. The architects, therefore, provided special insulation to minimise air and noise pollution from high-impact laboratories such as geological rock crushing. The fish laboratories were located on the top floor to prevent the migration of bad odours or contaminating substances, using prevailing wind patterns to aid building ventilation. Eco-efficiency is the key to the interior design, providing occupants with a healthy open-plan office environment that allows natural daylight to penetrate into even the deepest recesses of the building.

The color code for the building materials was chosen to complement the chromatic pallet of the surrounding countryside, while simultaneously invoking images of the departments in which they are used: blue for Fisheries, green for Forestry, and rose-pink for Agriculture. The visually soothing blend of natural light, open layouts and panoramic views creates a bright office environment, further embellished by plants and greenery. The choice of exterior building materials was dictated by durability and maintenance considerations. The pre-cast concrete - forming a weather-tight, energy-efficient skin - marbles and native non-threatened hardwoods are designed to provide lasting finishes that require very little maintenance. Viewed in its entirety, the building's architecture respects the symbiotic relationship between nature, environment and occupants, while providing an enduring structure that integrates human activities in a safe, non-threatening, physical and spiritual environment. The Natural Resources Building is built in an holistic, state-of-the-art design that views man and the environment as one single system.

Opposite, a detail of the
construction. Bottom of
page and opposite page,
site plan of the building
and plans.

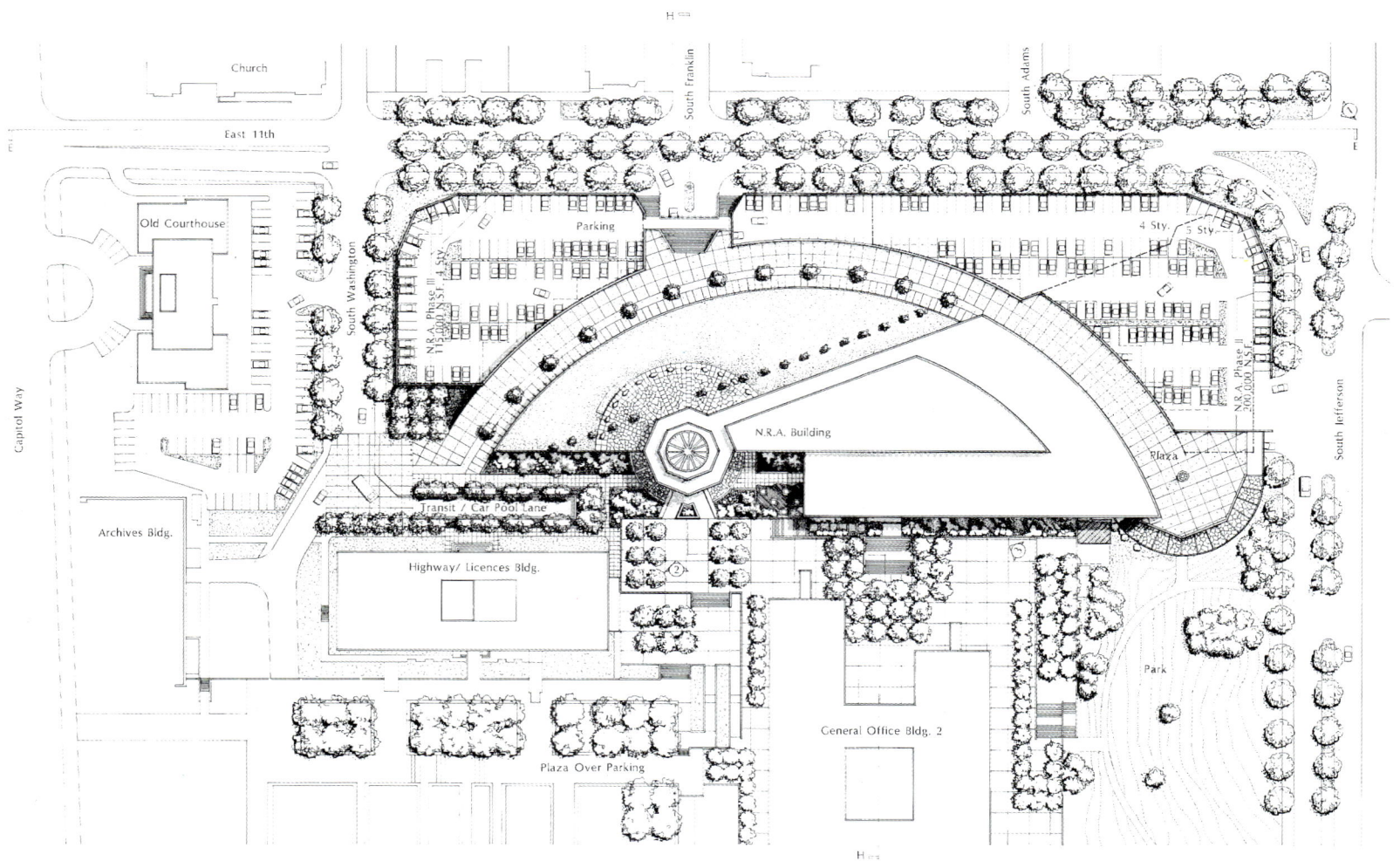

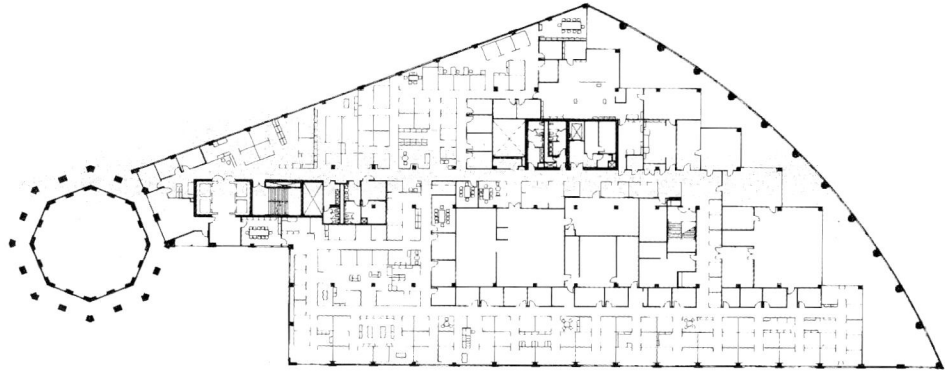

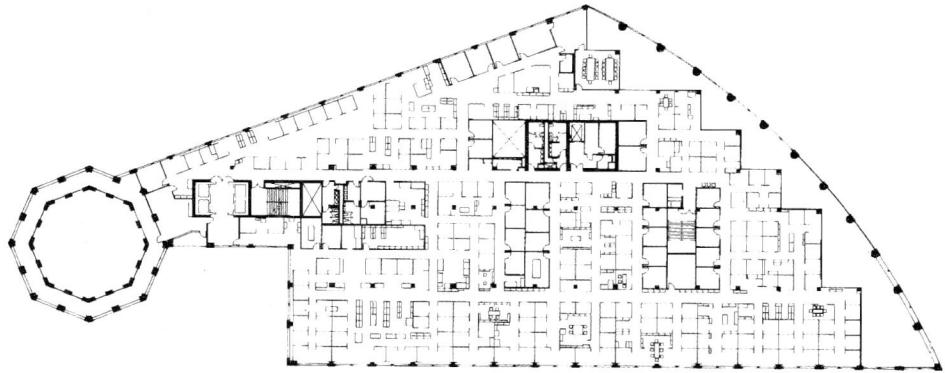

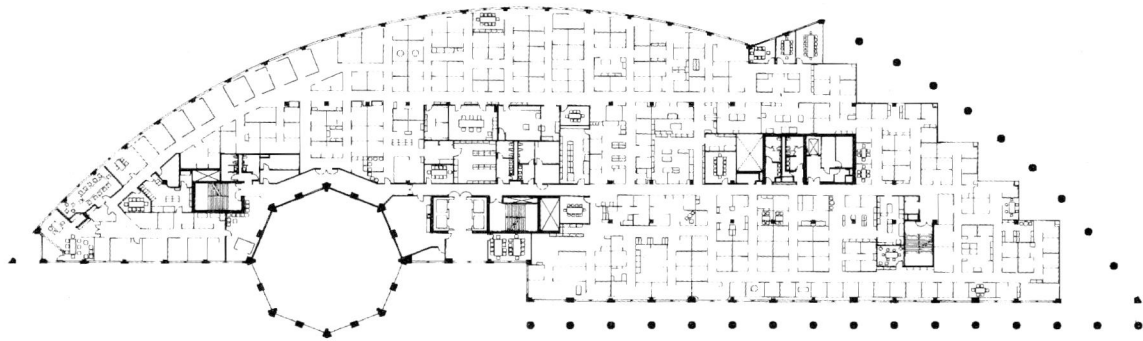

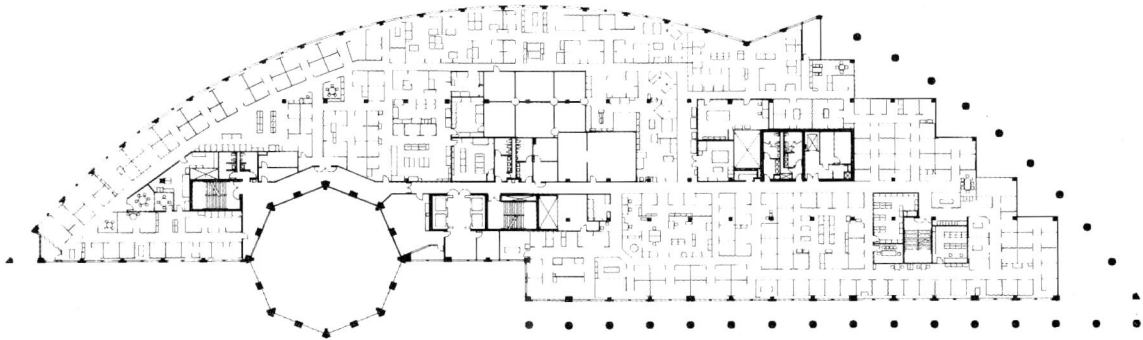

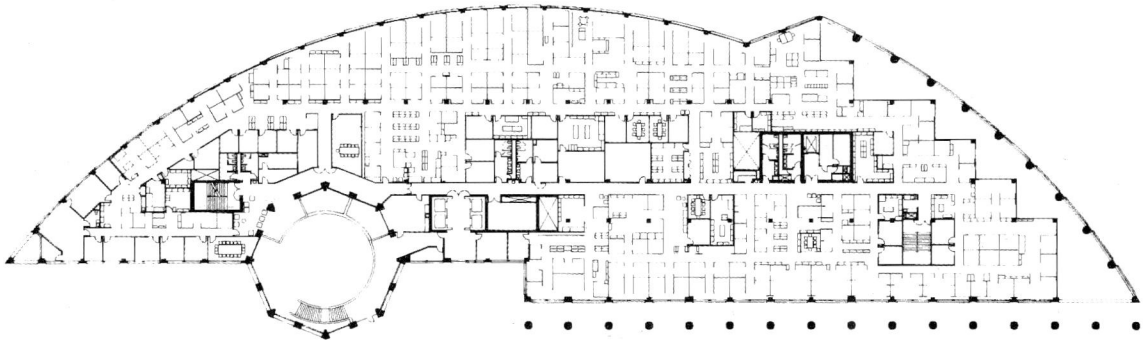

Previous and following pages, four views of the building showing structural details and design features.

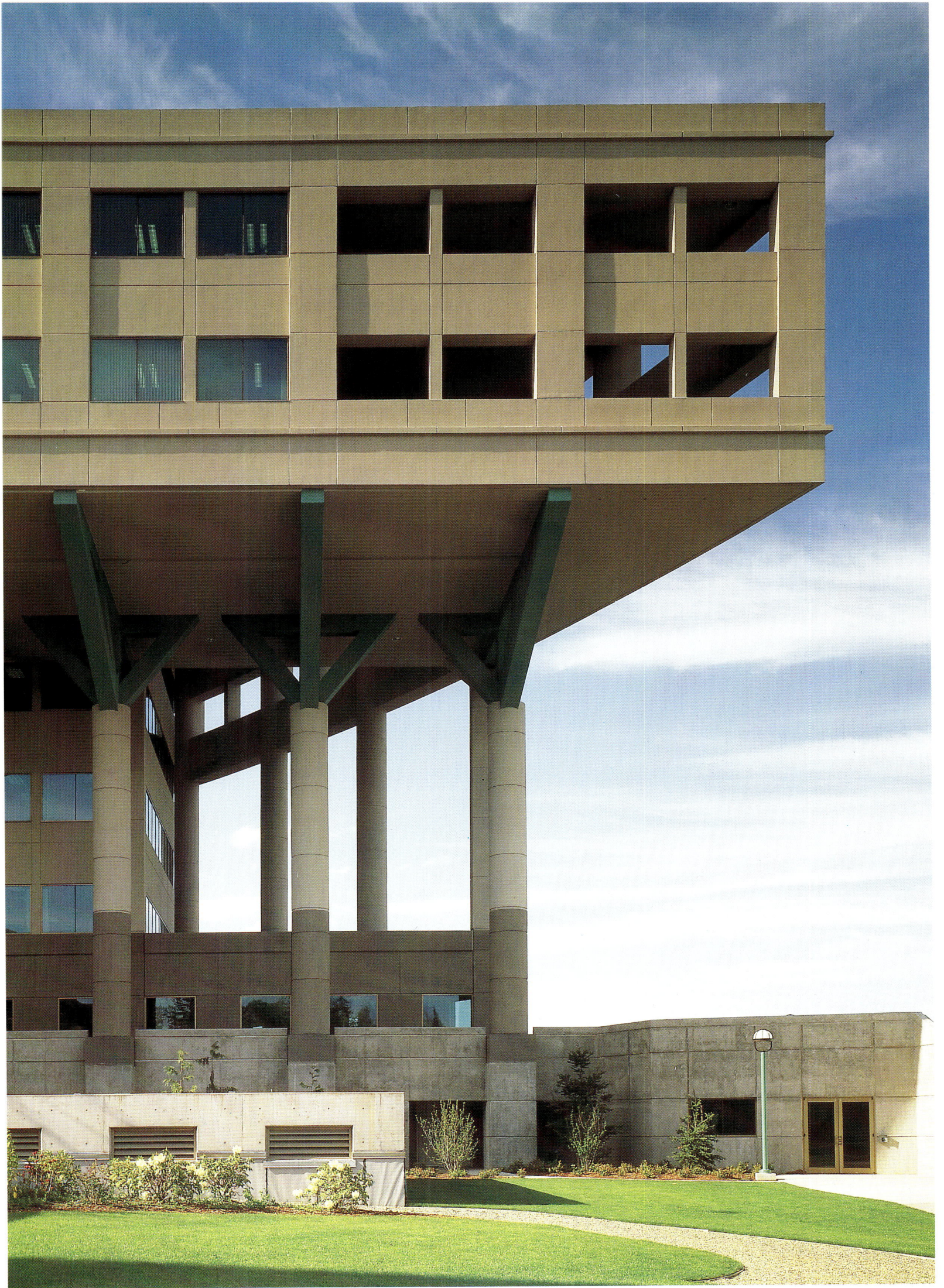

The large glass entrance
lobby is the focal point
of the entire
construction.

New Seoul International Airport

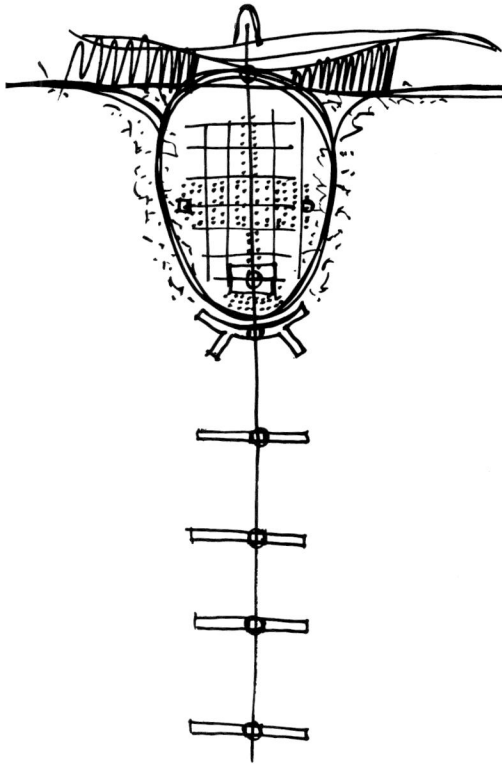

The Korean Ministry of Transportation and the Airports Authority were looking for a powerful architectural statement for an airport to be built on the reclaimed land of Young-jong Island in the bay alongside Seoul to meet what they described as "a rapidly increasing air transportation demand". The master plan included an approximately 291,963-square-metre terminal building and an adjacent business campus called the International Business Center.

Fentress Bradburn's terminal design, which clearly caters for the fact that the NSIA will be a worldwide hub airport and new gateway to Korea, attempts to harmonise cosmopolitan ideas with the traditional beauty of Korea.

The hub of the complex is the Great Hall that serves as a central location for transportation facilities, customer service amenities and airport handling operations. The 46-gate main terminal is designed with a variety of people-mover systems to ensure passengers do not have to walk distances of over 400 metres. Expansion plans provide for a satellite terminal and four remote concourses north of the main terminal complex, creating an additional 128 gates should air-travel needs require extra facilities. The structurally beautiful roof design is authentic enough to be taken as a model for a new generation of airports. The sheer size of the roof, covering three times the area of the Denver terminal, called for a catenary scheme that not only evokes the masts of passing freighters in the local harbour, but also alludes to the cultural language of Korea. As Curtis Worth Fentress himself pointed out:

"The graceful sweeping roof lines become a modem interpretation of traditional historic Korean architecture." This approach may hardly be described as post-modern pastiche and represents a 180-degree about-turn from the notions of post-structuralism or deconstructivism. Modern technology has been used to express the local language in what might be termed contextual regionalism. This term is intended to evoke a certain sensitivity to the sociology, ecology and cultural evolution of a given location. This cultural sensitivity can clearly be detected in the Korean-garden style interior landscaping, the patterning of the floor that conjures up images of the stripes of the Asian tiger, and the subtle detailing of the columns and trusses. A whole range of influences were drawn from the country's ancient culture and then translated into structural forms using national materials, colours and art forms.

Like other air projects the company has worked on, the NSIA features grand spaces, panoramic views and sweeping, aerodynamic forms designed to express motion. The company aims to highlight the fact that airports are gateways to cities and countries, providing travellers with their first and last impressions of a region and its people.

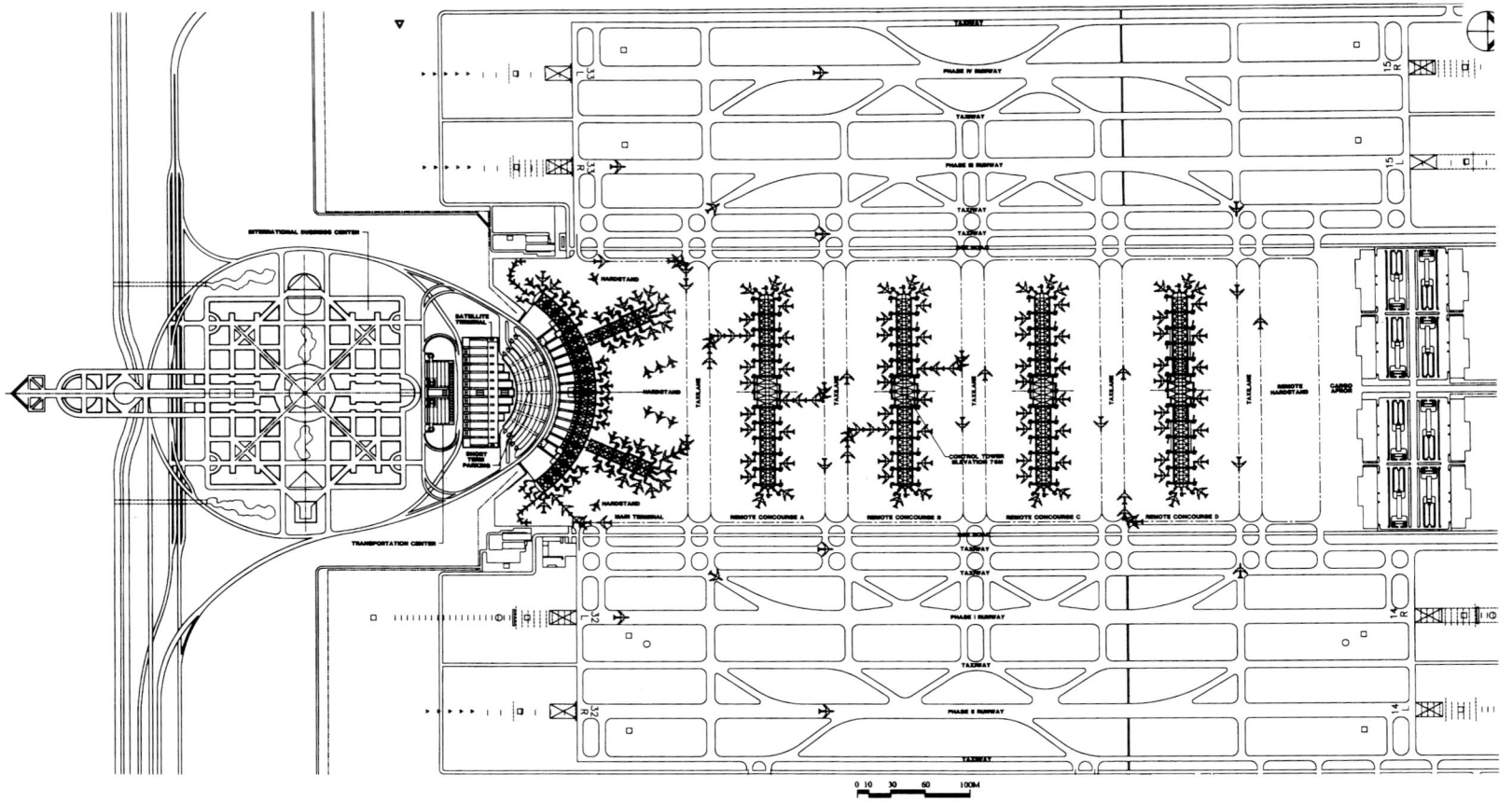

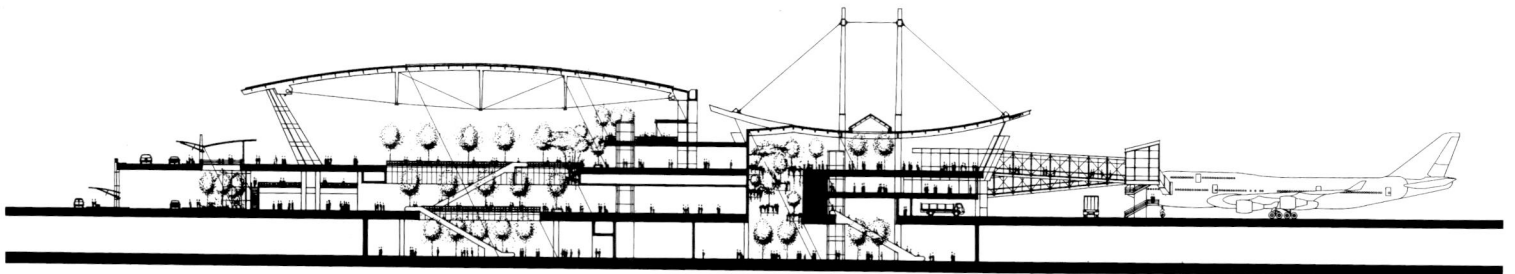

Above, the airport
master plan with one
section. Opposite page,
an overall view of the
model.

Two pictures of the
model giving an idea
of the technical standard
of the architecture.

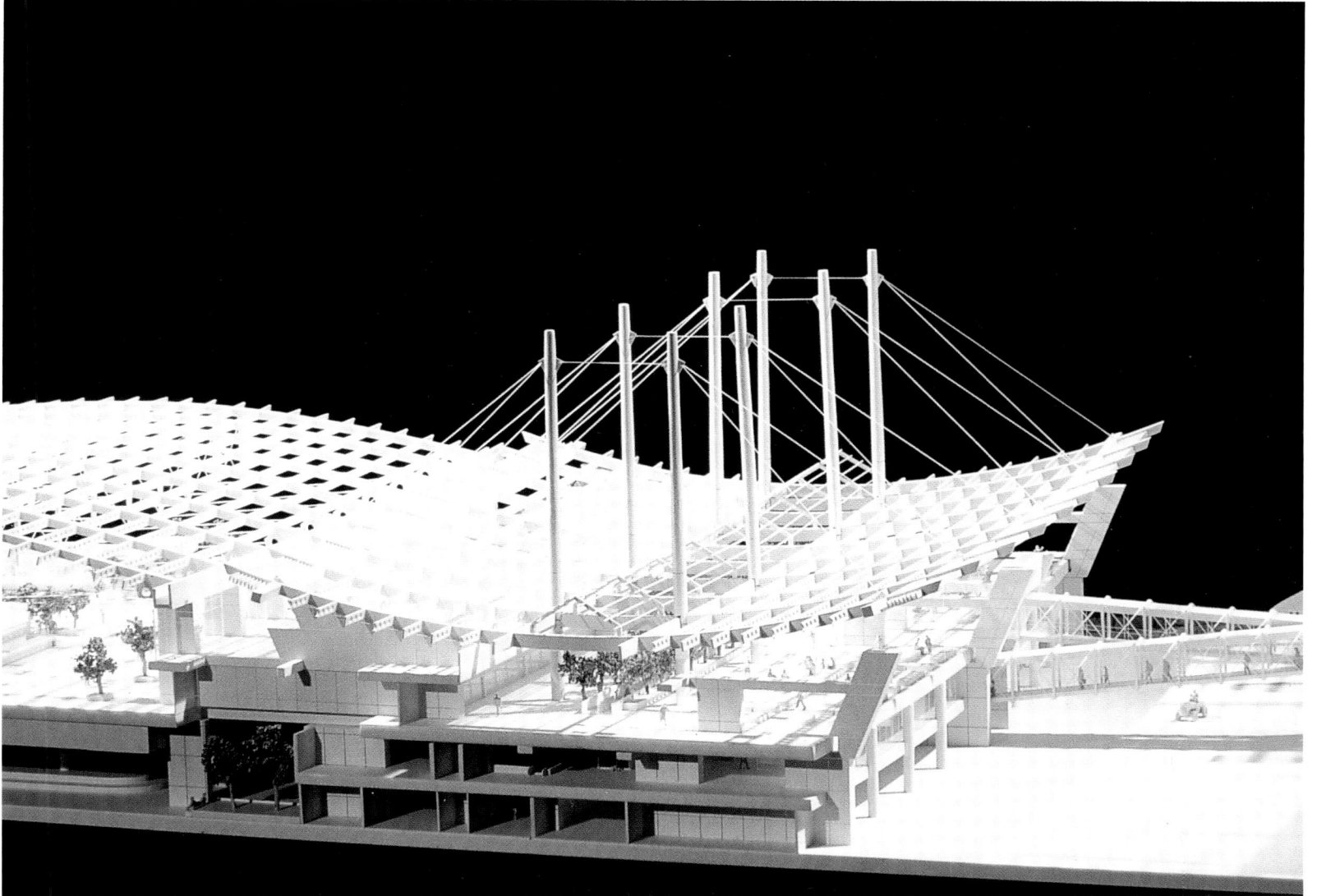

A detail of the model showing the designer's efforts to represent the main cultural features of its site location.

These drawings
emphasise the
international nature
of the airport and its
technological intricacy.

The layout of the vast
interiors in the services
area is dictated
by a thick colonnade
creating a distinct sense
of welcome.

National Museum of Wildlife Art

Three miles outside the town of Jackson, Wyoming, a 53,000-square-foot museum rests unobtrusively one hundred feet above the East Gros Ventre Butte, gently silhouetted against the Grand Teton Mountains in the background. Plans to develop the museum were viewed rather sceptically at first, in view of the damage caused to the area by previous commercial development projects. Soil erosion due to poor grading and inadequate vegetation had devastated the winter grounds of the mule deer habitat, and tourist-oriented commercial exploitation had visually and functionally wreaked havoc on a large portion of land at the base of the butte. This left Teton County grappling with the difficult issues of growth and preservation of the natural environment.

Fentress Bradburn realised that no conventional architectural form would be compatible with this natural context, so they opted for a building design reminiscent of the kind of rock outcrops found on the Butte. The rough stone cladding and irregular configuration naturally co-exist with the surrounding rock formations. The approach and entry to the building allow visitors to experience a "sense of discovery" as they are drawn into the building and given glimpses of the canyon-like lobby with its animal tracks etched into the stone floor. Setting the building in the hillside to completely cover the west elevation and partially cover the north and east elevations allowed notable energy savings and, at the same time, enhanced the museum's outcropping form and symbiotic relationship with the butte. Museum facilities include collection storage spaces, exhibit galleries, education classrooms, curatorial and administration spaces, a gift shop and cafeteria.

The building, which provides a rare opportunity to view wildlife in its natural habitat and enjoy a notable collection of fine art, is designed to reflect the natural beauty of its site. Its irregular lines and the use of native stone allow it to blend smoothly into the jagged landscape. Extensive reclamation work was also carried out to repair the severe damage that had been caused to the ecological balance by previous development work.

The design of the National Museum of Wildlife Art responds to many of the most import challenges facing architects today. Issues such as developmental pressures and impact on the natural environment and plant/animal communities have been solved through the creation of a warm and humanistic building that embodies the spirit of its delicate site, while setting new standards of quality and architectural design sensitivity in the Jackson area.

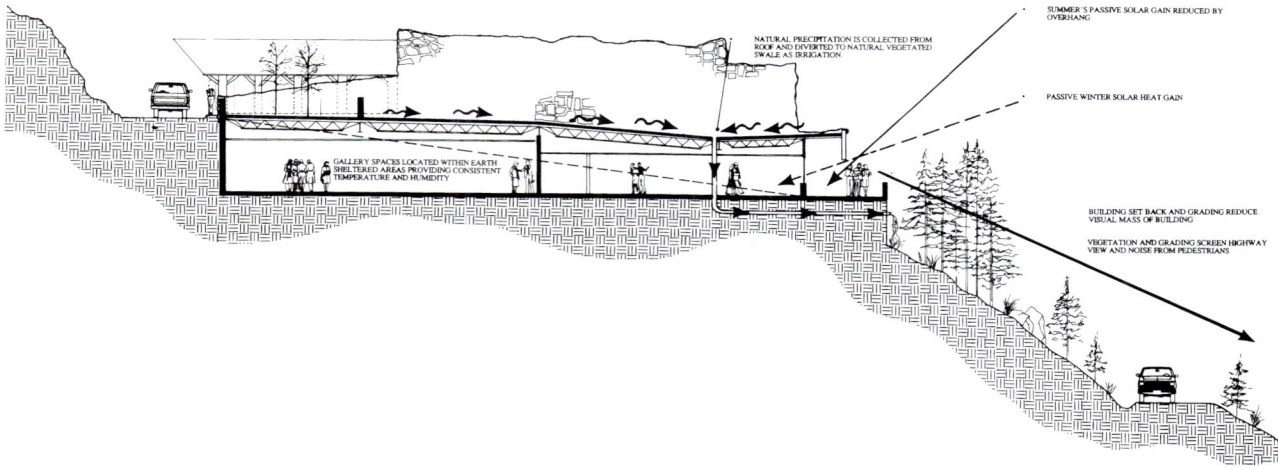

The drawings and overall view of the National Wildlife Museum show how finely it has been incorporated in the surrounding environment.

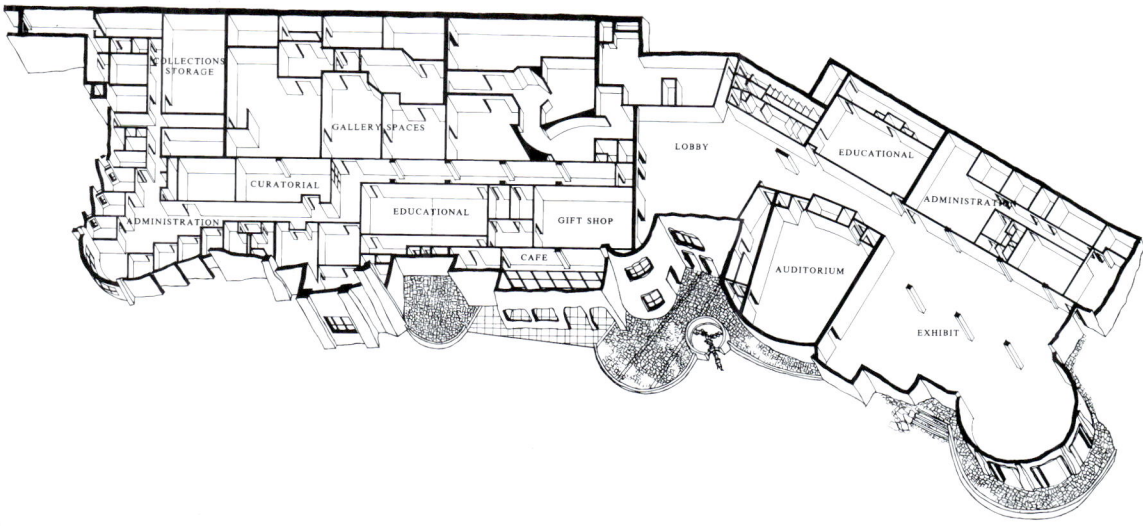

This page and previous pages, exterior views of the National Wildlife Museum.

Two interior views of the Museum. The design of the interiors alludes to the exterior image of the entire complex.

Kwangju Bank Headquarters

Prior to the design of the 35-story Kwangju Bank Headquarters, contextual regionalism had rarely been applied to high-rise buildings. Regionally-oriented projects and contextual motivations had never previously been combined in an extrapolated elevation.

Here in Kwangju, the historical agricultural centre of south east Korea, the extrusion of forms springs directly from Korean cultural traditions in terms of both its coloration and patterning. The way the facade is articulated at the multiple cornices evokes the past in its application of bowed Asian beams, just as the rhythm of the glass and natural stone courses recalls the patterns of traditional Korean dress. The mass of the building, which is reminiscent of a huge Asian castle, is thus deconstructed through the Yin and Yang relationship between historical past and projected future.

This dichotomy produces a practical, 700,000-square-foot office block, including four floors of retail and banking space and parking room for 400 vehicles, that is at once strikingly new and at the same time deeply entrenched in a positive sense of place.

Characteristically, contextual regionalism has driven the project design to a certain indefinable quality that treats viewers to the pleasure of a strangely familiar site - a cultural *je ne sais quoi.*

This creates a feeling of intense familiarity without actually aping history. A totally new experience of architecture cleverly conjured up without apparently offending the building's surroundings or the people who will inhabit it.

The creation of this new symbol of prosperity speaks directly to that burgeoning international business complex that South Korea is now becoming, helping transform Kwangju from an agricultural centre into a major trade and business centre.

Bottom of page, street
level floor plan and,
above, typical floor plan.
Opposite page,
a view of the model.

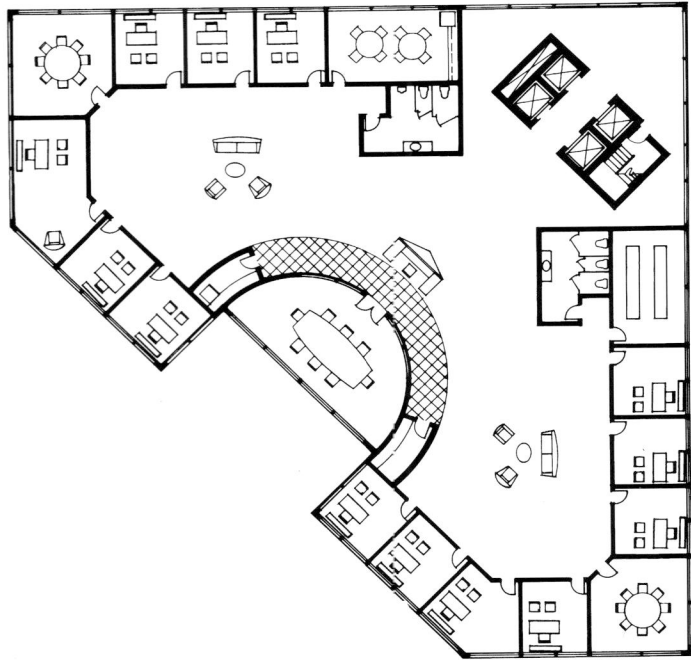

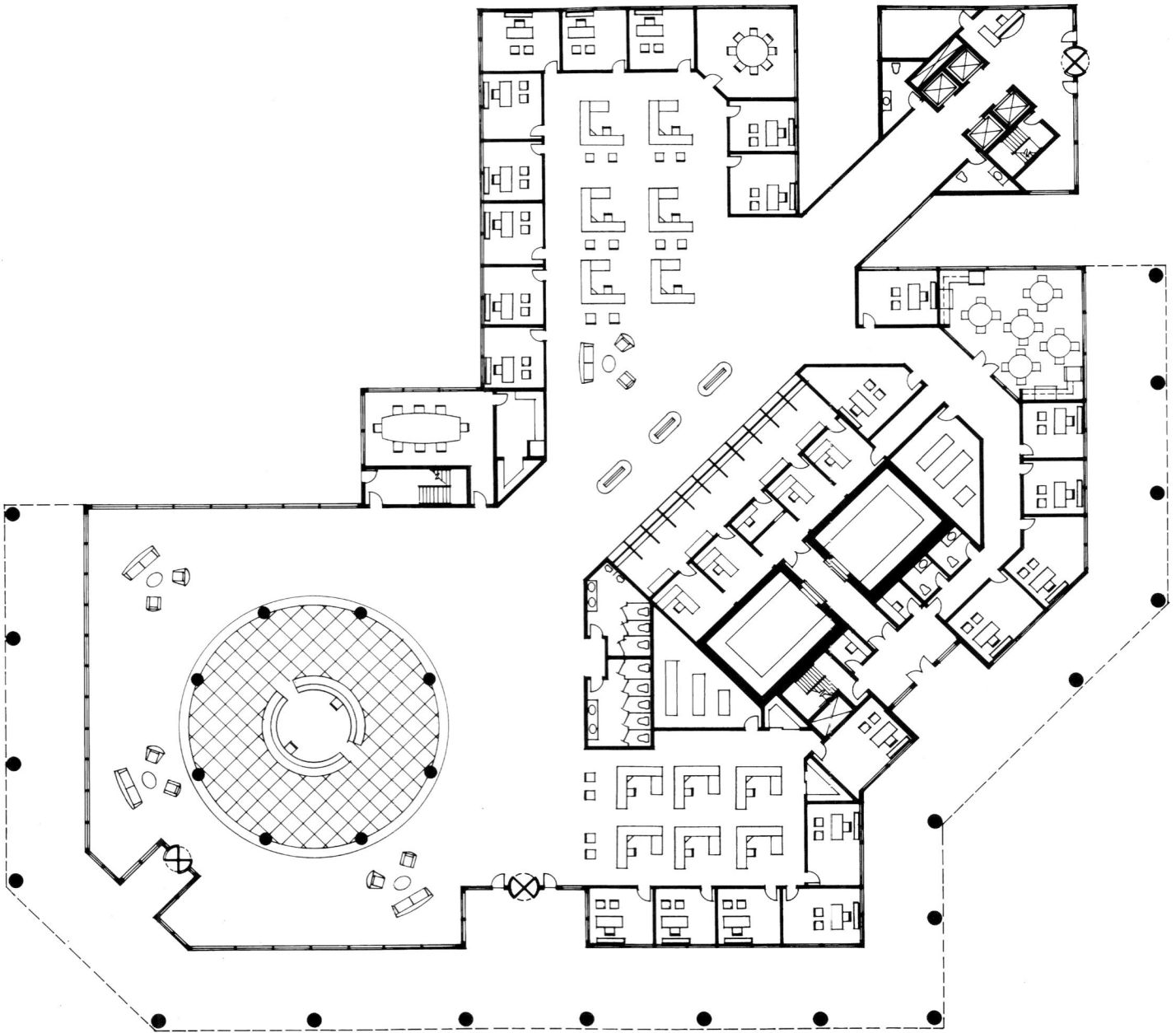

210

Second Bangkok International Airport

Bangkok Airport is designed to serve as an international gateway to South East Asia, embodying the excitement of travel and spirit of the Thai people. The final design, geared to the demands of a modern international airport, includes a passenger terminal building, elevated front roads serving landside traffic, a parking facility adjacent to the passenger terminal, offices and other support facilities, provisions for future rail access to the terminal, and carefully gauged landscaping. The project brief, stipulating that all aircraft gates be useable for international and domestic traffic, provided an added challenge for the design team, forcing them to scrutinise a variety of traffic patterns.

Constructed on a landfill in a swampy region outside the city, Bangkok Airport is rich in symbolic images of the Thai people and their native traditions. The runways, taxiways and concourses create the kind of linear progression associated with the waterways of Bangkok. The airside terminal is designed in the form of a simple, abstract, lotus flower, a revered symbol of life in the Buddhist religion reflected in much of the nation's sculpture and architecture.

The upsweeping form of the airside terminal building, reminiscent of the roof designs of traditional Thai structures, creates a sense of lift-off and flight, while the gracefully downward-curving roof conjures up images of the gentle petals of the lotus blossom. On the other hand, the landside terminal roof evokes the sinuous line of a closed lotus bud through an intricate combination of high technology and native materials.

The exterior structures are made of cast-in-place and pre-cast concrete in warm and earthy white tones, integrated with glass and steel constructions for the exterior walls. The roof tiles allude to the rich soils of Thailand through the choice of golden ochres and soothing greens, symbolising the lush vegetation that covers the entire nation. The granite and carpet floor patterns are designed in accordance with the Buddhist philosophy of the four components of life: wind, water, fire and earth.

The importance of the Thai landscape in the nation's history is clearly evoked in the dual notion of locating the airport in lavish garden settings and of incorporating the colours, fragrances and natural beauty of the local landscape inside the building. Extensive daylighting, through a series of skylights running across the entire structure, ensures the perfect growth and sustenance of natural flora.

This world-class airport, equipped with all the latest passenger conveniences and comforts, is designed to reflect the excitement of travel and spirit of the Thai people in a new global aviation gateway to the East and beyond. The airport is also intended to become a treasured national landmark and source of pride for the entire nation, as a universal showcase of the arts, traditions and cultures of Thailand.

Plans of the two levels
of the Second Bangkok
International Airport.

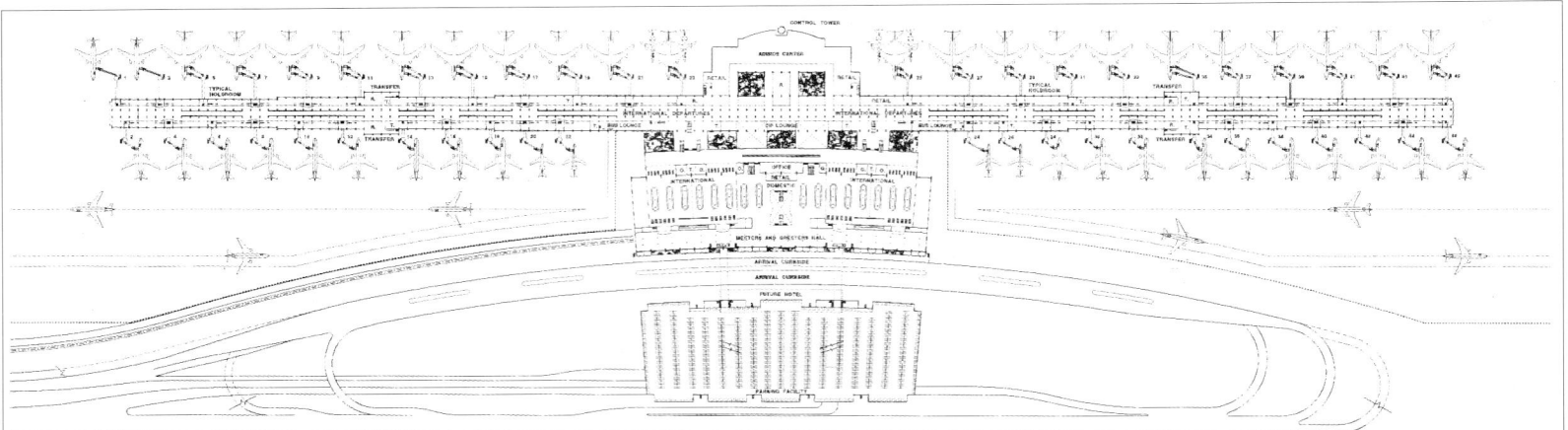

PASSENGER TERMINAL COMPLEX-LEVEL 2 PLAN

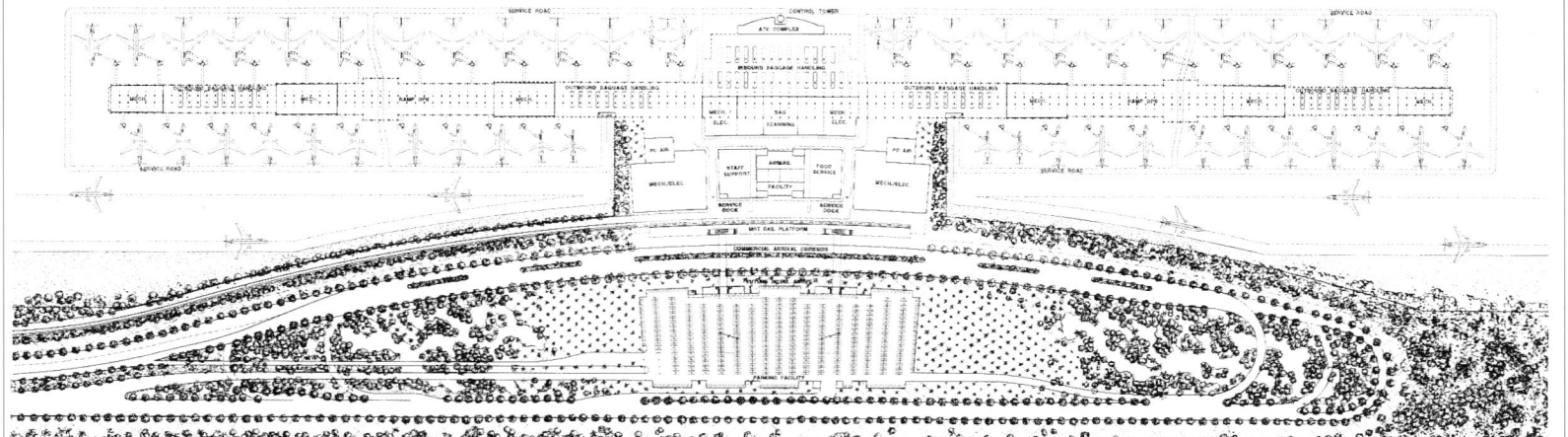

PASSENGER TERMINAL COMPLEX-LEVEL 1 PLAN

Two diagrams of flow
charts of passengers
and baggage inside the
airport.

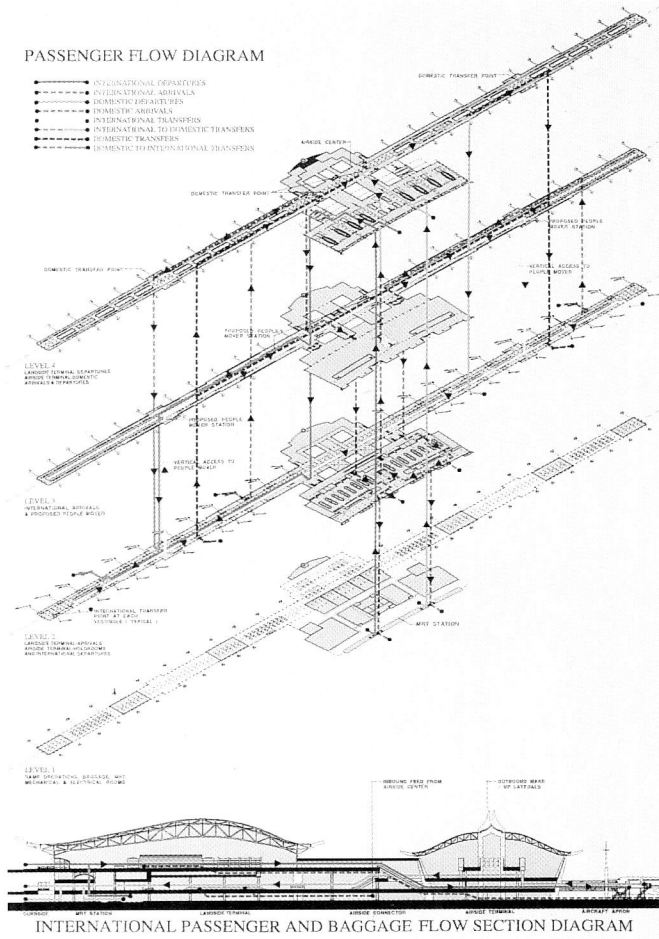

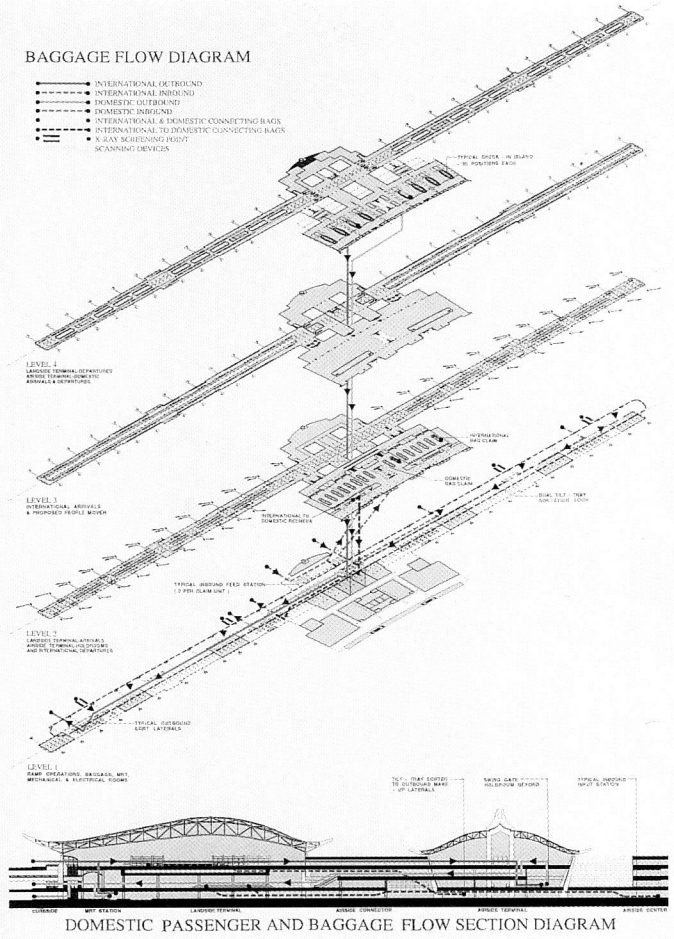

PASSENGER FLOW DIAGRAM

BAGGAGE FLOW DIAGRAM

INTERNATIONAL PASSENGER AND BAGGAGE FLOW SECTION DIAGRAM

DOMESTIC PASSENGER AND BAGGAGE FLOW SECTION DIAGRAM

THE SECOND BANGKOK INTERNATIONAL AIRPORT

C.W. FENTRESS J.H. BRADBURN AND ASSOCIATES, P.C., ARCHITECTS
with
COMPLEMENT CO., LTD.
McCLIER AVIATION GROUP
K. ENGINEERING CONSULTANTS CO., LTD.
S B CONSULTANT CO., LTD.

An overall view of the
model showing how
the combination
of high-tech structures
and architectural designs
is designed to be
expressive of the local
culture.

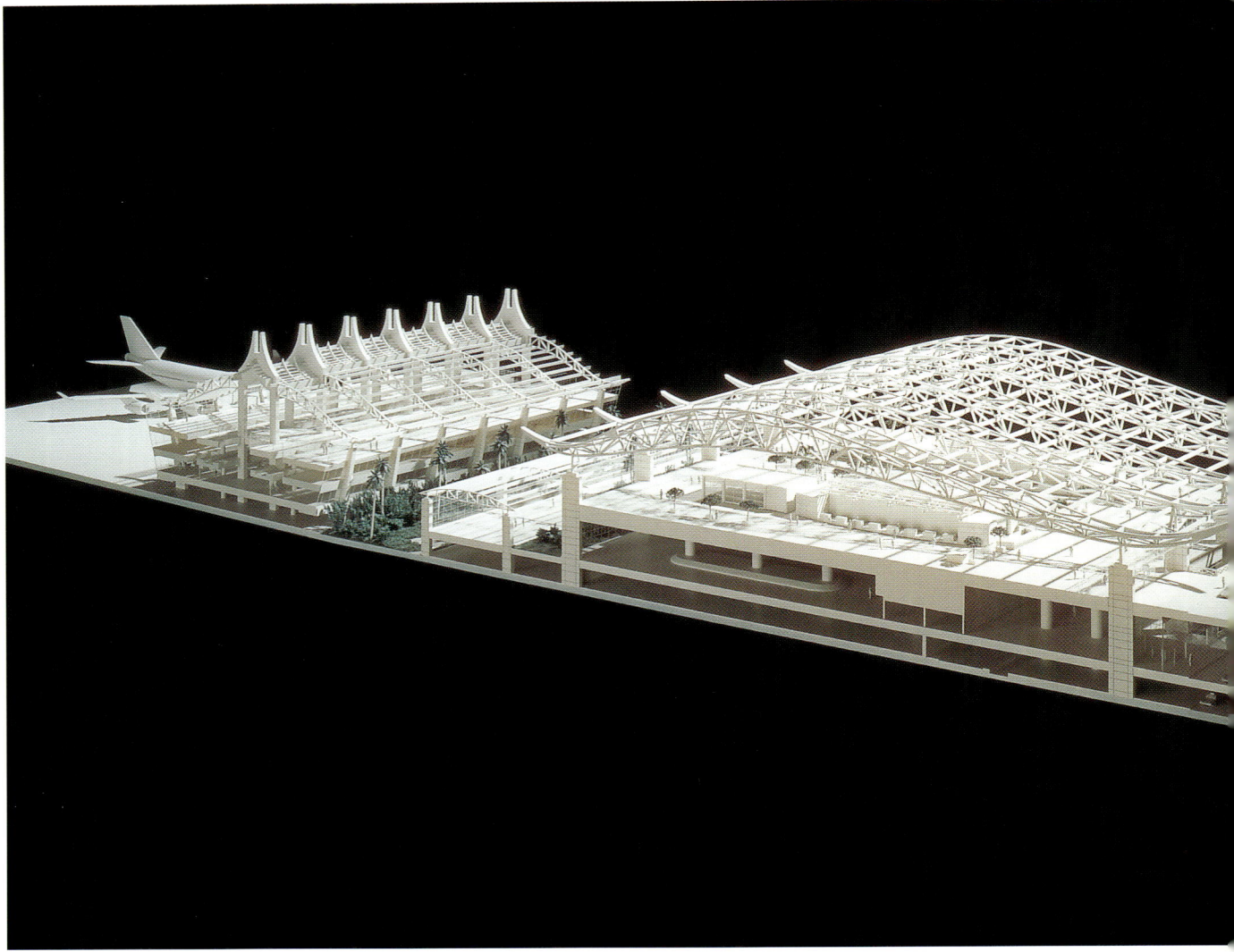

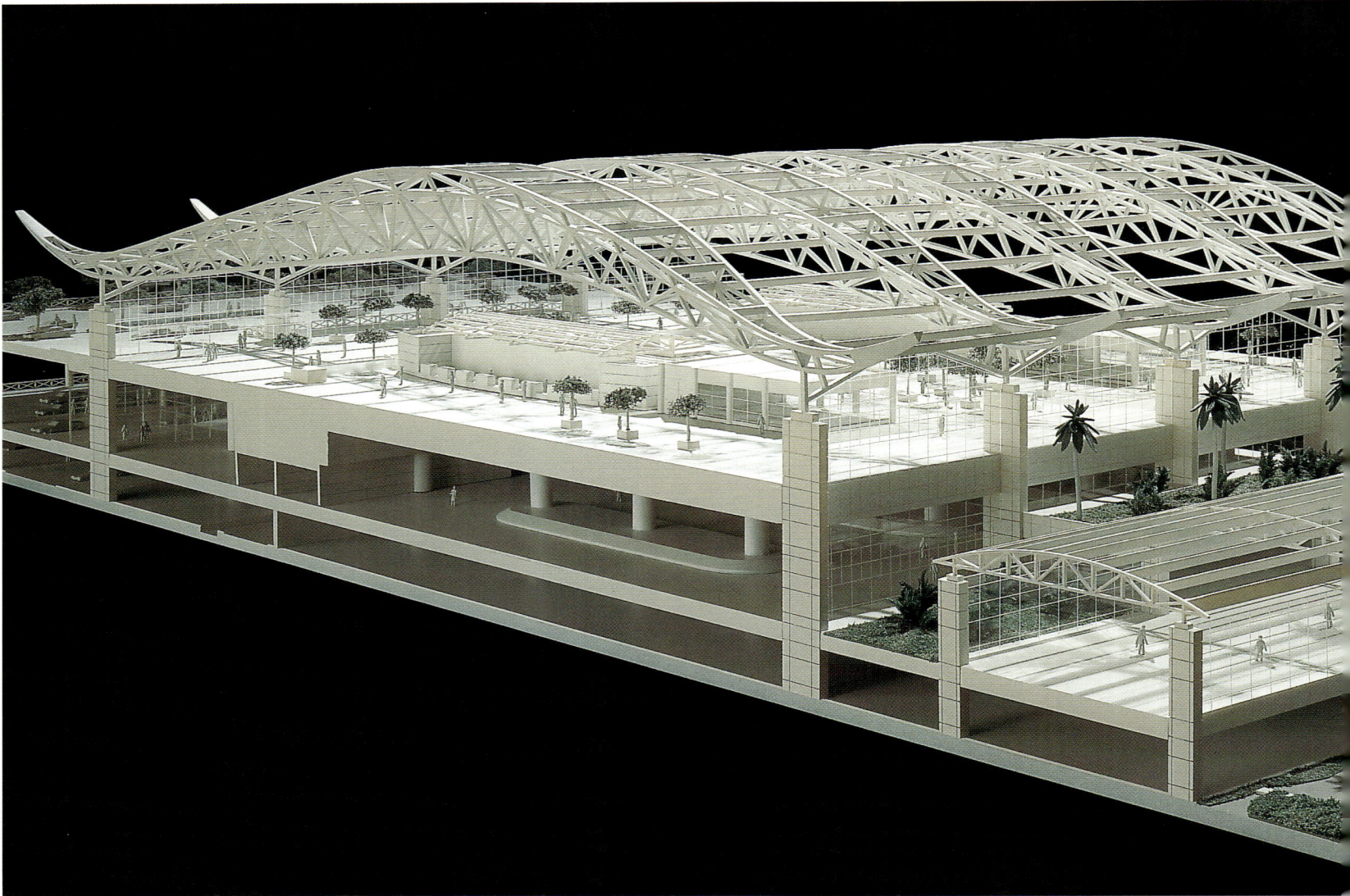

The three pictures of the model illustrate the cleverly gauged balance of functionality and symbolic/linguistic features.

This drawing illustrates
the building's outside
appearance and its
allusions to local culture.

A sketch of an interior
environment reiterating
the linguistic features
of the exterior.

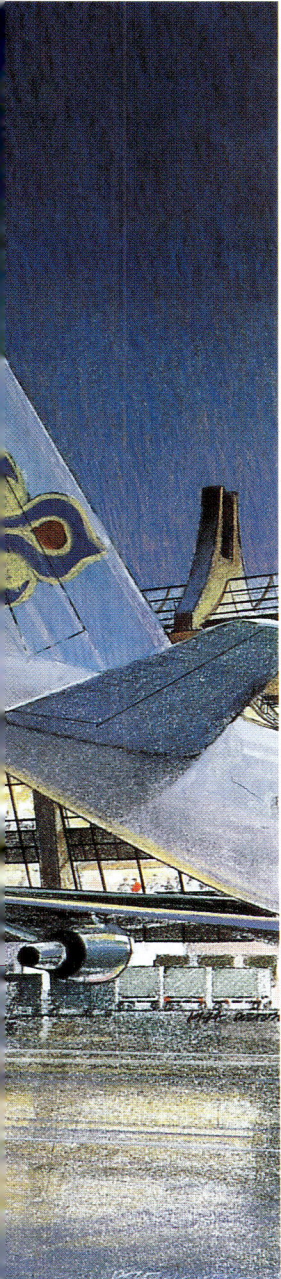

Clark County Government Center

Fentress Bradburn and Associates won the national design competition to design and construct a government center for Clark County in association with Domingo Cambeiro Architects from Las Vegas, Nevada. The competition also encompassed a master plan of the area to include space for a law enforcement complex, performing arts complex, child care facility and structured parking.

The 350,000-square-foot complex contains a single-story auditorium, pyramid-shaped cafeteria and cylindrical, six-story reception hall linking together the two curved office buildings. The design physically embodies Clark County's philosophy of providing an open, accessible government in a new, civic, cultural centre. After intricate design studies, the team elected to house the government centre in what is essentially a four-building structure that wraps around an exterior courtyard to form a circular composition. The fragile surrounding ecosystem of the native desert environment provides the underlying inspiration behind each of the four buildings. The oasis or "county courtyard" transforms into an outdoor amphitheatre, which may be used as a community amenity in an informal park-like setting. The circular plan, detailed with a colonnade enclosing the amphitheatre, imbues the complex with civic status and provides a centering device for the existing building and any future additions.

A distinctive outdoor stage provides a focal point from which performances and public addresses can be viewed. The architectural forms and courtyard design allude to natural phenomena in the delicate desert ecosystem. The architecture metaphorically embodies the underlying essence of the region by emphasising the sculptural qualities of the physical environment. A natural sandstone exterior with rose tinted windows captures the natural textures, colours and patterns of the surrounding landscape, projecting a timeless sense of permanence instilled by a high-quality stone building.

The cafeteria, reflecting the angular rock formations of the desert, is shaped in the form of a pure pyramid. The entry rotunda and county room lobby draw on the desert's spiraling sculptural rock strata, while the commissioners' chamber auditorium incorporates an intricate web of clerestory lights reminiscent of prickly pear cactus spines. The combined formation blocks out intense direct sunlight and allows cooler, indirect light to filter through to the interiors.

The harsh exterior climate is further mitigated by densely planted rows of pines that enhance shading in the busiest outdoor areas. The centrally located lobby, where the information desk and building directory are, may be entered from different directions, providing easy access to all the public facilities and functions. The overall building design constantly reinforces a combination of project objectives developed along three main lines: a carefully constructed sense of place embodied in the county courtyard; the concept of open accessible government symbolised by the building shape in the form of outstretched arms encircling the visitor and enticing him towards the main entrance; and the functionally logical and straightforward design epitomising civic order and creating a sense of community spirit.

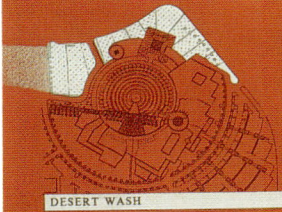

DESERT WASH
A Sinuous Line in the Desert, Evidence of Flash Floods, Exposing Boulders, Nurturing Ash Trees, and Providing Contrast to the Desert Floor

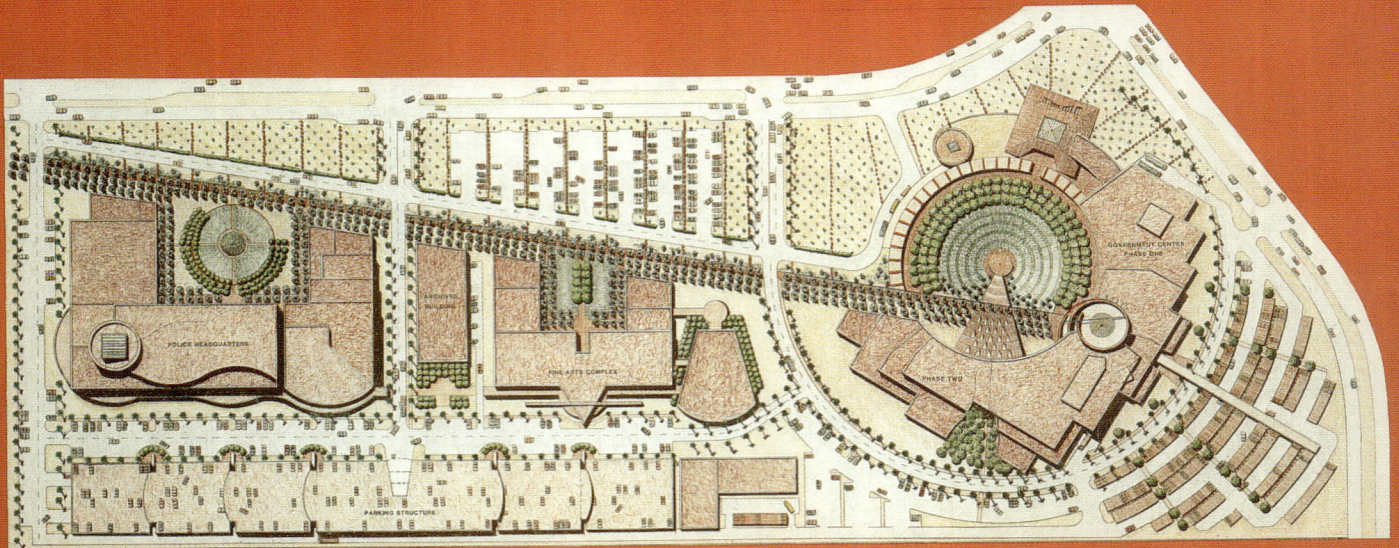

SITE MASTER PLAN

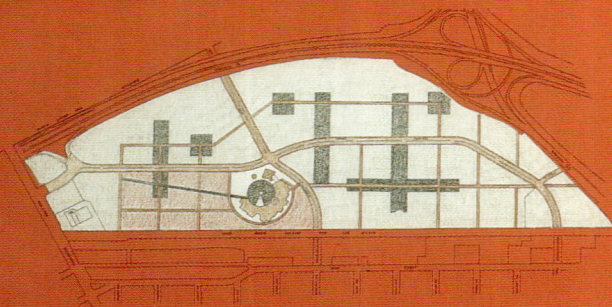 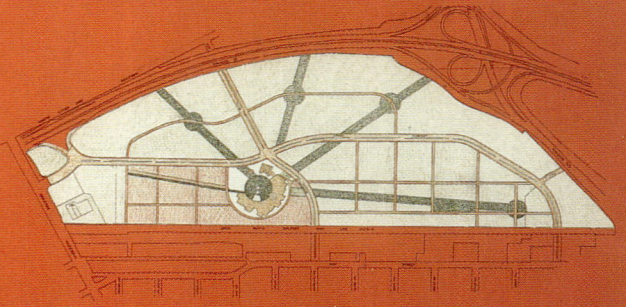

AREA MASTER PLAN 1

AREA MASTER PLAN 2

PHASE ONE

PHASE TWO

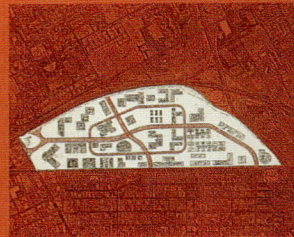 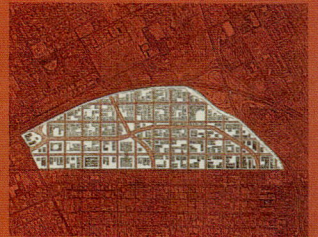

URBAN PATTERN

SUBURBAN PATTERN

CLARK COUNTY GOVERNMENT CENTER
CLARK COUNTY, NEVADA

C.W. FENTRESS   J.H. BRADBURN   and   ASSOCIATES, P.C.

CANYON WALLS

Textured Edifice Etched by Time are a Sculptured Definition of Volumes in Space, of Valley Boundaries, and of Landscape Color

VIEW FROM ALTA DRIVE

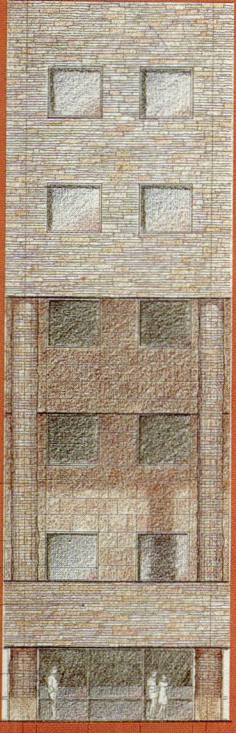

ELEVATION/SECTION AT COURTYARD GARDEN/BREAKOUT SPACE

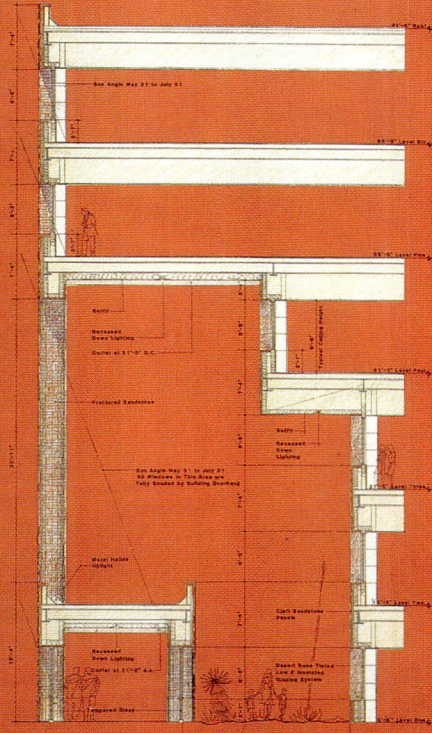

ELEVATION/SECTION AT TYPICAL SIX STORY FACADE

CLARK COUNTY GOVERNMENT CENTER
CLARK COUNTY, NEVADA

C.W. FENTRESS   J.H. BRADBURN   and   ASSOCIATES, P.C.

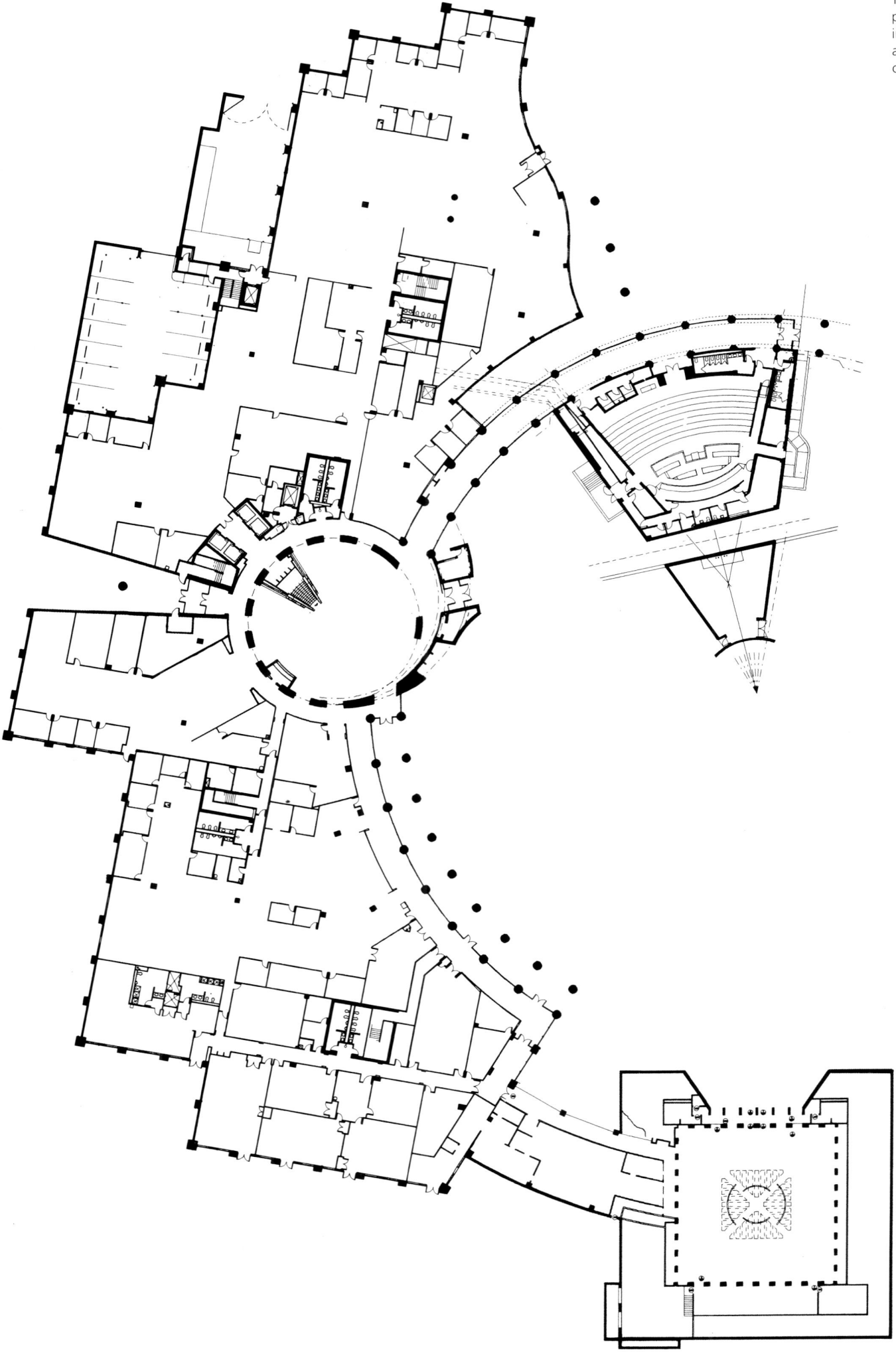

Two views of the
amphitheatre showing
how the building is
integrated into the
surrounding
environment.

The drawings carved into the perimetral wall embody the historic images of the region.

Left, the pyramid containing the cafeteria; below, the colonnade enclosing the amphitheatre. Opposite, detail of the main entrance tower.

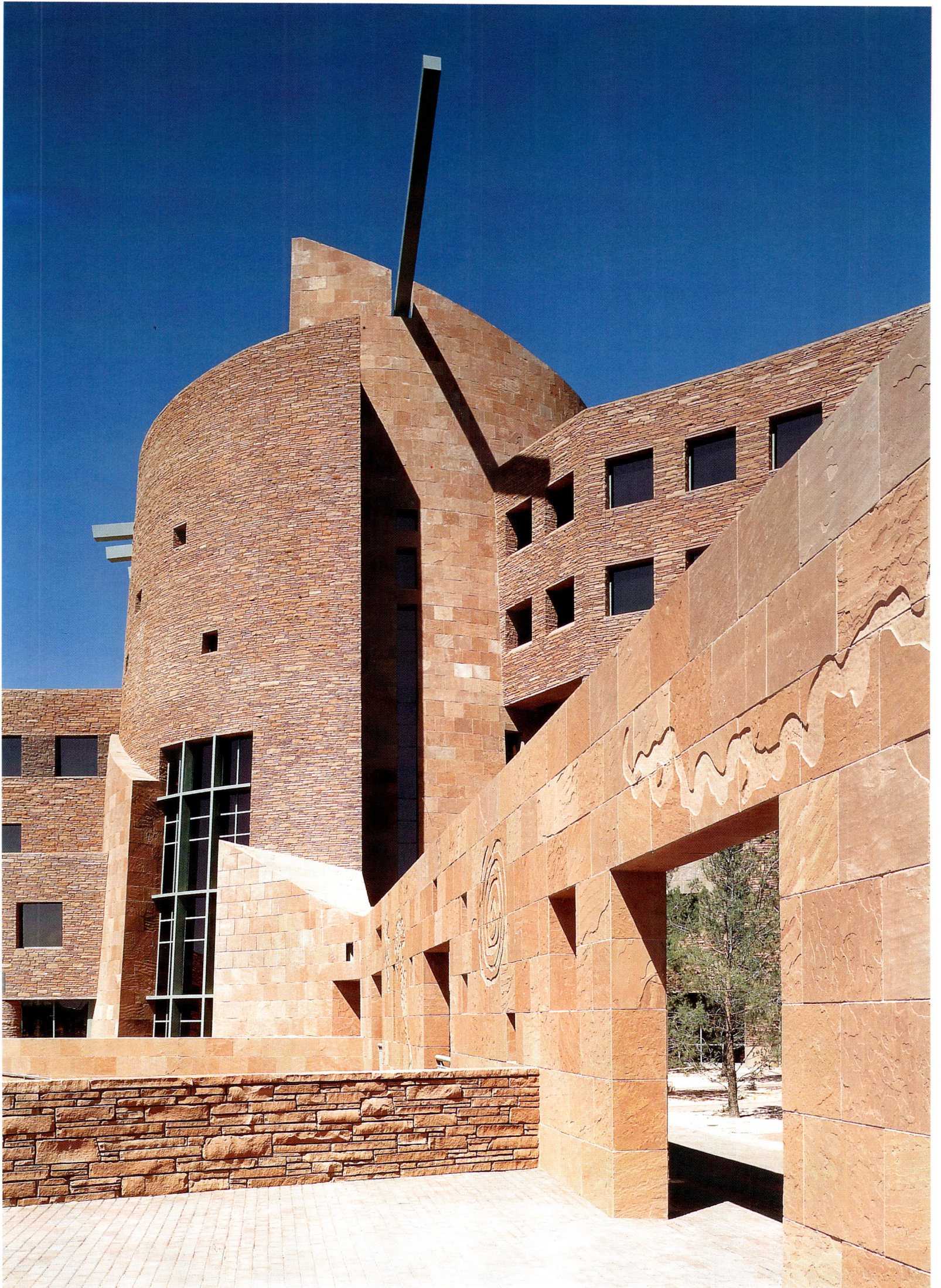

Two views of the interior
of the building, where
the combined formation
blocks out direct
sunlight and allows
cooler, indirect light to
filter through.

C. W. Fentress J. H. Bradburn and Associates

Denver International Airport

The Denver International Airport Passenger Terminal Complex is designed to create an iconographic symbol for the city of Denver, a breathtaking showcase of local pride and sense of place. The terminal building's symbolic roof structure of white peaks is a visual homage to the majestic Rocky Mountains.

Denver International Airport is the largest integrated tensile fabric structure in the world, covering almost 660,000 square feet or over fifteen acres. Its undulating fabric roof of thirty-four peaks, each rising to a height of approximately 120 feet, encloses the "Great Hall", whose design is mirrored in the curbside canopies of the drop-off and pick-up areas. The high-tech roof serves a variety of both functional and aesthetic uses. Its gently undulating curves imbue the interior with its own special character, while at the same time allowing in a flood of natural light. The wonderfully luminous balance of direct and diffuse sunlight brings the indoor and outdoor environments into close symbiosis. In the evening, interior lighting in the Great Hall illuminates the roof structure, creating a beacon of light visible for miles.

On a practical level, the intricately articulated waterproof building skin allows savings on both lighting and cooling costs by reducing the number of air-conditioning systems required to compensate for the additional heat generated by artificial lights. The entire passenger terminal complex is designed using state-of-the-art building materials to create a user-friendly facility of the highest comfort, convenience and efficiency.

Its key features include runways designed to allow simultaneous take-offs and arrivals, computerised runway lighting to guide pilots in conditions of low visibility, de-icing areas for accommodating up to six planes prior to take-off, and advanced wind shear detectors to warn of microbursts or sudden downdrafts.

The terminal is arranged along a north-south axis with three linear east-west concourses to the north. The south end of the terminal is characterised by a large glass wall providing panoramic views of the surrounding Colorado landscape.

The towering, translucent peaks of the fiberglass roof and huge expanse of the Great Hall conjure up the grandeur of the great railway stations of the past, reviving in one stroke the past sense of awe and romance once associated with travel.

This gateway to Denver is a one-of-a-kind place that will leave a lasting mark on international airport design.

The key feature
of the entire complex
is the centrally-located
Great Hall with its
34-peak tensile structure
covering an area
of 21,000 square metres.
Opposite page, general
site plan.

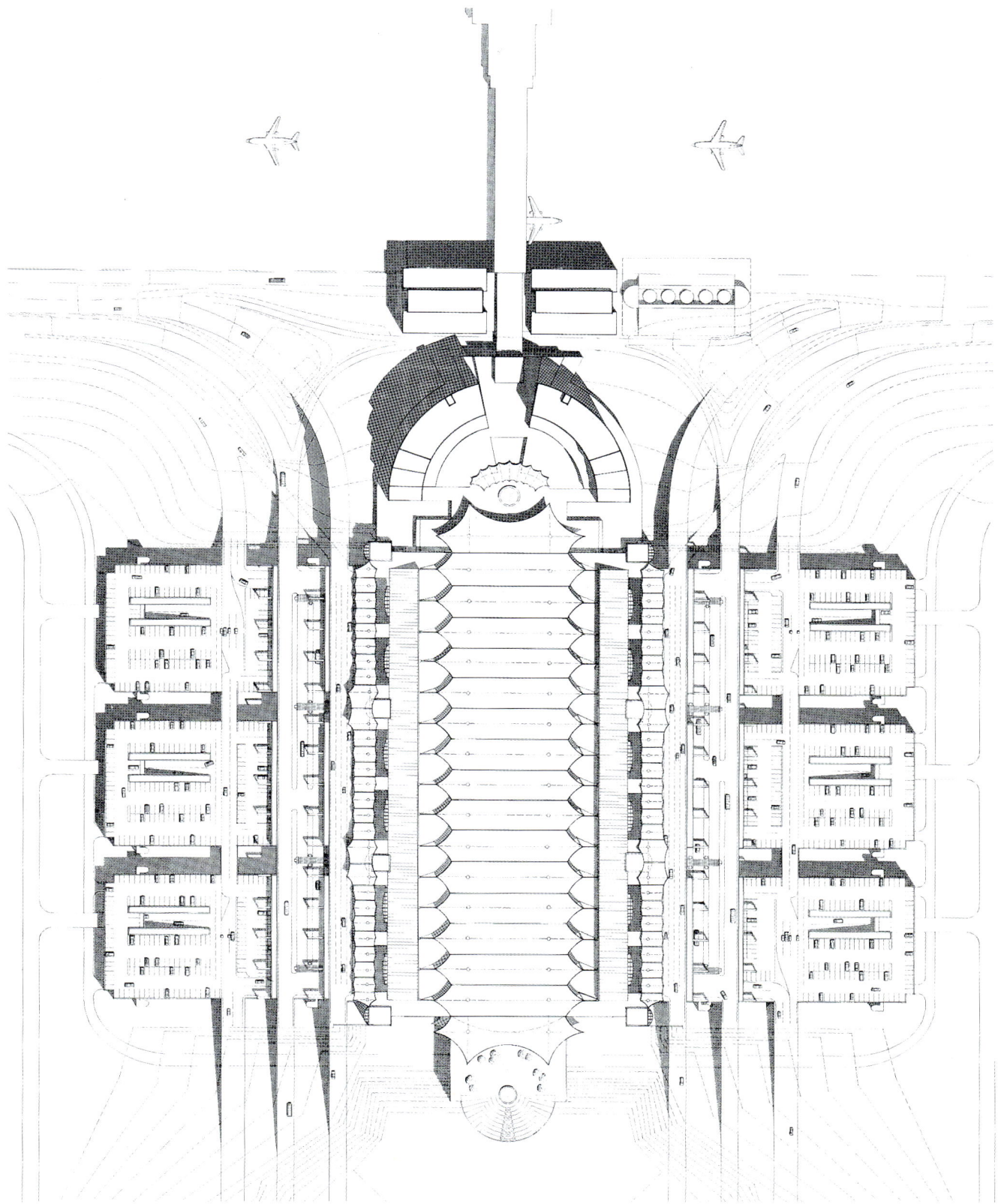

Below longitudinal
section; opposite page,
south elevation
and cross section of
the complex. Bottom
of page, overall view
showing details
of the roof.

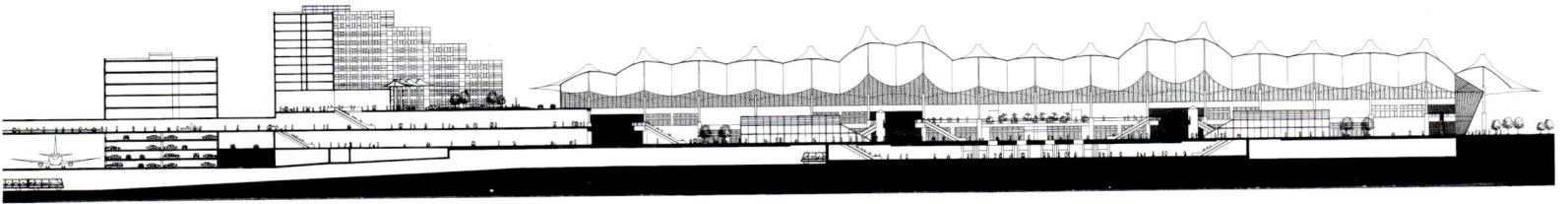

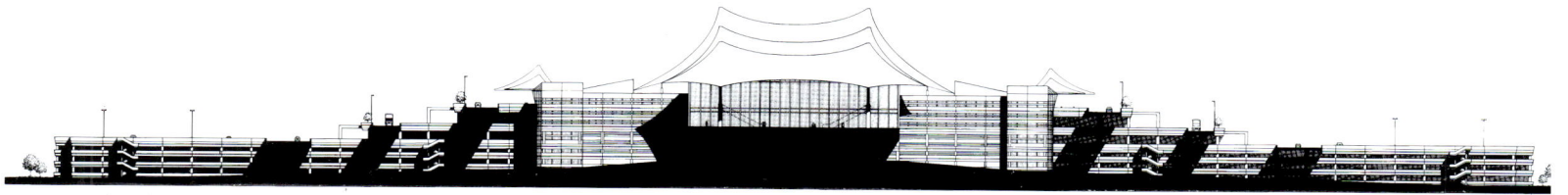

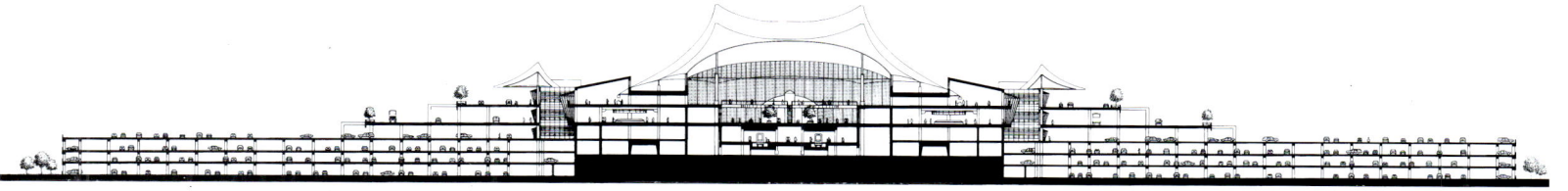

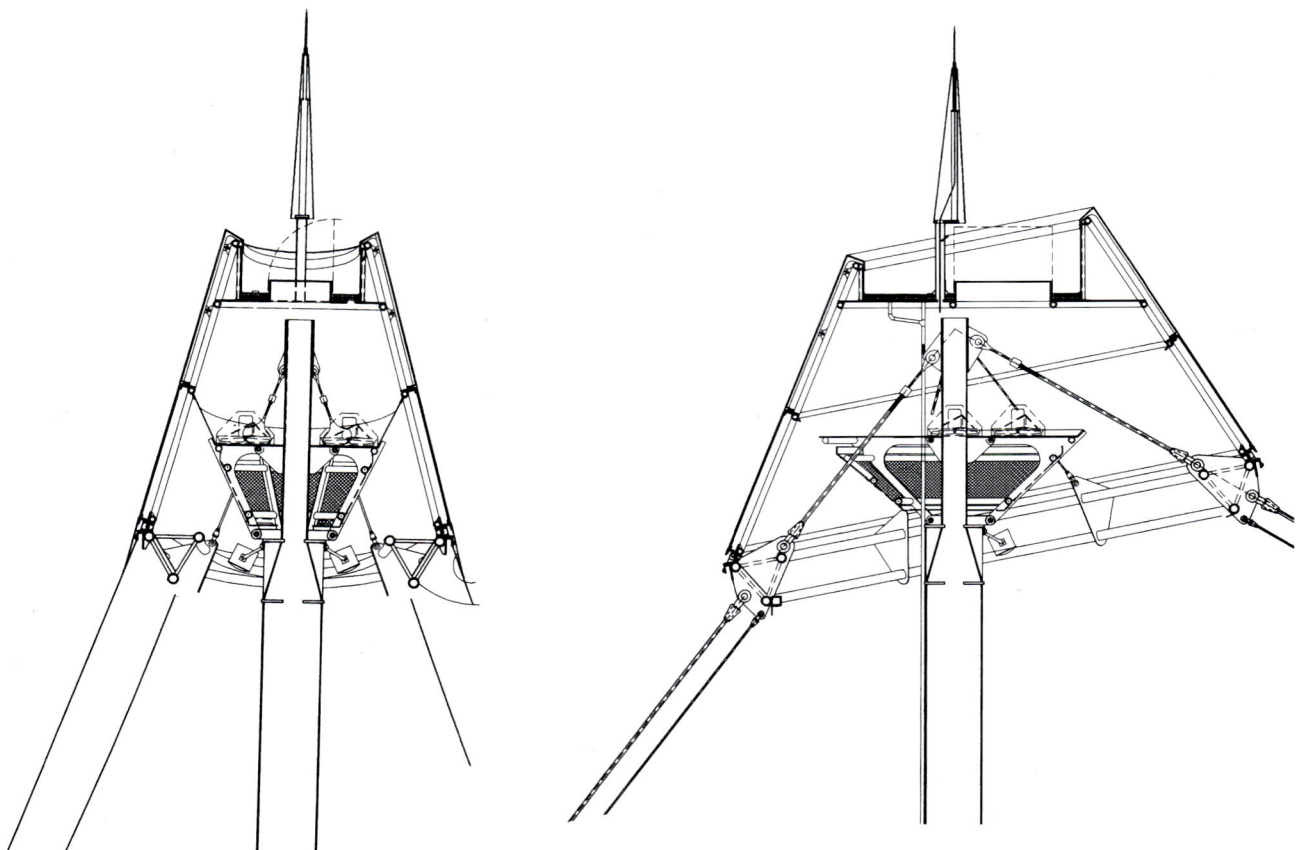

Detail of the airport
entrance.

The panoramic walkway showing the tie-rods supporting the tensile roof that reflect the structural synthesis of this expressive architectural structure in high-tech language.

A particularly welcoming atmosphere is created in the interiors of the Great Hall by the permanent natural lighting flowing through the large glass surfaces, and the fiber glass fabrick roof coated with Teflon.

High technology
and research into space
and forms are the main
features of this project.

ATKINSON DRIVE

KAPIOLANI BOULEVARD

KAHAKAI DRIVE

KALAKAUA AVENUE

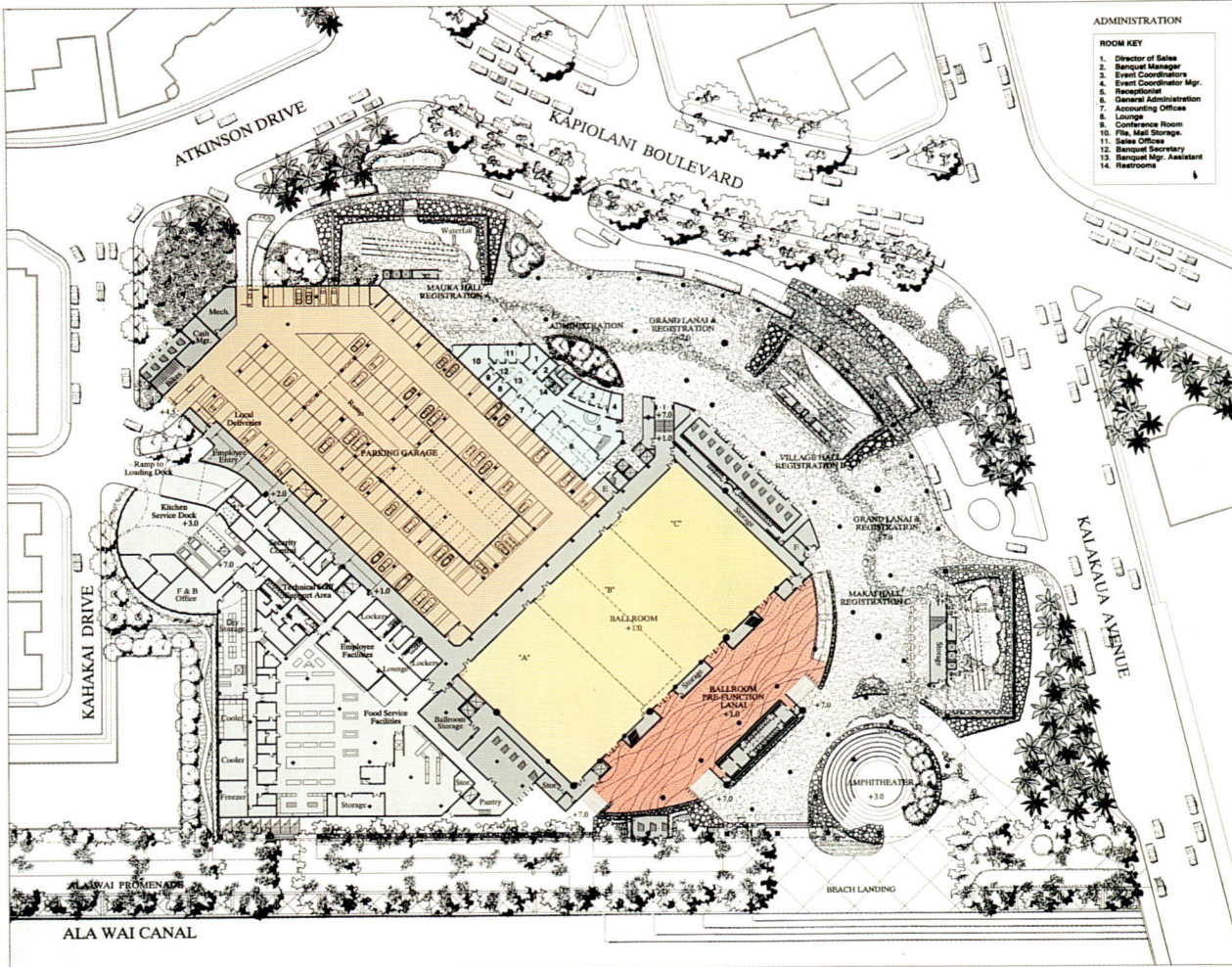

ADMINISTRATION

ROOM KEY
1. Director of Sales
2. Banquet Manager
3. Event Coordinators
4. Event Coordinator Mgr.
5. Receptionist
6. General Administration
7. Accounting Offices
8. Lounge
9. Conference Room
10. File, Mail Storage
11. Sales Offices
12. Banquet Secretary
13. Banquet Mgr. Assistant
14. Restrooms

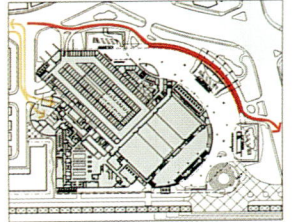

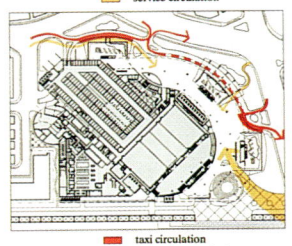

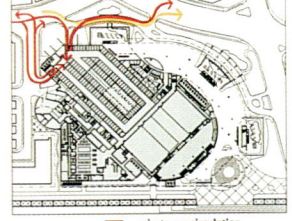

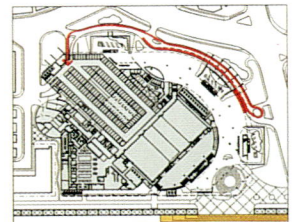

Waterfall

MAUKA HALL REGISTRATION

ADMINISTRATION

GRAND LANAI & REGISTRATION A

Mech.

Mgr.

Local Deliveries

Employee Entry

PARKING GARAGE

Ramp to Loading Dock

Kitchen Service Dock

VILLAGE HALL REGISTRATION D

GRAND LANAI & REGISTRATION

F & B Office

"C"

MAKAI HALL REGISTRATION C

Technical Staff Banquet Area

"B"

BALLROOM

Cooler

"A"

Employee Facilities

Lockers

Lockers

BALLROOM PRE-FUNCTION LANAI

Food Service Facilities

Cooler

Ballroom Storage

Storage

Cooler

Pantry

AMPHITHEATER

Freezer

Storage

ALA WAI PROMENADE

BEACH LANDING

ALA WAI CANAL

bus circulation
service circulation

taxi circulation
pedestrian circulation

private car circulation
waikiki people mover

valet circulation
boat landing

Hawaii Convention Center

The challenge underlying this project was to design a practical, functional convention center of great aesthetic beauty that might be described as embodying that state of mind and feeling of well-being and acceptance associated with what is known as the "Aloha Spirit". The final design drew from the very best of Hawaii's rich cultural history and varied landscape, while setting new standards for architectural excellence and sensitivity.

The three-level building incorporates a generous amount of open space, outdoor landscape, water features and a large 400-seat outdoor amphitheatre on the first level. The second level contains 100,000 square feet of meeting room space divided into four banks of rectangular rooms. The third level houses a 200,000-square-foot exhibition hall. The essence of the design is the relationship between interior and exterior space, exploiting the local climate to marry indoors with outdoors and eliminating doors, windows, exterior walls and any other potential barriers to evoke a strong sense of warmth and hospitality.

The high ceilings and wide corridors at the meeting room level allow sunlight and cool trade winds to flow through the corridors refreshing the entire environment.

High waterfalls, pools, streams, ponds, and rows of trees and shrubs are all paramount to the overall site plan, alleviating the bulk of building masses and alluding to natural elements of pre-contact Hawaii in a carefully construed symbiosis of technology and tradition. These leitmotivs are reinforced in the choice of building materials and their colors and textures. The main facade elements are embellished with a stucco finish and the light-grey pre-cast columns and beams are reminiscent of the weathered woods along Hawaii's coastline. The terrazzo floor patterns simulate the coral beaches and turquoise waters in a combination of large and small stones.

The shades of jade and turquoise recreate the subtle colour variations of water as it travels down from mountain to ocean, from Mauka to Makai. The interior design is a synthesis of the functional need for durable, easily maintained finishes and a more intimate extension of the building's exterior concepts. The landscape elements incorporated in the design are important as the building is truly set within the landscape. The convention center's careful design heightens an awareness of Hawaii's unique sense of place, thereby differentiating this low-impact building from hundreds of other similar centres around the world.

Two details of the
exterior architecture of
the Hawaii Convention
Center.

Site plan of the entire
complex.

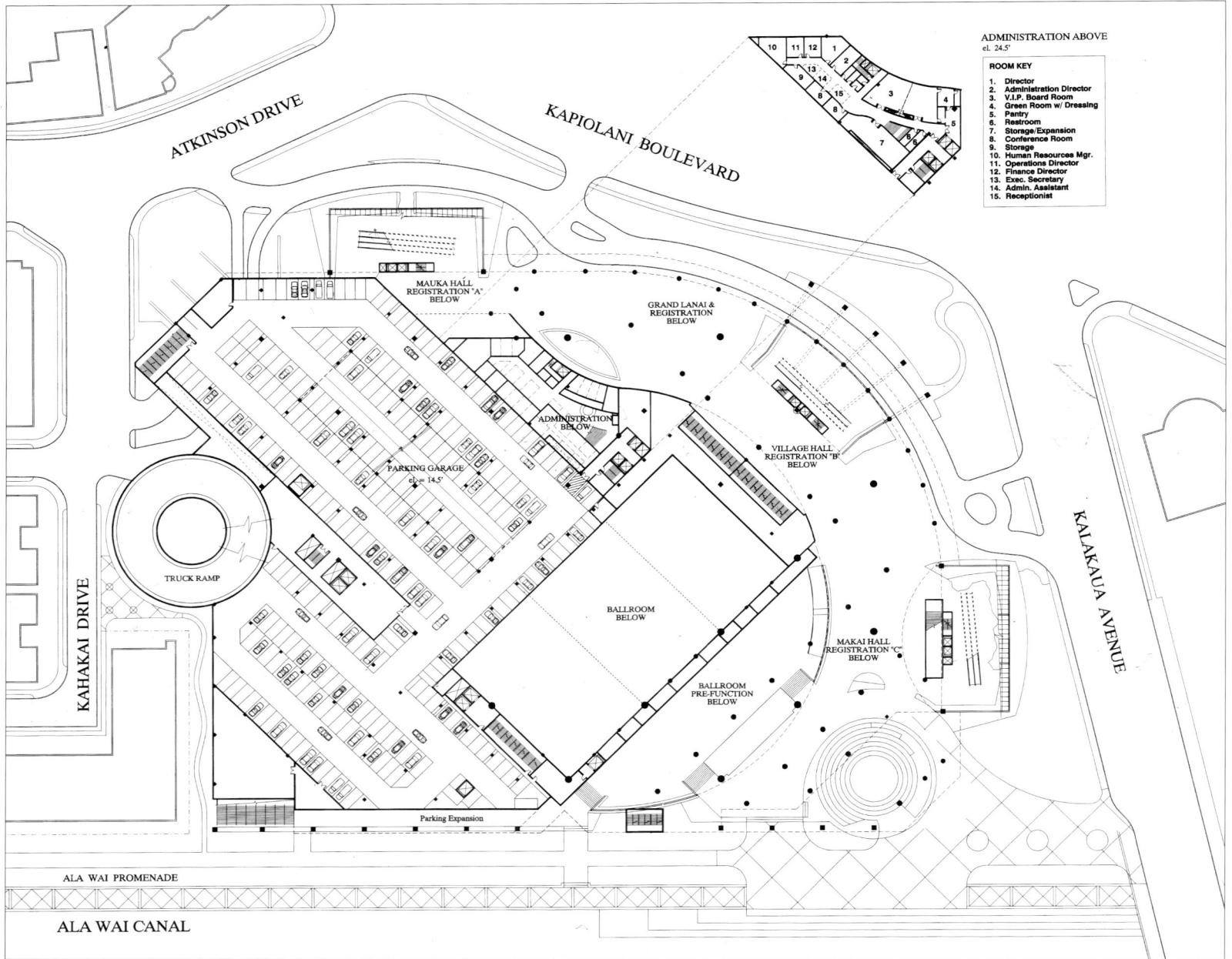

ATKINSON DRIVE

KAPIOLANI BOULEVARD

ADMINISTRATION ABOVE
el. 24.5'

ROOM KEY
1. Director
2. Administration Director
3. V.I.P. Board Room
4. Green Room w/ Dressing
5. Pantry
6. Restroom
7. Storage/Expansion
8. Conference Room
9. Storage
10. Human Resources Mgr.
11. Operations Director
12. Finance Director
13. Exec. Secretary
14. Admin. Assistant
15. Receptionist

MAUKA HALL
REGISTRATION "A"
BELOW

GRAND LANAI &
REGISTRATION
BELOW

ADMINISTRATION
BELOW

VILLAGE HALL
REGISTRATION "B"
BELOW

KALAKAUA AVENUE

PARKING GARAGE
el. = 14.5'

TRUCK RAMP

KAHAKAI DRIVE

BALLROOM
BELOW

MAKAI HALL
REGISTRATION "C"
BELOW

BALLROOM
PRE-FUNCTION
BELOW

Parking Expansion

ALA WAI PROMENADE

ALA WAI CANAL

Overall view of the
model and two building
sections.

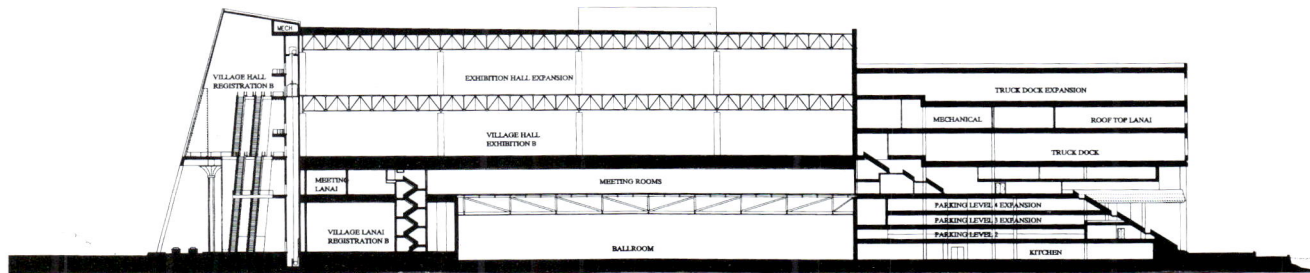

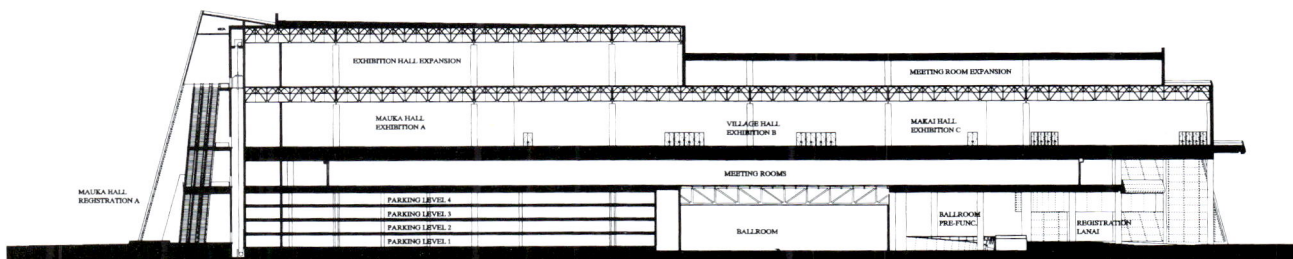

Moscow Redevelopment Center

Experimenting with capitalistic constructs in a burgeoning democracy is usually a tenuous business, particularly if the new democracy in question is emerging from a totalitarian regime. In the case of Russia, subsequent to the collapse of the former Soviet Union, the desire to launch a programme of free creation has often far outpaced the nation's physical ability to do so. Liaisons with foreign countries have become one of the most successful means of achieving these aims with little capital investment.

For its part, the foreign firm in question uses this new liaison to establish a beachhead in a new and potentially lucrative market. In the case of the Moscow Redevelopment Center, the Russian entrepreneurs who launched the project certainly were not lacking in either capital or creativity, but what they were looking for was an influx of extra-Russian design work.

Fentress Bradburn soon recognised the project's latent potential to further test the international breadth of their philosophical concept of contextual regionalism while distilling new life into the bland sterility of conventional Soviet architecture. The infusing of true Russian life back into a society in the process of becoming was clearly evident in the new designs.

The new complex of apartments, a hotel and office-retail space is a fine example of co-mingling designed to unite and not segregate. Intertextual figures have created a variety of building masses that are calming rather than confrontational, introducing new soothing elements into local society. Human concerns, such as comfort and ease-of-use, were given paramount importance, driving ideology into a state of inconsequence. As this new project gradually develops, it will undoubtedly take on the status of a monument of cooperation between the architectural communities of the United States and a new Russia.

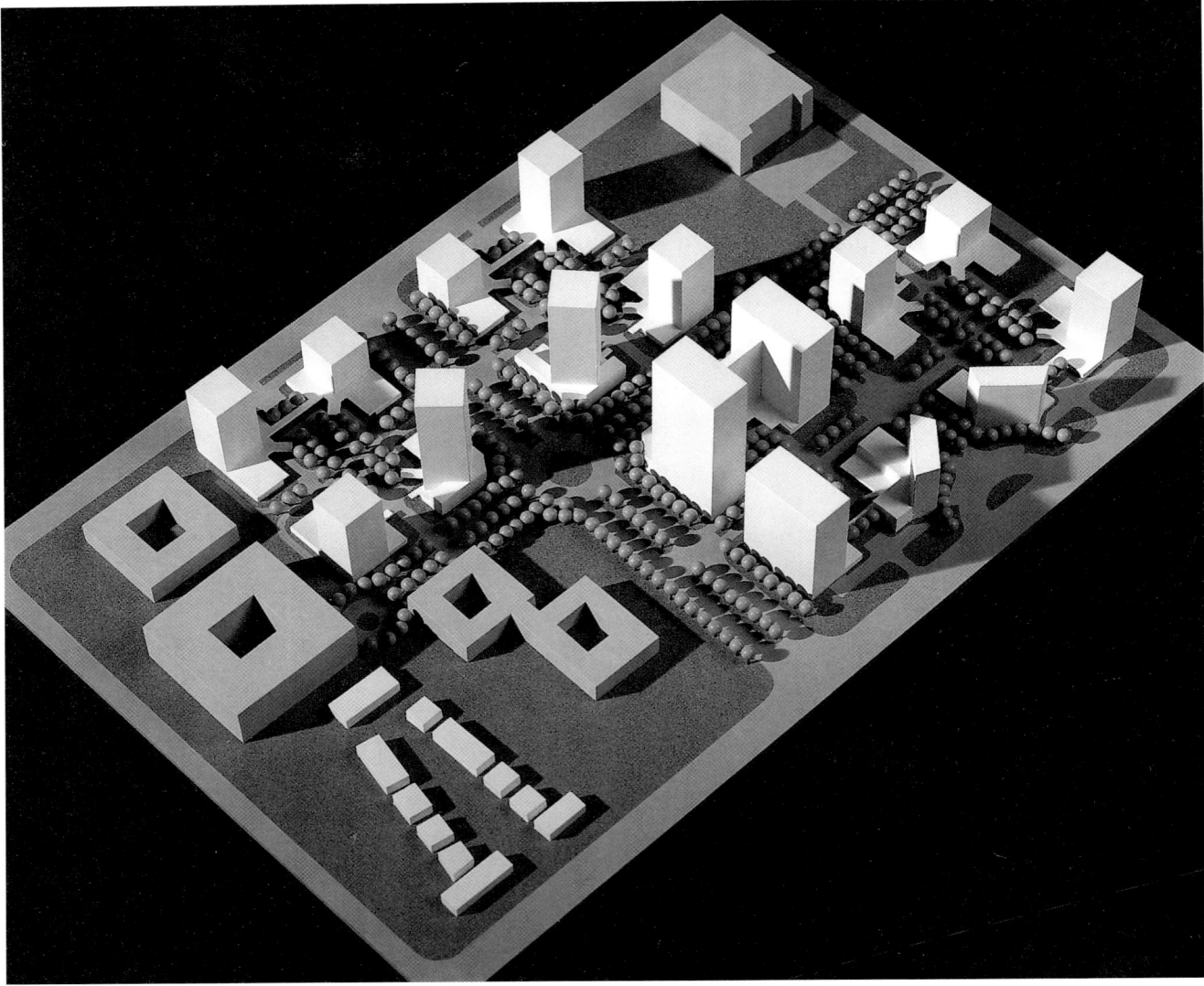

Two pictures of the
model. The building's
intricate, flat
architectural forms
blend incisively into the
environment with great
ease. Opposite page,
site plan.

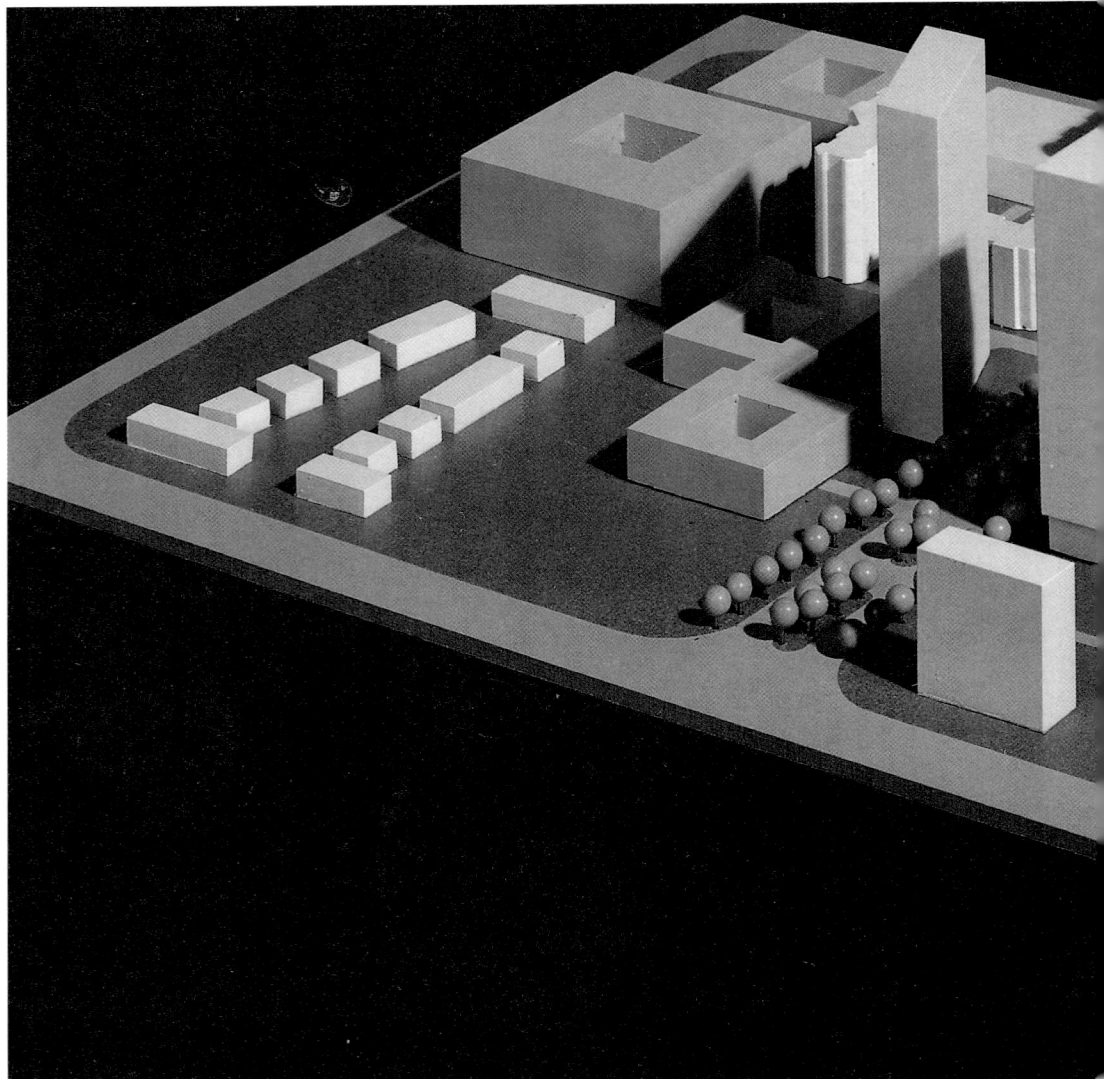

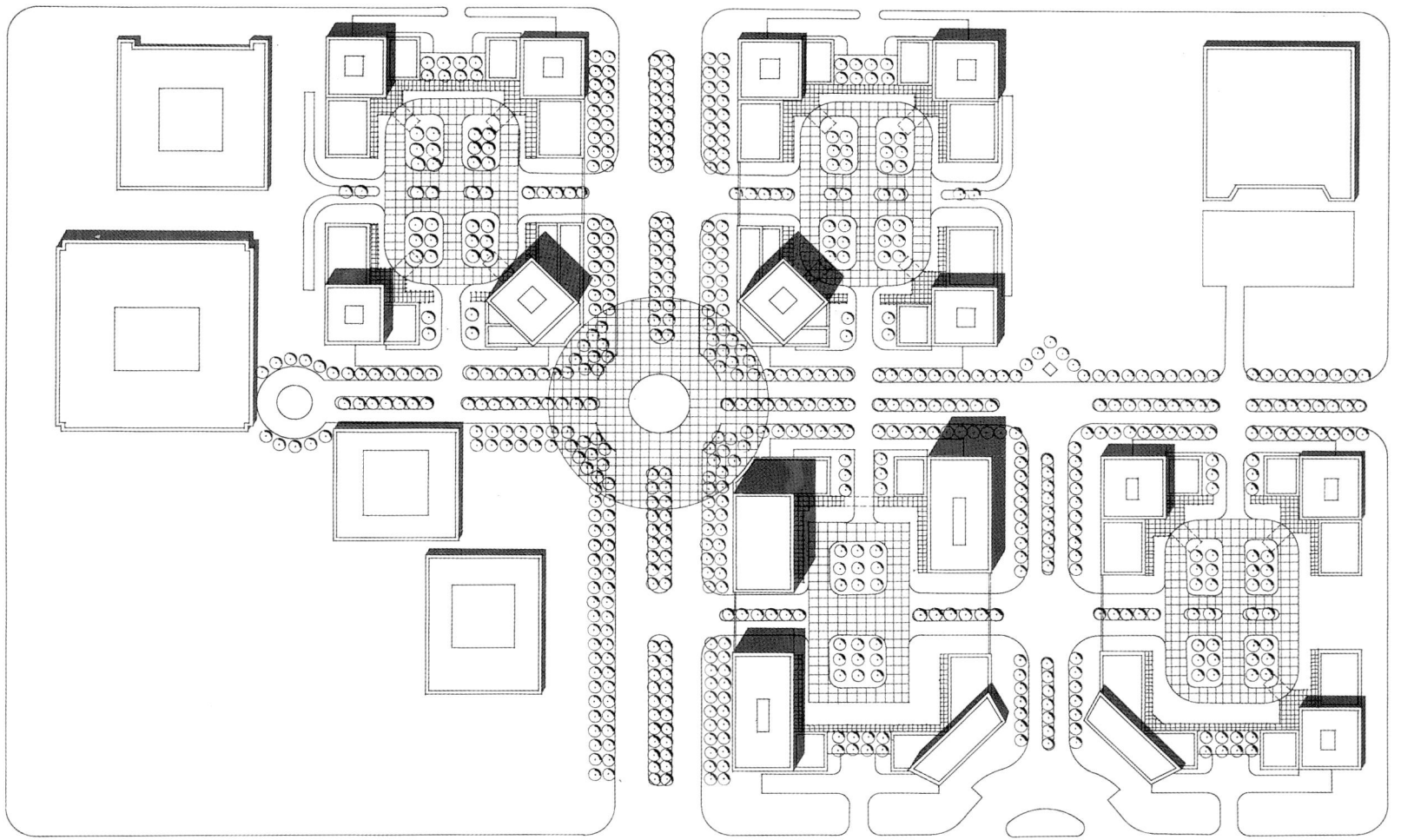

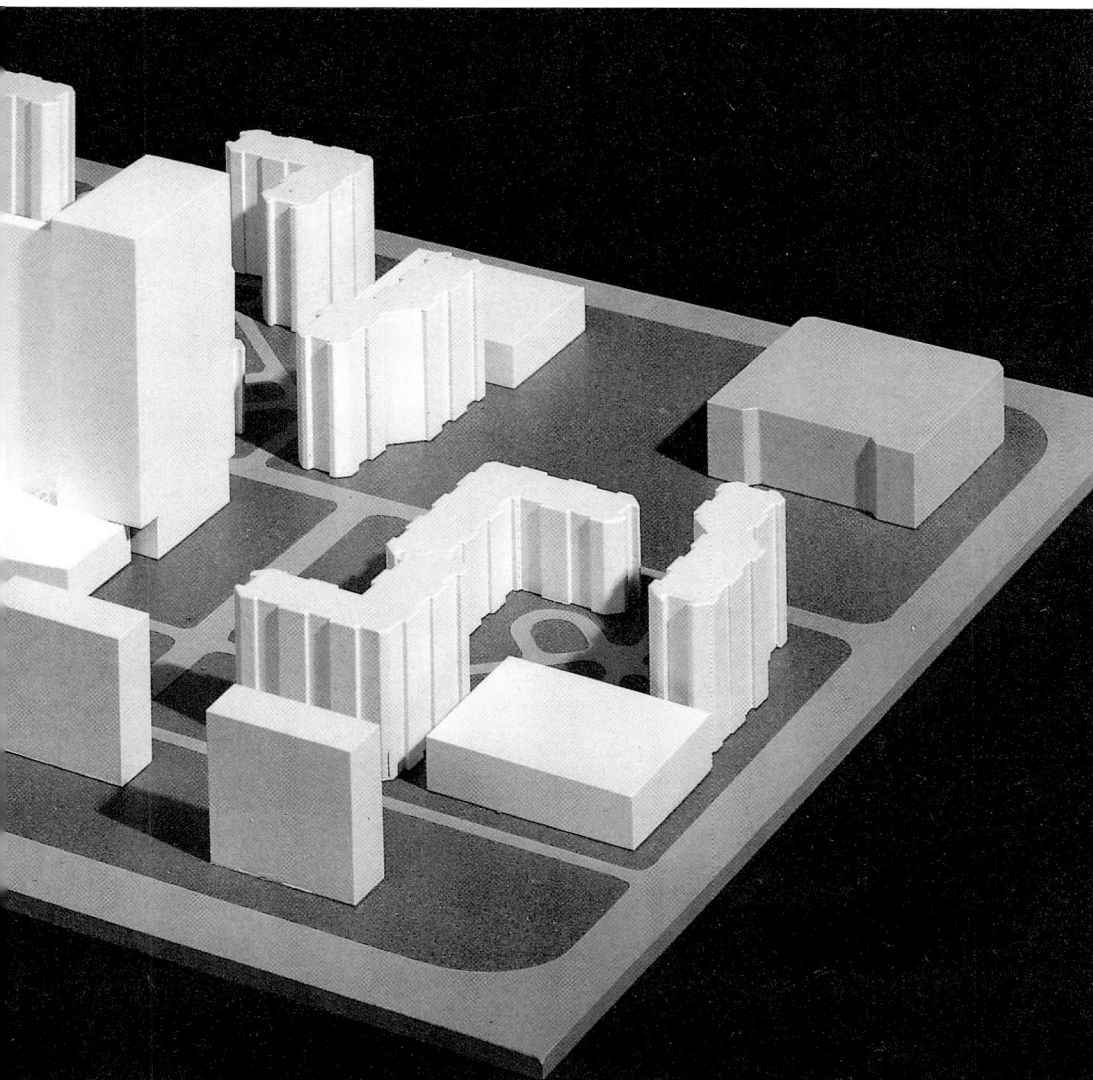

Vladivostok City Center

Bowing to the rapid growth and development of the international communities on the Pacific rim, Russia has recently revised its isolationist position and begun the process of attracting visitors from all over the world. This is why the seaport of Vladivostok leapt at the challenge of creating a new center around which a tourist driven economy would have a great chance to flourish. Fentress Bradburn's response to this challenge was to create a huge complex, including a 300-room hotel, 600 luxury apartments and yachting slips, one million square feet of office space and parking facilities for two-thousand vehicles, designed to revitalise and breathe life into the undeveloped potential of this pristine location. The complex's concrete structure has an exterior finish of precast concrete and glass, and interiors made of gypsum and lined with carpets.

The Russian naval seaport of Vladivostok, located just 640 miles from Tokyo on the Sea of Japan, provided the company with a unique opportunity to create an image of new Russia. A definite late-modern influence is clearly visible in the overall project design of the new complex, which rises up from the shoreline in a series of virtual steps accentuating the sloping hillside on which it is grounded. The figure-ground relationships of the site plan, extrapolated from Russian cultural imagery, create a portrait of the new around which the old city forms a strikingly colorful mosaic.

A proposed site plan
for Vladivostok.

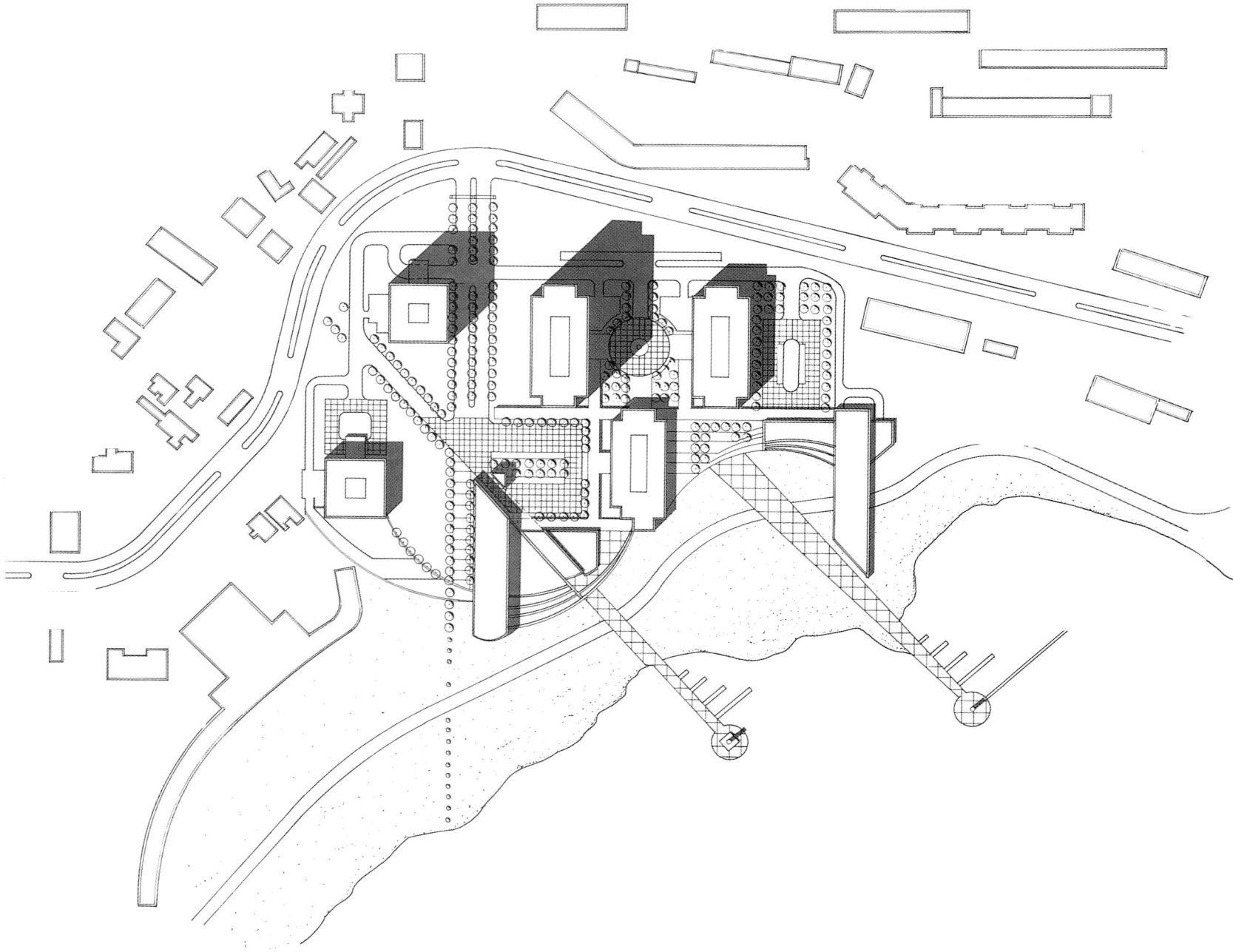

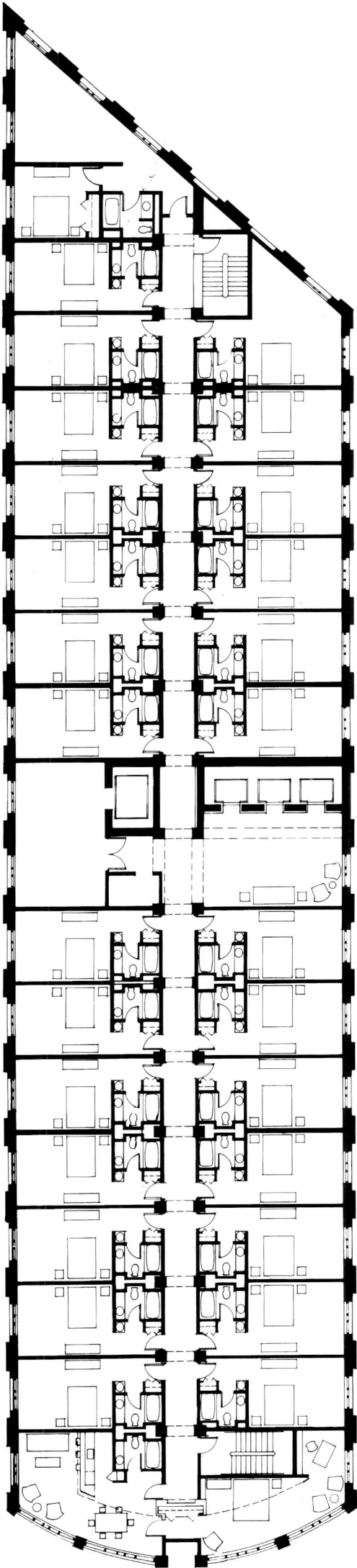

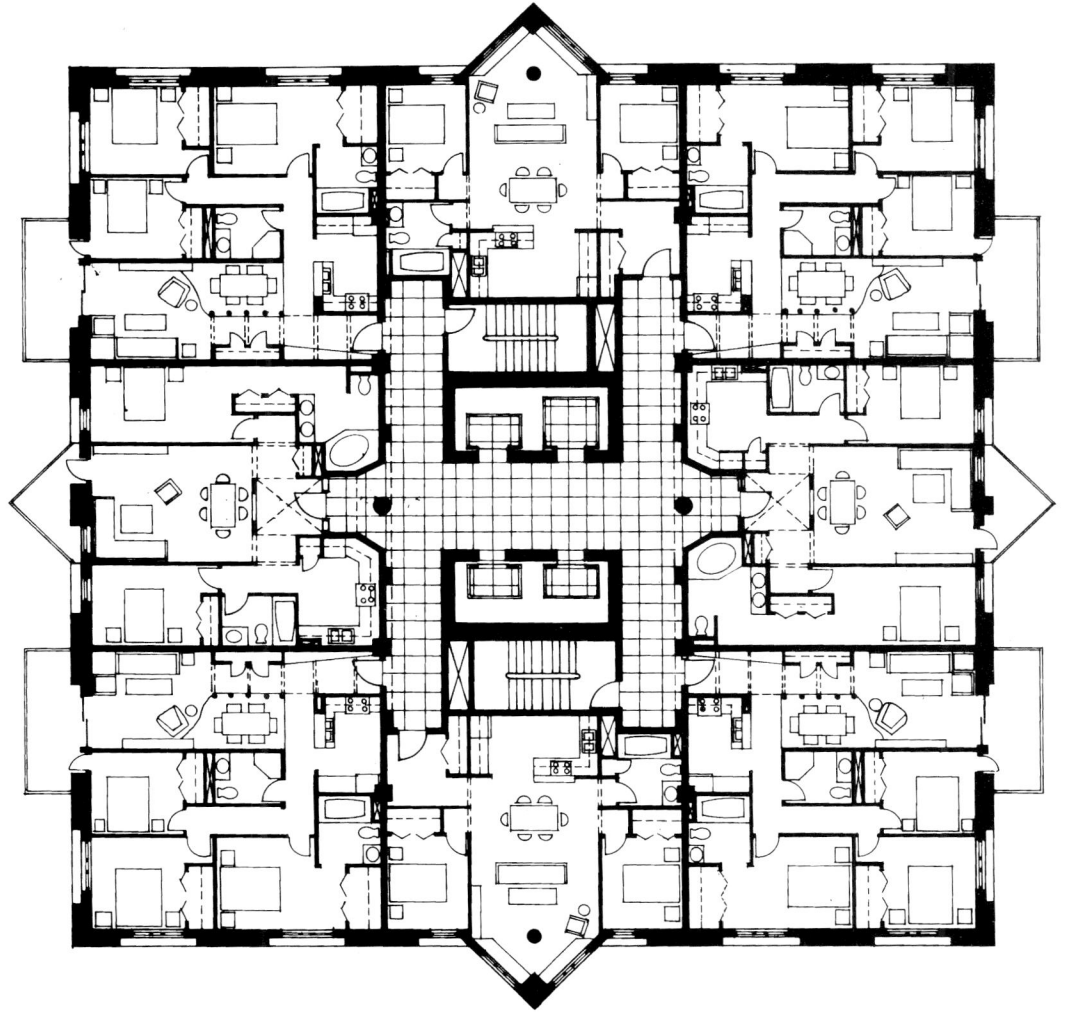

Two standard plans
of the proposed hotel
complexes.

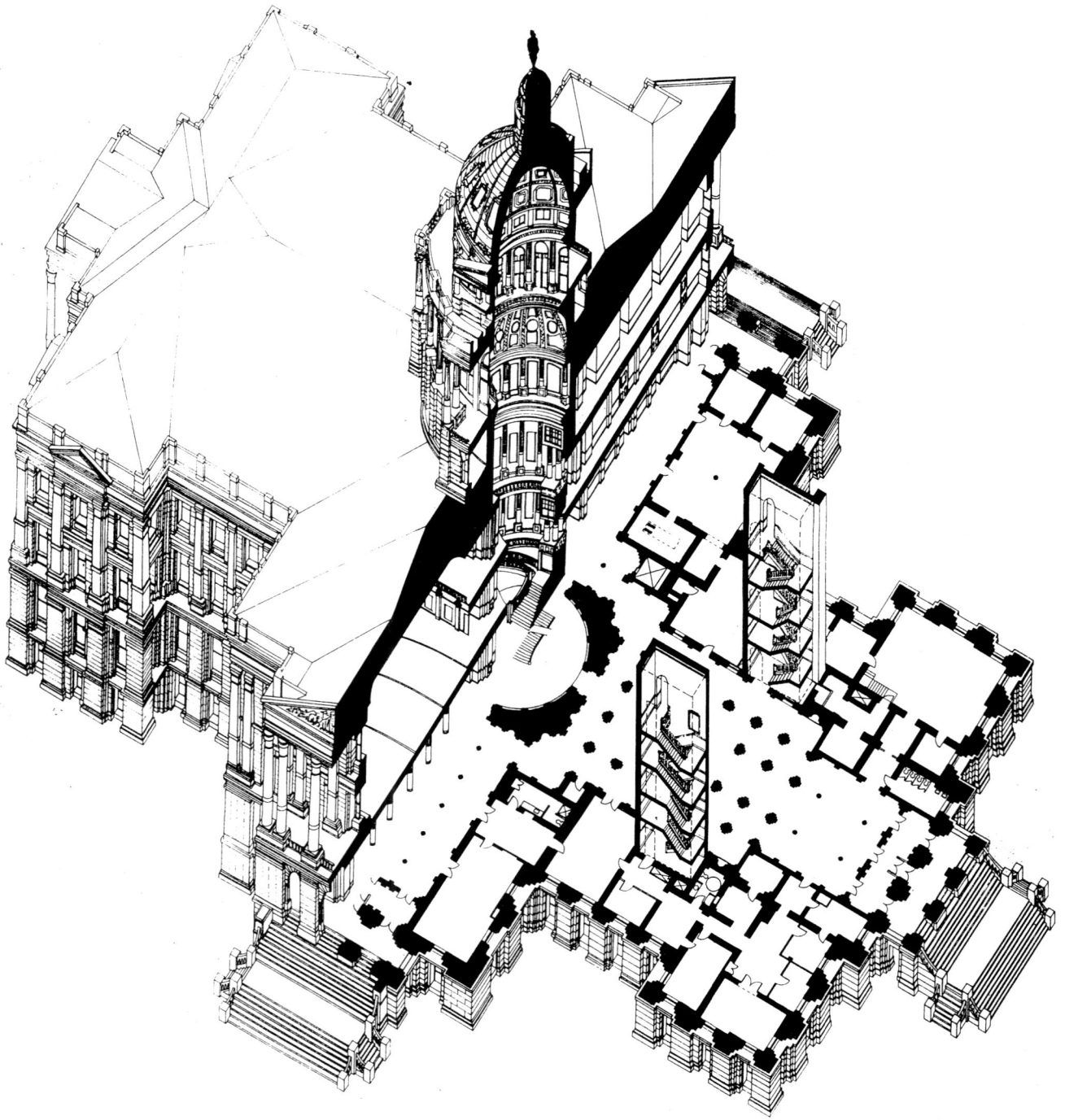

Colorado State Capitol

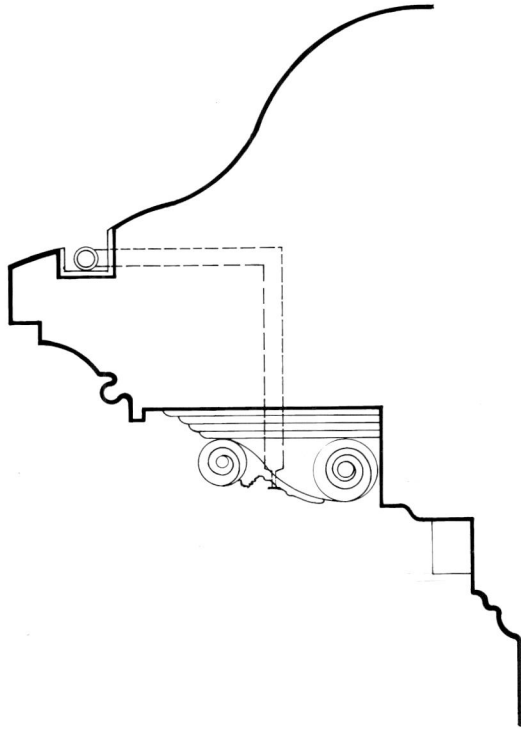

The Colorado State Capitol is Colorado's most significant architectural landmark and one of its citizens' most treasured historic artifacts.

Historians have stated that the building embodies the true essence of Colorado in its predominantly native materials: epitomised by its Ft. Collins' sandstone foundations, grey Gunnison granite exterior walls, ornate marble floors and stairs from Marble, Beulah rose onyx wainscoting, and Michelangelesque dome, leafed in Colorado gold.

The Capitol was originally designed by Detroit architect Elijah E. Meyers and first inhabited by Governor Davis H. Waite in 1894, housing the Tenth General Assembly in 1895. The building has undergone numerous modernization operations during its first century of service, but many of these changes have had negative repercussions on the Capitol's historic features, safety standards and functionality.

The Colorado State Capitol renovation project is a multi-year programme of phased restoration and building system improvements. The key to the entire project is an Historic Building Preservation Plan (HBPP) designed to guide renovation operations.

The entire project's design philosophy hinges around uncompromising respect and sensitivity for the historic character of this national landmark. Any missing or damaged original fabric is restored with matching materials and construction techniques. New high profile elements, such as extended stairways and access corridors to the dome observation desk, are carefully designed to blend in with the original architecture, creating a harmonious family of architectural elements, all related but not identical. New utilitarian accessories, such as fire sprinklers and smoke detectors, are positioned and detailed so that they can hardly be noticed at all. Although the century-old structure is made of iron, masonry, concrete and marble, a number of essential safety-related modifications are required to reduce the risk of potentially devastating fires and bring the building in line with stringent safety standards.

The renovation work is divided into a series of phases: Phase One, involving the installation of a sprinkler system for the dome and sub-basement. Sub-phases Two-Five include the restoration of the original vaulted ceilings of the House and Senate chamber, the renovation of the original east entrance and new work on stair extensions, dome access corridors, smoke control, fire sprinklers and fire alarm systems for the rest of the building. The project's underlying intention is to allow Colorado's most important architectural landmark to regain its full historic grandeur for the benefit of future generations.

Below, plan
of work on the old
building. The centre-
page picture shows
a longitudinal section
of the Colorado State
Capitol.
Opposite page, section
of the main staircase.

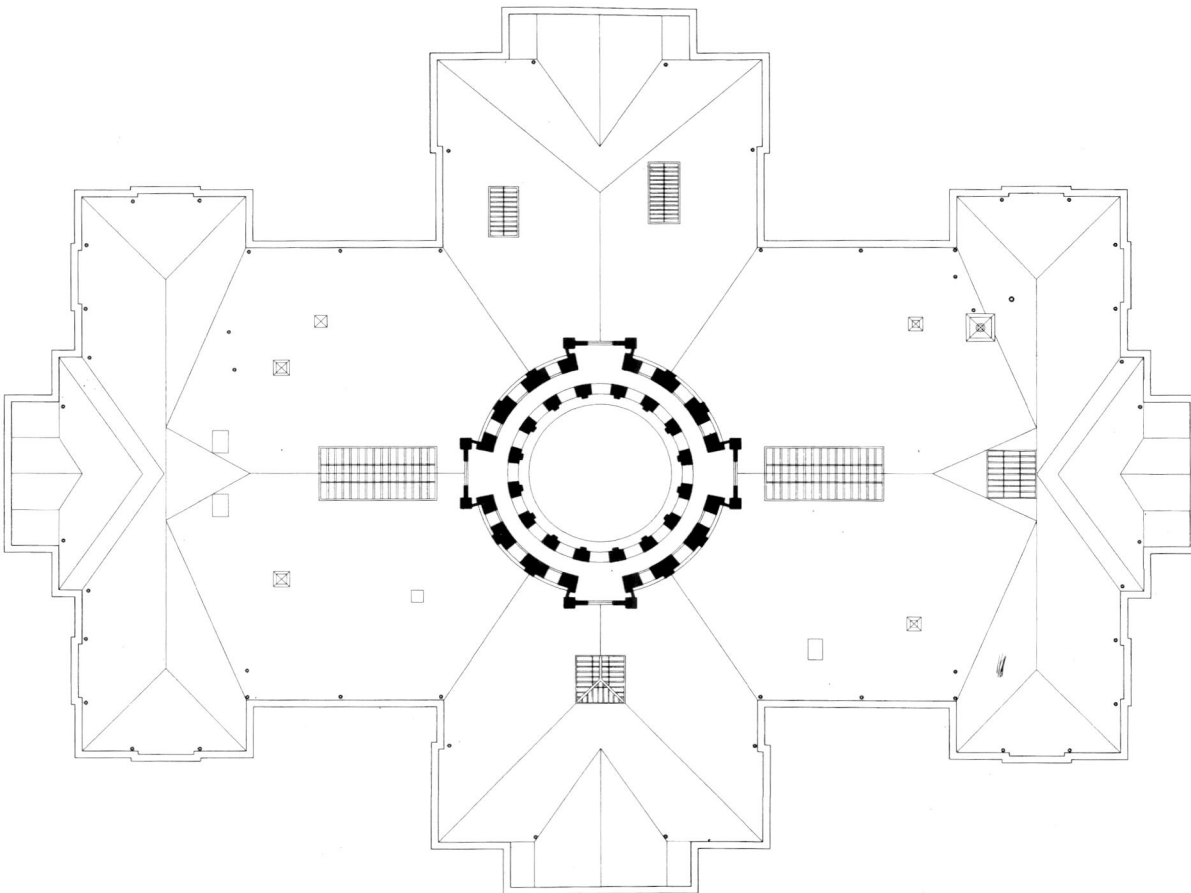

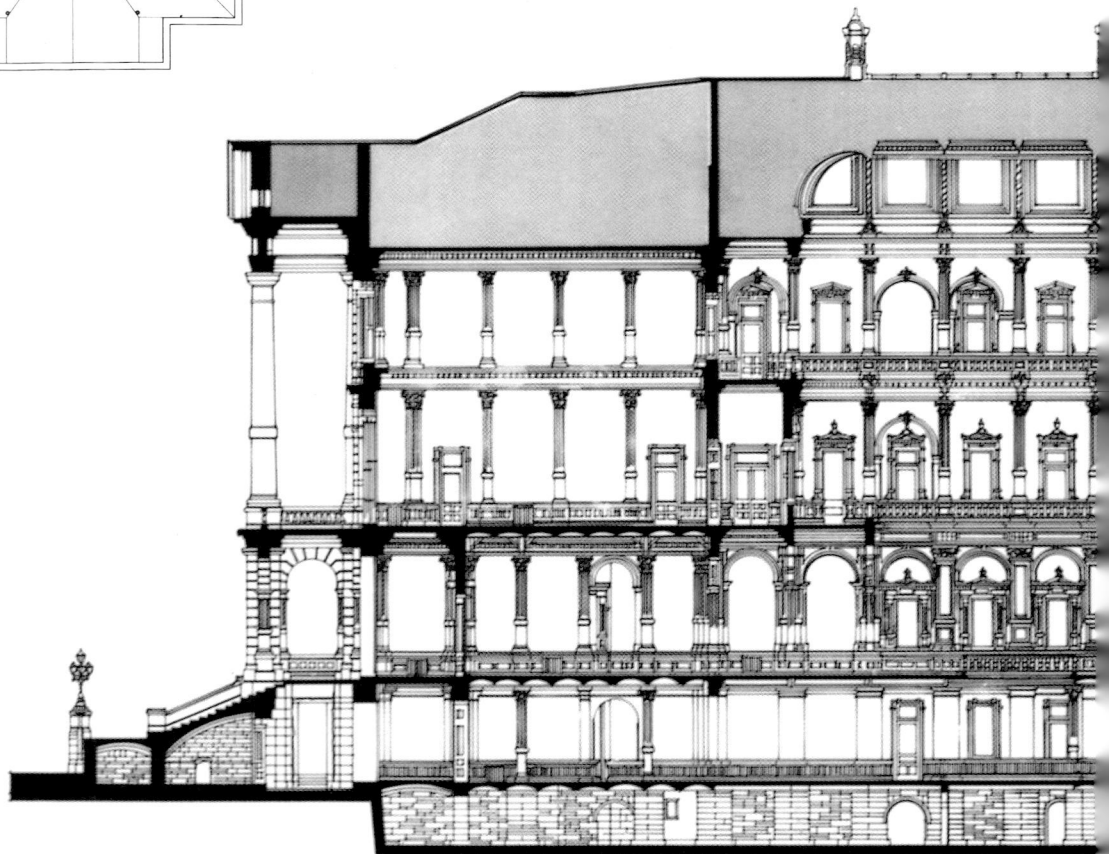

270

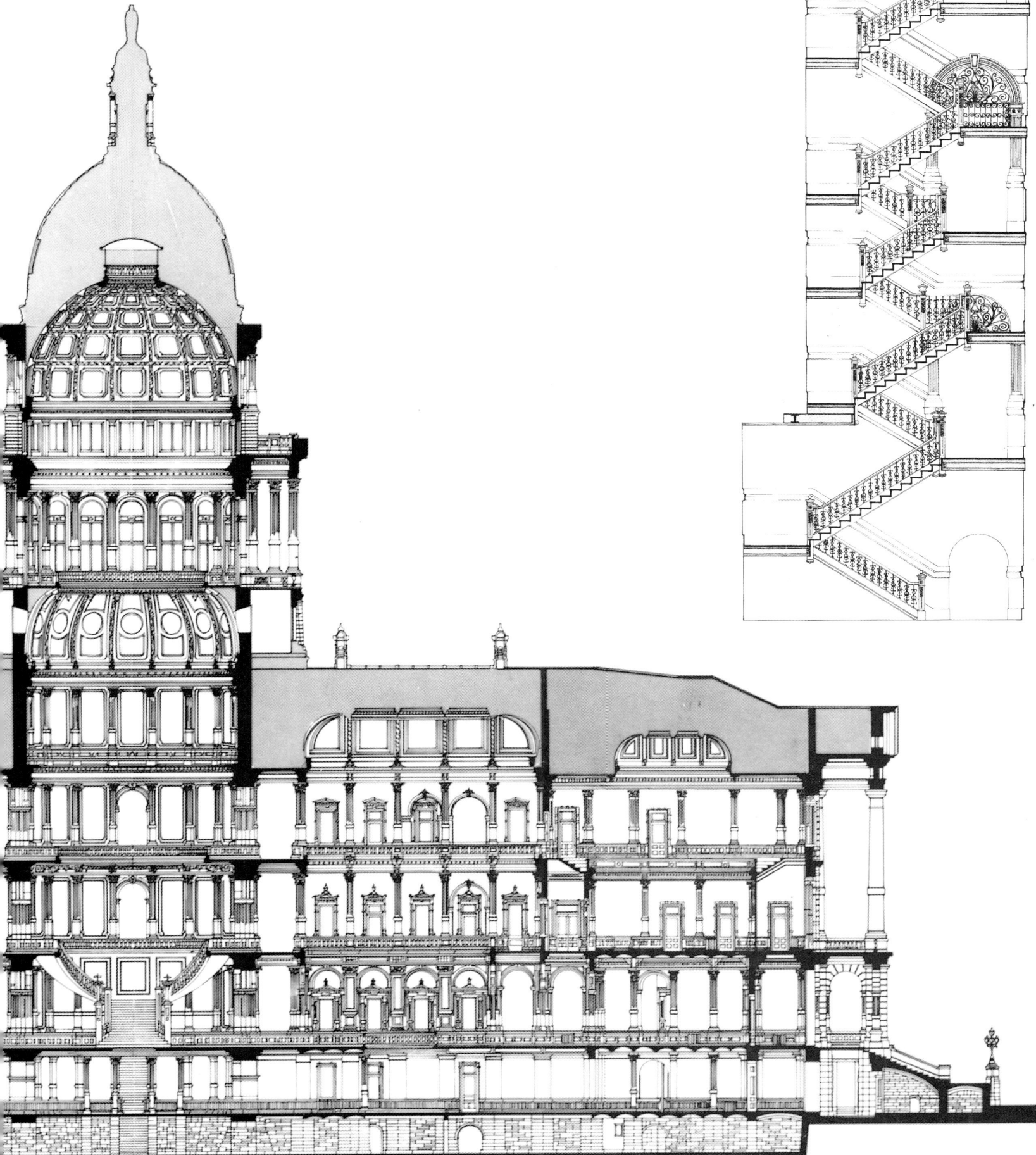

City of Oakland Administration Complex

Since the destruction caused by the Loma Prieta earthquake in 1989, the City of Oakland has invested considerable money and energy into struggling for survival and into an aggressive campaign to rebuild, repair and recapture its sense of permanence and spirit of place.

The two new City office buildings combine with the old City Hall to form a new City Government Complex. The focus of this new complex is the City Hall Building, skilfully designed to allow City Hall to retain its historical prominence thanks to a carefully gauged use of scale and massing, in similar colors and materials. The main entrances to each of the new buildings are deliberately accentuated for easy public recognition and carefully positioned to simplify interrelationships.

In the best democratic tradition, this fine example of civic architecture expresses stability, honesty and purpose. As with many of the nation's civic structures, the new City administration buildings look to the Renaissance for their underlying architectural idiom. Classical architecture symbolises the stability of the government process, exploiting logic and order to make it easily comprehensible. The tripartite ordering of the facade into base, middle and top gives the structure this clear sense of scale.

The combined walls of the existing and new buildings also mark the boundaries of Frank H. Ogawa Plaza. Generally speaking, the new buildings have been carefully constructed to respect the style and scale of existing structures, but like all good neighbours they do not ape or mimic, standing on their own thanks to their clearly defined detailing and articulation.

The goals and ideals underpinning this visionary project have been pursued with great skill and craftsmanship.

The new buildings, each with its own definition and personality, enrich Oakland's urban fabric, while creating a cohesive civic spirit and stimulating economic revitalisation.

Site plan of the City of
Oakland Administration
Complex. Opposite page
another view of the
model.

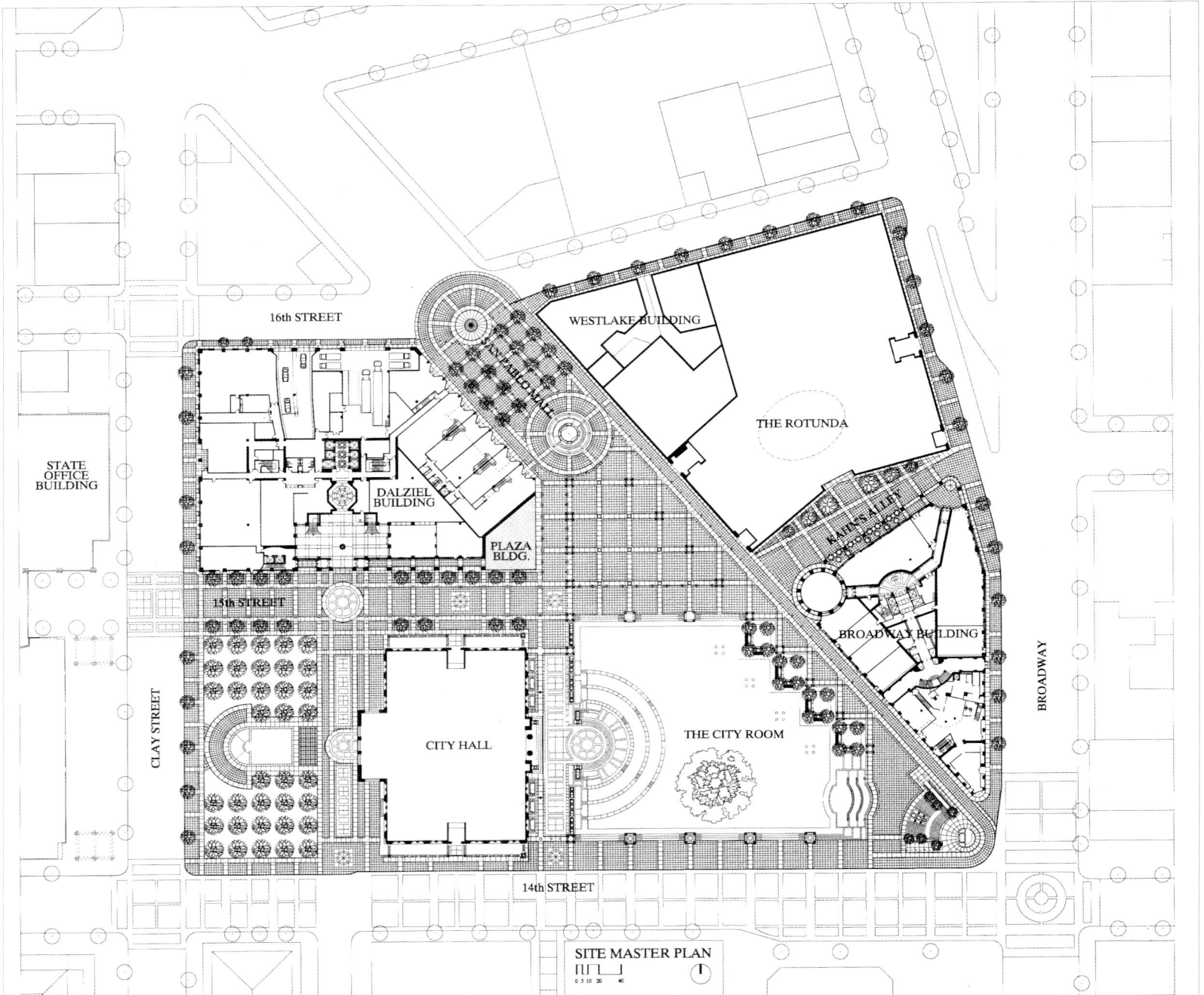

16th STREET

WESTLAKE BUILDING

STATE
OFFICE
BUILDING

THE ROTUNDA

DALZIEL
BUILDING

PLAZA
BLDG.

KAHN'S ALLEY

15th STREET

BROADWAY BUILDING

CLAY STREET

CITY HALL

THE CITY ROOM

BROADWAY

14th STREET

SITE MASTER PLAN

0 5 10 20   40

Roatan Resort
Camp Bay-Port Royal Resort

The Camp Bay-Port Royal Resort is one of the world's greatest natural environments, so the primary purpose of this development scheme was to devise an overall model of sustainable environmental growth for the island of Roatan.

The environmental plans incorporated proper land use patterns, natural resource utilization, non-depletion of the existing water aquifer and maintenance of waste disposal procedures. Natural features such as the steep hills, wetlands and drainage basins were carefully preserved by restoring the vegetation to its natural tropical forest state.

The rich colours of the island are reflected in the gardens and natural surroundings, forming a perfect backdrop for the buildings and social activities. The architecture itself is a contextual vernacular expression of the best of local architecture on the Bay Islands and the surrounding geographical region. These influences range from Victorian architecture with porches and verandas to the handcrafted details of early Paya-Indian and African artifacts.

A key architectural characteristic of the island is its rooflines, bestowing a sense of security and shelter against the weather and symbolising the local architectural idiom. The buildings' pitched roofs create a layering effect with overhangs at the upper levels to help create a cooling cycle while blending in with the natural surroundings.

The basic design incorporates numerous well-ventilated features to exploit natural breezes, providing daylight and ventilation for every room. Louvered doors, lattice work, transoms and high ceilings increase the air flow at the top of wall partitions. Smaller architectural features like closets, bathrooms and pantries are also well ventilated to prevent moisture and mildew from forming. All the hotel rooms have their own observation decks to provide visitors and guests with dramatic views of the natural landscapes, gardens and sea.

A sense of continuity between the interior and exterior environments is fostered by the large doors and windows fitted with louvered wood shutters to control daylight and let in the sea breezes.

The porches or sheltered entrances are another important aspect of the architectural vocabulary, linking both indoor and outdoor space while separating the heat and brightness of the exterior environment from the coolness of the interior areas.

All the hotels, recreational, residential and multi-purpose facilities are designed to create low-level visual impact and blend in with the picturesque surroundings. All the structures are no more than three stories high and actually lower than the canopies of mature palm trees. Higher density clusters are located in flatter areas of the site and screened with lush vegetation.

Once again Fentress's policy of contextual regionalism has created an environmentally compatible high-quality architectural project that actually enhances the local surroundings.

This page and opposite page, a series of sketches showing the development scheme devised to create an enviromentally compatible architectural project for the island of Roatan.

air view of site

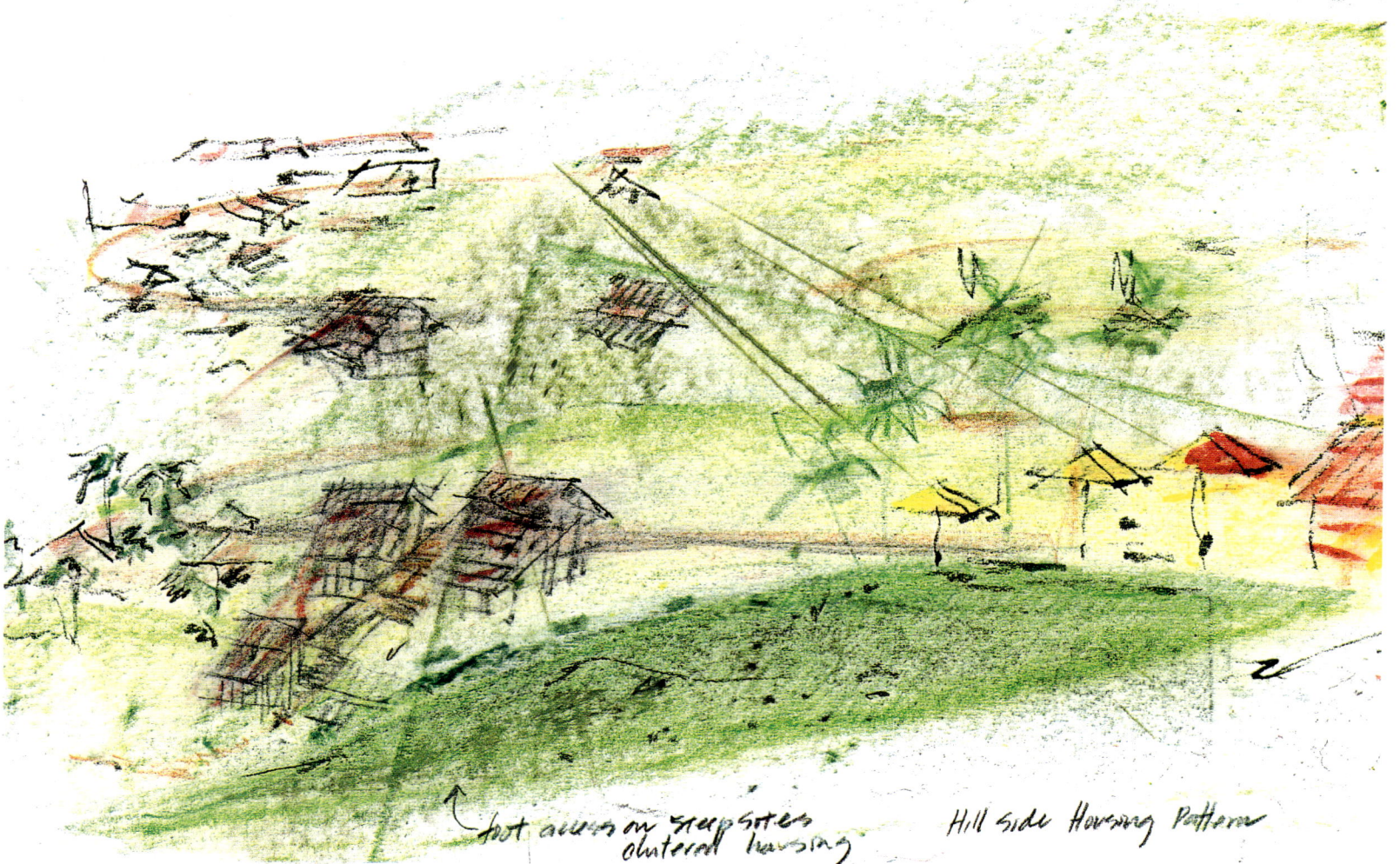

foot access on steep sites
clustered housing

Hill side Housing Pattern

Hotel w/ hill beyond

Birds eye - hotel/pool at Beach

Project Assistants

Principals:
Curtis Worth Fentress   1980-present
James Henry Bradburn   1980-present

Associate Principals:
Ronald R. Booth   1988-present
Michael O. Winters   1981-present
Christopher A. Carvell   1988-95
Barbara K. Hochstetler   1986-93
Brit Probst   1982-91

Senior Associates:
James F. Hartman   1980-present
John M. Kudrycki   1983-present
Thomas J. Walsh   1989-present

Ellen Flynn-Heapes   1982-86
John K. McCauley   1981-87
Sandy Prouty   1985-91
Robert Root   1986-91

Associates:
Todd R. Britton   1982-present
Brian Chaffee   1981-present
Arthur A. Hoy, III   1989-present
Jack M. Mousseau   1990-present
Mark A. Wagner   1993-present

B. Edward Balkin   1983-89
Frederic M. Harrington   1980-87
John L. Mason   1981-91
Frederick R. Pax   1983-92
Leslie Sudders   1984-87

Ana Acosta, Luis O. Acosta, Don Adams, Mary Adkins, Deborah R. Allen, Lyle R. Anderson, Jacqueline Y. April, Judy Arkulari, David Arnoth, Debbie Atencio, LeAlta Ayers, Galen Bailey, Antoinette Colonel Baines, Mary Baird, Linda I. Barclay, Melissa Bare, Margorie Bates, Karen Bauman, Nina Bazian, Nina Beardsley, Karen R. Beasley, Brian Beckler, Benjamin Berg, Jane Bertschinger, Gregory Biggs, Gregory D. Billingham, Susan Blosten, Blake Booth, James M. Boucher, Betty Lou Bowers, Barbara Bowman, Bill Bramblett, Sandy Brand, Daniel Braun, Charlotte C. Breed, Mark Brinkman, Rosanne Brock, Robert T. Brodie, Andrew Bromberg, Russell Brown, Kristine Brundige, Carla Brunstead, Elizabeth Buckman, Richard Burkett, Robert Busch, David Caldwell, Katharine Capra, Peter D. Carlson, James Carney, James Carpenter, Carol A. Carr, Gary Chamers, Dr. Roger A. Chandler, Marilynn Charles, Deborah Chelemes, Garrett M. Christnacht, Arpie Christianian Chucovich, Andrew Clements, Roslyn Clinton, Jayne Coburn, Melanie Colcord, Martin Cole, Jacqueline Collard , Melora Collette, Pamela Combs, Sonia Rocio Contreras, Cheryl Cooper, Vicky Cooper, Ruth Cramer, Delores Cuba, Jennifer Cuney, Ava Dahlstrom, Carl J. Dalio, Eric Dalio, James Daniels, Robert G. Datson, Philip Davis, Donald W. DeCoster, Janet Delaney, Joanne Delude, Lawrence Depenbusch, Kimberly Devore, Douglas Dick, Dalas Disney, Stan Doctor, MaryJane Donovan, Petr Dostal, Mary Claire Downing, Michael Driscoll, Catherine Dunn, Diane Durane, Douglas Eichelberger, Michael Eltrich, Annette English, Brian Erickson, Kristine K. Ewoldt, Carolyn S. Fedler, Ray Fedler, Coleen Fisher, Cydney Fisher, Margaret Fisher, Robert Fitzgerald, Josephine Flanagan, Lewis Fowler, Frank Fritz, Steven Fritzky, Peter Frothingham, Lisa K. Fudge, Marie Fulop, J. Scott Gabel, John Gagnon, Marjorie A. Gallion, Kathleen Corner Galvin, Michael Gengler, Haia Ghalib, Linda Ghannam, Gregory R. Gidez, Karen Gilbert, Mitchell Lee Gilbert, Dawn Givens, Edward Goewert, Ken Goff, Mitchell Gomez, David Goorman, Roxanne Gorrell, John Gossett, Stanley Gould, Jean L. Greaves, Randy Green, Stephen O. Gregory, Robert C. Grubbs, Gregory J. Guastella, D'Anne Gudeman, Susan Guinn-Chipman, Renata Hajek, Kristin Halstrum, Christie Halverson-Larson, Elizabeth Hamilton, Timothy Hanagan, Mark T. Harpe, Geoffrey B. Harris, Milan Hart, William Haskey, Ala F. Hason, Frank G. Hege, JoAnne Hege, Michael Henry, Richard A. Herbert, Sheryl Highsmith, Erin Hillhouse, Bridget Hilton, Kimble Hobbs, Warren Hogue, III, Kimberly J. Holmes, Brian Homerding, Jon Hooley, Laurie Horn, Ernest W. Howard, June Huhn, Doris Hung, Kelly Hynes, Lisa Jelliffe, Charles Johns, Kelly J. Johnson, Lynn Wisecarver Johnson, Ron Johnson, Greg Jones, Glenda Jordan, Judith Jump, J. Mike Klebba, Anthia Kappos, Jeff M. Kaufman, Kathy Diane Kavan, Jeffrey Keast, Andrew Kelmers, Nancy Kettner, Michael Kicklighter, Earl John Kincaid, Angeline C. Kinnaird, Ned Kirschbaum, Mary Jane Koenig, Loretta Konrad, Kathleen Krenzer, Stan Kulesa, Barbara Kusske, Rene L. Lancaster, Bere Lane, Lauren Lee, Linda Lee, Greg Lemon, Leslie Leydorf, Forrest A. Liles, Robert Louden, Harold O. Love, Christoph B. Lueder, Randy E. Macmillan, Robin Mahaffey, Renee Major, Colleen Marcus, Karin Mason, Sally Mason, Carla L. McConnell, John M. McGahey, Loren McGlone, Patrick M. McKelvey, Daniel F. McLaughlin, Geeta Mehta, Julia Mendelson, David Miller, Michael Miller, Pam Mills, Francis Mishler, Doni Mitchell, Mona Mohney, Daniel L. Monger, Wilbur Moore, Gary Morris, Ned Morris, Bruce R. Mosteller, Rodney Mowry, Jacqueline Murray, Richard D. Myers, Dan Naegele, Sonja Natter, James Niemi, Minh (Mark) Nguyen, Kathy Nightengale, Lyn K. Oda, Marnie Odegard, Clement Okoye, A. Chris Olson, Christian Olson, Jeff Olson, Brian Ostler, Kathy O'Donnell, Robert J. O'Donnell, James W. O'Neill, Teri Paris, Michel Pariseau, Wee Park, Wendy Paulson, Beverly G. Pax, John Petro, W. Harrison Phillips, Elisabeth Post, Dorothy Potter, Gary Prager, Gerard Prus, Clay Pryor, Michelle Ray, Robert Reedy, Heather Richardson, Sherri Riepe, Shannon Riley, Penelope Roberts, Blaine Rodgers, David Robb, Brigette Rothfuss-Moore, William Rosebrook, Lou Ann Roses, Tim Roush, Raymond L. Rupert, Alexander S. Ryou, Janice M. Sadar, Robin Sakahara, John M. Salisbury, Carol Scheibe, Laura M. Schumacher, Stuart A. Schunck, Anthony F. Serratore, Lisa Shelton, Jyh-Lin Michael Shen, Aleksandr Sheykhet, Catherine Shields, Harold T. Small, Carol Ann Smith, Jill Smith, Jim Snyder, Amy Solomon, Joseph Solomon, Jessica Sommers, Christy Sorrese, Joy Spatz, Eric A. Spielman, John J. Stein, Byron Stewart, Maggie Stienstra, Carolyn S. Stojeba, Donald Strum, Les Stuart, Voraporn (Mai) Sundarupura, Randy Swanson, Nathaniel A. Taiwo, John R. Taylor, Thomas P. Theobald, Debbie Thurgood, David Tompkins, Chris Tons, Samuel Tyner, Virginia Valocchi, Karen E. Volton, Patricia Walton, Chris Weber, Kristen Wehrli, Dave B. Weigand, Neil Weigert, Richart T. Weldon, Dale White, Marilyn White, Deanna Williams, Catherine Wilson, Michael Wisneski, Lynda Woodhall, Wendy Woodhall, Kevin Wright, John C. Wurzenberger, Jr., Jun Xia, John S. Yanz, Ivy Yau, Mark Young, Robert Young, Billy F. Zamora, Anna M. Zemko, Monica Zorens

List of works

1980
Crystal Center, Denver, Colorado
with Brian Chaffee, Lisa K. Fudge

1981
Kittredge Building, Denver, Colorado
with Deborah R. Allen, Brian Chaffee, Peter Frothingham, Gregory R. Gidez, Frederic M. Harrington, James F. Hartman, JoAnne Hege, Patrick M. McKelvey, Robert J. O'Donnell, John R. Taylor

1981
Terrace Building, Englewood, Colorado
with Robert T. Brodie, Brian Chaffee, Mary Jane Donovan, Lisa K. Fudge, Frederic M. Harrington

1981
Southbridge One, Littleton, Colorado
with Robert Brodie, Lisa K. Fudge, Elizabeth Hamilton, Frederic M. Harrington, Robert J. O'Donnell

1981
One Mile High Plaza, Denver, Colorado
with Brian Chaffee, Mary Jane Donovan, Lisa K. Fudge, Chris Weber

1981-86
Milestone Square Master Plan, Englewood, Colorado
with James H. Bradburn; Robert Busch, Brian Chaffee, Gregory R. Gidez, Michael Kicklighter, Stuart A. Schunck, Byron Stewart, Dave B. Weigand

1982
116 Inverness Drive East, Englewood, Colorado
with James H. Bradburn; Gregory R. Gidez, James F. Hartman, Dan Naegele, James Niemi

1982
Milestone Tower, Englewood, Colorado
with James H. Bradburn; Benjamin Berg, Donald W. DeCoster, Mary Jane Donovan, Robert C. Grubbs, John L. Mason

1982
Reliance Center, Denver, Colorado

with James H. Bradburn; Robert T. Brodie, Brian Chaffee, Gary Chamers, Lisa K. Fudge, Gregory R. Gidez, JoAnne Hege, John K. McCauley, Patrick M. McKelvey, James Niemi, Michael O. Winters

1982
Capitol Tower/J.D. Tower, Denver, Colorado
with Gary Chamers

1983
Odd Fellows Hall, Denver, Colorado
with James H. Bradburn; Deborah R. Allen, Frederic M. Harrington, James F. Hartman, JoAnne Hege, Leslie Leydorf, Carla L. McConnell, Patrick M. McKelvey, James Niemi, Nathaniel A. Taiwo, Richard T. Weldon, Dave B. Weigand, Toshika Yoshida

1983
YMCA, Denver, Colorado
with Gary Chamers

1983
Museum of Western Art/The Navarre, Denver, Colorado
with James H. Bradburn; Deborah R. Allen, Donald W. DeCoster, Douglas Dick; John Prosser

1984
Englewood Mixed-use Center, Englewood, Colorado
with James H. Bradburn; B. Edward Balkin, Douglas Dick

1984
Southbridge Plaza, Littleton, Colorado
with James H. Bradburn; Elizabeth Hamilton, Kimble Hobbs, Bruce R. Mosteller, W. Harrison Phillips, Brit Probst, Bryon Stewart

1984
Tuscon City Center Master Plan, Tuscon, Arizona
with James H. Bradburn; Michael O. Winters

1984
Castlewood Plaza Master Plan, Englewood, Colorado

with James H. Bradburn; B. Edward Balkin, Steve Nelson

1984
Mountain Bell Special Services Center, Denver, Colorado
with James H. Bradburn; Deborah R. Allen, Donald W. DeCoster, Annette English, Gregory R. Gidez, Frank G. Hege, JoAnne Hege, James W. O'Neill, Frederick R. Pax, Toshika Yoshida

1984
Balboa Company Corporate Headquarters, Denver, Colorado
with James H. Bradburn; Deborah R. Allen, Donald W. DeCoster, Gregory R. Gidez, JoAnne Hege, Stan Kulesa, James W. O'Neill, Toshika Yoshida

1984
Pioneer Plaza Hotel, Denver, Colorado
with James H. Bradburn; Gary Chamers, Lisa K. Fudge, Gregory R. Gidez, Michael O. Winters

1984
Greenville Park Tower, Dallas, Texas
with James H. Bradburn; Garrett M. Christnacht, Steven O. Gregory, Clement Okoye, James W. O'Neill, John R. Taylor, Michael O. Winters

1984
Temple Sinai, Denver, Colorado
with James H. Bradburn; B. Edward Balkin, Ava Dahlstrom, Dalas Disney, John K. McCauley, John R. Taylor

1985
1999 Broadway, Denver, Colorado
with James H. Bradburn; Robert T. Brodie, Robert G. Datson, Donald W. DeCoster, Lawrence Depenbusch, Douglas Dick, Frederic M. Harrington, Gregory R. Gidez, Michael Kicklighter, John M. Kudrycki, John L. Mason, John K. McCauley, Patrick M. McKelvey, James Niemi, Frederick R. Pax, Brit Probst, Sandy Prouty, Clement Okoye, John R. Taylor, Mark A. Wagner, Michael O. Winters, Toshika Yoshida

1985
Holy Ghost Roman Catholic Church, Denver, Colorado
with James H. Bradburn; Elizabeth Hamilton, John M. Kudrycki, John L. Mason, Patrick M. McKelvey, Bruce R. Mosteller, John R. Taylor, Michael O. Winters

1985
Welton Street Parking Garage, Denver, Colorado
with James H. Bradburn; Douglas Dick, Frederic M. Harrington, Kimble Hobbs, John L. Mason, John K. McCauley, Patrick M. McKelvey, Brit Probst, Michael O. Winters

1985
1800 Grant Street, Denver, Colorado
with James H. Bradburn; Deborah R. Allen, Brian Chaffee, Gregory R. Gidez, Renata Hajek, James F. Hartman, JoAnne Hege, John K. McCauley, Mark A. Wagner, Toshika Yoshida

1985
Republic Park Hotel, Englewood, Colorado
with James H. Bradburn; Lyle R. Anderson, Brian Chaffee, John K. McCauley, Mark A. Wagner; Victor Huff and Associates

1985
One DTC Tower, Englewood, Colorado
with James H. Bradburn; Deborah R. Allen, Lyle R. Anderson, B. Edward Balkin, Gary Chamers, Garrett M. Christnacht, Dalas Disney, Gregory R. Gidez, Renata Hajek, Frederic M. Harrington, Stan Kulesa, James Niemi, Clement Okoye, Brit Probst, John R.Taylor, Toshika Yoshida

1985
Lexington Center, Colorado Springs, Colorado
with James H. Bradburn; Brian Chaffee, John K. McCauley, Patrick M. McKelvey

1985
Centennial Office Park Master Plan, Englewood, Colorado

with James H. Bradburn; B. Edward Balkin, Charlotte C. Breed

1985
Parkway Plaza Master Plan, Littleton, Colorado
with James H. Bradburn; Charlotte C. Breed

1985
Fiddler's Green Ampitheater, Englewood, Colorado
with James H. Bradburn; Galen Bailey, Todd R. Britton, Amy Solomon

1986
Norwest Tower, Tuscon, Arizona
with James H. Bradburn; Jane Bertschinger, Brian Chaffee, Garrett M. Christnacht, Douglas Dick, Donald W. DeCoster, Gregory R. Gidez, Frank G. Hege, Renata Hajek, Stan Kulesa, John L. Mason, James Niemi, James W. O'Neill, Jim Snyder, Michael O. Winters

1986
Terrace Tower II, Englewood, Colorado
with James H. Bradburn; Deborah R. Allen, Donald W. DeCoster, Frank G. Hege, John M. Kudrycki, James Niemi, Frederick R. Pax, Brit Probst

1986
Data General Field Engineering Logistics Center, Fountain, Colorado
with James H. Bradburn; B. Edward Balkin, Garrett M. Christnacht, Steven Fritzky, Frank G. Hege, Renata Hajek, John M. Kudrycki, Brit Probst

1987
Black American West Museum, Denver, Colorado
with James H. Bradburn; Mark Brinkman, Donald W. DeCoster, James F. Hartman, Mary Jane Koenig, Francis Mishler

1987
Sun Plaza, Colorado Springs, Colorado
with James H. Bradburn; Luis O. Acosta, Sandy Brand, Gregory R. Gidez, John K. McCauley, Patrick M. McKelvey, Frederick R. Pax, John R. Taylor

1987
West Hills Hotel, Keystone, Colorado
with James H. Bradburn; Gary Chamers,
Brit Probst, Mark A. Wagner, Michael O.
Winters

1987
Boise Civic Center, Boise, Idaho
with James H. Bradburn; Michael O. Winters

1988
Oxbridge Towne Center, Oxbridge, England
with James H. Bradburn; Douglas Dick,
Michael O. Winters

1988-90
Cherry Creek Plaza, Denver, Colorado
with James H. Bradburn; B. Edward Balkin

1989
Denver Permit Center, Denver, Colorado
with James H. Bradburn; James Carpenter,
Robert G. Datson, Philip Davis, James F.
Hartman, Beverly G. Pax, Frederick R. Pax,
Robert Root, John M. Salisbury, Les Stuart

1989
Western and American Galleries, Denver Art
Museum, Denver, Colorado
with James H. Bradburn; Michael Gengler,
John M. Salisbury, Robert Root

1989
Idaho Power Company Headquarters, Boise,
Idaho; CSHQA Architects
with James H. Bradburn; Robert G. Datson,
Karin Mason, Jack M. Mousseau, Sandy
Prouty, Michael O. Winters, Jun Xia

1989
Franklin and Lake, Chicago, Illinois
with James H. Bradburn; Michael O.
Winters, Jun Xia

1989-92
Jefferson County Master Plan, Golden,
Colorado
with James H. Bradburn; B. Edward Balkin,
Brian Chaffee

1989
Jefferson County Human Services Building,

Golden, Colorado
with James H. Bradburn; B. Edward Balkin,
Renata Hajek, Barbara K. Hochstetler, John
M. Kudrycki, John L. Mason, Mark A.
Wagner

1989
Colorado State Capitol, Life Safety Project,
Denver, Colorado
with James H. Bradburn; Garrett M.
Christnacht, James F. Hartman, Ala F.
Hason, Brian Ostler, John M. Salisbury,
Samuel Tyner

1990
Colorado Convention Center, Denver,
Colorado
with James H. Bradburn; B. Edward Balkin,
Richard Burkett, Brian Chaffee, Melanie
Colcord, Gregory R. Gidez, Barbara K.
Hochstetler, Nancy Kettner, John M.
Kudrycki, Lauren Lee, Greg Lemon, Beverly
G. Pax, Brit Probst, John M. Salisbury, Les
Stuart, Michael O. Winters, Mark A.
Wagner; Loschkey MarQuardt and
Nesholm; Bertram A. Bruton and Associates

1990
IBM Customer Service Center, Englewood,
Colorado
with James H. Bradburn; Robert G. Datson,
Donald W. DeCoster, Kathleen Corner
Galvin, John A. Gossett, Barbara K.
Hochstetler, Judith Jump, Sandy Prouty,
Michael O. Winters

1990
Colorado School of Mines, Golden,
Colorado
with James H. Bradburn; Robert G. Datson,
James F. Hartman, Nancy Kettner, Ned
Kirschbaum, Robert Root, Robert Young

1990
Westlake Residences, Seattle, Washington
with James H. Bradburn; Richard Burkett,
Peter D. Carlson, Christopher A. Carvell,
Mark A. Wagner

1990
809 Olive Way, Seattle, Washington

with James H. Bradburn; Ronald R. Booth,
Christopher A. Carvell, Robert Louden,
Mark A. Wagner

1990
Denver Central Library, Denver, Colorado
with James H. Bradburn; Arthur A. Hoy, III,
Michel Pariseau

1990-91
Union Station Redevelopment Plan,
Denver, Colorado
with James H. Bradburn; Galen Bailey, Todd
Britton, Arthur A. Hoy, III

1991
Ronstadt Transit Center, Tuscon, Arizona
with James H. Bradburn; Brian Chaffee,
James Carpenter, Robert Louden, John L.
Mason, Clement Okoye, Robert Root

1991
Cathedral Square, Milwaukee, Wisconsin
with James H. Bradburn; Peter D. Carlson

1991-94
Denver International Airport, Passenger
Terminal Complex, Denver, Colorado
with James H. Bradburn; Galen Bailey, Todd
R. Britton, Richard Burkett, James Carney,
James Carpenter, Brian Chaffee, Garrett M.
Christnacht, John Gagnon, Michael
Gengler, Gregory R. Gidez, Barbara K.
Hochstetler, Warren Hogue, III, Doris
Hung, Charles Johns, Anthia Kappos,
Michael Klebba, John M. Kudrycki, Lauren
Lee, Robert Louden, Colleen Marcus,
Michael Miller, Gary Morris, Jack M.
Mousseau, A. Chris Olson, Brian Ostler, Teri
Paris, Frederick R. Pax, Brit Probst, Robert
Root, Tim Roush, John M. Salisbury, Amy
Solomon, Joseph Solomon, Les Stuart, David
Tompkins, Samuel Tyner, Thomas J. Walsh,
Mark A. Wagner, Michael O. Winters, John
C. Wurzenberger, Jr., Jun Xia; Pouw and As-
sociates; Bertram A. Bruton and Associates

1991
Dinosaur Discovery Museum, Canyon City,
Colorado
with James H. Bradburn; Brian Chaffee,
Wilbur Moore

1992

Jefferson County Judicial and Administrative Building, Golden, Colorado
with James H. Bradburn; Brian Chaffee, Gregory D. Billingham, Bill Bramblett, Sandy J. Brand, Richard Burkett, James Carney, James Carpenter, Douglas Eichelberger, Gregory R. Gidez, James F. Hartman, Barbara K. Hochstetler, Ala F. Hason, Judith Jump, Ned Kirschbaum, Lauren Lee, Robert Louden, John L. Mason, Clement Okoye, Beverly G. Pax, Brit Probst, Samuel Tyner, Mark A. Wagner, Lynn Wisecarver Johnson

1992

Gemmill Mathematics Library and Engineering Sciences Building, University of Colorado, Boulder, Colorado
with James H. Bradburn; Ronald R. Booth, Christopher A. Carvell, Douglas Eichelberger, Barbara K. Hochstetler, Nancy Kettner, Greg Lemon, Robert Louden, Gary Morris, Robert Root, Michael O. Winters, Jun Xia

1992

Natural Resources Building, Olympia, Washington
with James H. Bradburn; Ronald R. Booth, James Carney, Gregory R. Gidez, Milan Hart, Barbara K. Hochstetler, Arthur A. Hoy, III, Lynn Wisecarver Johnson, John M. Kudrycki, Lauren Lee, David Tompkins, Michael Wisneski

1992

New Seoul International Airport Passenger Terminal Complex, Seoul, Korea
with James H. Bradburn; Richard Burkett, Galen Bailey, Todd R. Britton, John Gagnon, Barbara K. Hochstetler, Arthur A. Hoy, III, Anthia Kappos, Ned Kirschbaum, Lauren Lee, John M. McGahey, Wilbur Moore, Gary Morris, Jack M. Mousseau, Minh Nguyen, Brian Ostler, Michelle Ray, Tim Roush, Amy Solomon, Les Stuart, Thomas J. Walsh, Michael O. Winters, John C. Wurzenberger, Jr.; Baum, Hi-Lim, Jung-Lim, Wodushi Architects (BHJW); McClier Aviation Group

1992

University Art Museum, University of California at Santa Barbara, Santa Barbara, California
with James H. Bradburn; Douglas Dick, Michael O. Winters; John Prosser

1992

Eastbank Conference Center and Hotel, Wichita, Kansas
with James H. Bradburn; Barbara K. Hochstetler, Mark A. Wagner

1992

Colorado Convention Center Hotel, Denver, Colorado
with James H. Bradburn; Galen Bailey, Todd Britton, Amy Solomon, Jun Xia

1992

Coors Stadium, Denver, Colorado
with James H. Bradburn; John A. Gossett, Michel Pariseau; Ellerbe Becket Inc.

1992

Kuala Lumpur Airport, Kuala Lumpur, Malaysia
with James H. Bradburn; Carl J. Dalio, Michael O. Winters

1992

Moscow Redevelopment Center, Moscow, Russia
with James H. Bradburn; Arthur A. Hoy, III, Jack M. Mousseau, Aleksandr Sheykhet, Michael O. Winters; Andrei Meerson & Partners

1992

Ogden-Weber State University Conference and Performing Arts Center, Ogden, Utah
with James H. Bradburn; Gregory D. Billingham, Ronald R. Booth, Peter D. Carlson, Christopher A. Carvell, Robert Herman, Laureen Lee, Minh Nguyen, Michael Sanders, Thomas P. Theobald, Mark A. Wagner; Sanders Herman Associates

1992

Catalina Resort Community Plan, Playa Dantita, Ocotal, Costa Rica
with James H. Bradburn; Barbara K. Hochstetler, Wilbur Moore, Jack M. Mousseau

1992-95

Clark County Government Center, Las Vegas, Nevada
with James H. Bradburn; Ronald R. Booth, John A. Gossett, Ala F. Hason, Barbara K. Hochstetler, Warren Hogue, III, Arthur A. Hoy, III, Anthia Kappos, John M. Kudrycki, Ned Kirschbaum, Lauren Lee, Robert Louden, Gary Morris, Joy Spatz, Michael O. Winters, Michael Wisneski, John C. Wurzenberger, Jr.

1992

National Cowboy Hall of Fame, Oklahoma City, Oklahoma
with James H. Bradburn; Ronald R. Booth, Gregory D. Billingham, Peter D. Carlson, John Gagnon, Barbara K. Hochstetler, John M. McGahey, Gary Morris, Jack M. Mousseau, Teri Paris, Thomas P. Theobald, Mark A. Wagner

1992

General Services Administration Federal Building, National Oceanic and Atmospheric Administration Headquarters, Boulder, Colorado
with James H. Bradburn; Ronald R. Booth, Peter D. Carlson, Gregory R. Gidez, Ala F. Hason, Barbara K. Hochstetler, Warren Hogue, III, Robert Louden, Jeff Olson, Teri Paris

1992

Estes Park Convention Center, Estes Park, Colorado
with James H. Bradburn; Christopher A. Carvell, Barbara K. Hochstetler, Lynn Wisecarver Johnson, Roger Thorpe, Mark A. Wagner

1993

National Museum of Wildlife Art, Jackson Hole, Wyoming
with James H. Bradburn; Brian Chaffee, Gregory R. Gidez, Barbara K. Hochstetler, Anthia Kappos, Gary Morris, Brian Ostler, Tim Roush

1993

Second Bangkok International Airport, Bangkok, Thailand
with James H. Bradburn; Galen Bailey, Nina Bazian, Todd R. Britton, Catherine Dunn, David Goorman, John A. Gossett, Barbara K. Hochstetler, John M. McGahey, Doni Mitchell, Jack M. Mousseau, Minh Nguyen, Brian Ostler, Michelle Ray, Amy Solomon, Voraporn Sundarupura, Thomas J. Walsh, Michael O. Winters; McClier Aviation Group

1993

Vladivostok City Center, Vladivostok, Russia
with James H. Bradburn; Arthur A. Hoy, III, Doni Mitchell, Aleksandr Sheykhet

1993

Kwangju Bank, Kwangju, Korea
with James H. Bradburn; Arthur A. Hoy, III

1994

Colorado State Capitol, Denver, Colorado
with James H. Bradburn; Garret Christnacht, Petr Dostal, James Hartman, Ala F. Hason, Michael Miller, Brian Ostler, John Salisbury, Joseph Solomon, Jacqueline Wisniewski

1994

Hawaii Convention Center, Honolulu, Hawaii
with James H. Bradburn; Nina Bazian, Cydney Fisher, Michael Gengler, Haia Ghalib, John A. Gossett, Ala F. Hason, Anthia Kappos, John M. Kudrycki, John M. McGahey, Michael Miller, Jack M. Mousseau, Gary Morris, Minh Nguyen, Aleksandr Sheykhet, Voraporn Sundarupura, Thomas J. Walsh, Michael O. Winters, John C. Wurzenberger, Jr.; DMJM Hawaii; Kauahikaua and Chun Architects

1994

Montrose Government Center, Montrose, Colorado
with James H. Bradburn; Christopher A. Carvell, Brian Chaffee, Barbara K. Hochstetler, John Gagnon, Charles Johns, Doni Mitchell, Aleksandr Sheykhet

1994

The Reconstruction of the Souks of Beirut: An International Ideas Competition, Beirut, Lebanon
with James H. Bradburn; Nina Bazian, Dr. Roger A. Chandler, Jamili Butros Copty, Mark T. Harpe, Ala F. Hason, Barbara K. Hochstetler, Jack M. Mousseau, Minh Nguyen, Voraporn Sundarupura, Michael Wisneski

1995

Colorado Christian Home - Tennyson Center for Children and Families
with James H. Bradburn; John Gagnon, Gregory R Gidez, Warren Hogue, Arthur A. Hoy, III, Teri Paris, Aleksandr Sheykhet

1995

City of Oakland Administration Complex, Oakland, California
with James H. Bradburn; Galen Bailey, Ronald R. Booth, Todd Britton, Peter D. Carlson, Mark Dietrick, Catherine Dunn, John A. Gossett, Barbara K. Hochstetler, Arthur A. Hoy, III, Laureen Lee, Jack M. Mousseau, Jeff Olson, Amy Solomon, Michael O. Winters; Gerson/Overstreet; Muller & Caulfield

1995

Camp Bay-Port Royal, Roatan Island, Honduras
with James H. Bradburn; Galen Bailey, Minh Nguyen, Aleksandr Sheykhet, James Sobey, Amy Solomon

Selected bibliography

"AIA Colorado design award winner." *Daily Journal* 89, no. 149 (December 23, 1985): AIA section, 16.

"AIA honors Fentress Bradburn for design of government building." *Daily Journal* 94, no. 195 (March 1, 1991): 1

"AIA Western Mountain Region, 1985 Honor Award, 1999 Broadway, Denver, Colorado." *Daily Journal* 89, no. 127 (November 20, 1985): Western Mountain Region section, 11.

Acosta, Lois O. "Convention Center rides on flexibility." *Rocky Mountain News* October 30, 1984, 7.

"Architect played a key role." *Rocky Mountain News* August 29, 1987, 30.

"Architecture and energy building excellence in the northwest: 1993 Design Awards." *Architecture* 82, no. 5 (May 1993): 113.

Arnaboldi, Mario Antonio. "Airport on the Water." *l'Arca* 71 (May 1993): 24–29.

"Associates with principles: Fentress Bradburn team strong on values." *Daily Journal* 94, no. 44 (July 24, 1990): section 2, 5.

"Awards." *Denver Post* January 6, 1992, C5.

"Awards." *Denver Post* September 28, 1992, C5.

Barrett, Marjorie. "Odd Fellows Hall lends character to downtown." *Rocky Mountain News* May 14, 1984, 48.

Berger, Horst. "Modern Basilica." *Fabrics in Architecture* 5, no. 3 (May–June 1993): 10–21.

—. and Edward M. De Paola. "Tensile Terminal." *Civil Engineering* 62, no. 11 (November 1992): 40–43.

BirdAir Tensioned Membrane Structures (Amherst, New York: BirdAir, Inc.), January 1992.

Blaha, Bill. "Denver Dandy." *Concrete Products* 94, no. 9 (September 1991): 16–18.

"Boulder campus gets new math library." *Daily Journal* 94, no. 220 (April 5, 1991): 1.

Boyd, Charlie. "New attachment technique: Alternative to traditional stone cladding systems." *Modern Steel Construction* 21, no. 4, (4th Quarter 1981): 14–15.

Bradley, Jeff. "Landmark Navarre holds gems of old West." *Denver Post* November 5, 1989, D1.

Brown, Daniel C. "Reviving an architectural pioneer." *Building Design and Construction* 24, no. 10 (October 1983): 40–43.

"Building designer discusses Amoco Building." *Amoco Building News* December 21, 1979, 1.

"Building intelligently: One DTC." *Construction Specifier* 39, no. 11 (November 1985): 103.

"Buildings on the rise." *Colorado Offices and Design* 2, no. 1 (Summer 1983): 8.

Bumgarner, Kevin. "Proposed Sheraton Hotel would hold commanding views of Arkansas River." *Wichita Business Journal* 5, no. 22 (August 6, 1990): section 1, 8.

"C.W. Fentress and Associates: Denver landmark: Odd Fellows Hall." *Interiors* 142, no. 9 (April 1983): 22.

"C.W. Fentress designs Denver's Reliance Center." *Architectural Record* 170, no. 4 (March 1982): 41.

"C.W. Fentress J.H. Bradburn and Associates: A 1991 AIA Denver design award winner." *AIA Denver Newsletter* (July–August 1992): 1.

"C.W. Fentress J.H. Bradburn and Associates: Old and new." *Daily Journal* 94, no. 150 (December 24, 1990): AIA Colorado section, 9.

"C.W. Fentress named largest Denver architectural firm in 1988." *Daily Journal* 92, no. 233 (April 24, 1989): 1.

"Cambridge Group plans Odd Fellows Hall restoration." *Denver Business World* 5, no. 22 (February 7, 1983): 8.

Canty, Donald. "Building with a checkered past renovated as a museum." *Architecture* 75, no. 11 (November 1986): 78–79.

Cattaneo, Renato. "A canopied air terminal." *l'Arca* 73 (July–August 1993): 19–23.

Chalmers, Ray. "Mullion-free exterior enhances office views: Four-sided structural silicone glazing first in the Rocky Mountain Region." *Building Design and Construction* 25, no. 3, (March 1984): 176–79.

Chandler, Mary V. "Architectural icon rises from the plains." *Rocky Mountain News* June 6, 1993, A38.

—. "Artistic project plans on light at the

new Denver airport." *Rocky Mountain News* June 16, 1993, C17.

—. "Fourteen artists turning Denver's new airport into a work of art." *Rocky Mountain News* February 23, 1992, 115.

—. "Historic temple building faces modern dilemma." *Rocky Mountain News* May 17, 1992, 140–41.

—. "Jeffco center radiates power." *Rocky Mountain News*, January 9, 1993, 8.

—. "New CU biochemistry building has classic feel of rural Italy." *Rocky Mountain News* April 29, 1990, 80.

Chandler, Roger A. "Learning from Las Vegas? The Clark County Government Center." *Competitions* 2 (Winter 1992): 31–39.

—. "Variations on a theme: Americans win airport competitions on the Pacific rim." *Competitions* 3 (Summer 1993): 30–39.

Cheek, Lawrence W. "Look up in the sky, this tower is Tucson's first respectable high rise." *Tucson Citizen* December 10, 1986, C1.

—. "Taking the high road." *Tucson Citizen* July 1, 1991, B1.

Cohen, Edie. "Curtis Fentress, the architect restricts intervention in an historically significant Denver house." *Interior Design* 65, no. 4 (March 1994): 112–15.

"Colorado architects receive awards." *Denver Post* December 10, 1984, B3.

"Colorado Convention Center" *Daily Journal* 92, no. 136 (Dec 5, 1988): 98–101.

"Colorado Convention Center: A dream come true." *Daily Journal* 94, no. 142. (December 12, 1990): 16.

"Colorado projects win ten Gold Nugget Awards." *Daily Journal* 90, no. 23 (June 24, 1984): 1.

"Colorado projects win building awards." *Denver Post* July 3, 1983, G3.

"Colorado's showcase to the world opening in Denver." *Daily Journal* 93, no. 230, (April 18, 1990): Real Estate section 2, 1.

"Convention center offers dramatic design." *Sun Coast Architect–Builder* 56, no. 11 (November 1991): W section, 28–30.

Cooper, Jerry. "Balboa Company: Fifty-seven floors above the Mile-High City, C.W. Fentress and Associates creates art-inspired corporate offices for a Denver investor." *Interior Design* 58, no. 10 (August 1987): 188–92.

Couch, Jan. "The Verdict's in on Jeffco's new facility: 'Magnificent.'" *Jefferson Sentinel* August 10, 1993, Jeffco's New Home section, 6.

"County business and nature harmonize in new facility." *Daily Journal* 93, no. 240 (May 2, 1990): 1.

Crain, Jan. "New convention center design sets tone for state, architecture." *Denver Business Journal* 39, no. 50 (September 5, 1988): section 1, 16–17.

—. "New Jeffco building suits needs of workers, clients." *Denver Business Journal* 39, no. 18 (January 25, 1988): section 1, 16.

—. "Office designers start the process by determining the client's style." *Denver Business Journal* 40, no. 46 (August 7, 1989): section 1, 14–15.

"Curtis Worth Fentress." *Denver Business Journal* 13, no. 4 (December 1985): 23.

Della Corte, Evelyn. "The Museum of Western Art: The interiors of Denver's newest museum win 1984 ASID project design award." *Interior Design* 55, no. 10 (October 1984): 204–9.

Delsohn, Gary. "Architect Fentress vows to design convention center as a showpiece." *Denver Post* September 8, 1987, B1.

"Denver airport design unveiled: The terminal will be capped by one of the nation's largest cable supported fabric roofs." *Building Design and Construction* 32, no. 1 (January 1991): 17.

"Denver buildings win interior awards." *Historic Denver News* 14, no. 1 (January 1985): 7.

"Denver firm wins national design competition for National Cowboy Hall of Fame." *Daily Journal* 96, no. 125 (November 18, 1992): 1–2.

"Denver International Airport: Colorado's bid for a transportation hub of the future." *Denver Business Journal* 45, no. 1 (September 17–23, 1993): B1–B24.

"Denver International: Design and mission of new airport usher in a new age for business and travel." *Denver Post* January 19, 1992, A14.

"Denver International shaping up." *Denver Post* January 19, 1992, A1.

"Denver landmarks honored by ASID and AIA." *Downtown* (February–March 1985): 10.

"Denver landmarks honored for interior design." *Intermountain Jewish News* 71, no. 50, December 14, 1984, B section, 24.

"Denver office tower cradles an historic church." *Building Stone Magazine* 1–2 (January–February 1988): 18–21.

"Denver Permit Center, Denver, Colorado." *New Mexico Architecture* 31, no. 3–4, May–August 1990: 17.

"Denver: Take a closer look." *Fortune* 127, no. 8 (April 19, 1993): 164–72.

"Denver terminal design approved." *Engineering News Record* 225, no. 13 (September 27, 1990): 40–42.

Dietsch, Deborah K. "Green realities: Architects must agree on standards to distinguish the green from the faux." *Architecture* 83, no. 6 (June 1993): 15.

Ebisch, Robert. "Response to location: Denver's Amoco Building compliments its angular site." *Building Design and Construction* 21, no. 10 (October 1980): 44–49.

Eng, Rick. "1999 Broadway establishes harmony between skyscraper and sanctuary." *Designers West*, 33, no. 6 (April 1986): 86–87.

"Fentress Bradburn designs the 'airport of the future.'" *Daily Journal* 95, no. 271 (June 17, 1992): Top 20 section, 1.

Fentress, Curtis Worth. "Architect explains design goals of new Colorado Convention Center." *Denver Post* June 18, 1990, B7.

—. "Convention center took its model from future." *Rocky Mountain News* June 18, 1990, 44.

—. "Design intelligence." *Sun Belt Buildings Journal* 9, no. 12 (April 1985): 7.

—. "Doughnut hole can coexist in city plan." *Rocky Mountain News* April 30, 1983, N32.

—. "Preservation requires skill." *Rocky Mountain News* January 31, 1984, B29.

— and Richard Weingardt. "One Denver Tech Center: Commanding views of earth and sky." *Modern Steel Construction* 27, no. 6 (November–December 1987): 23–27.

"Firm profile." *AIA Denver Newsletter* November 1986, 1–4.

Fisher, Thomas. "Projects: Flights of fantasy." *Progressive Architecture* 73, no. 3 (March 1992): 105–7.

"Five Colorado projects win design awards." *Daily Journal* 87, no. 27 (June 29, 1983): 1.

"Frankly speaking: Curt Fentress and Jim Bradburn talk about the practice of architecture." *Daily Journal* 94, no. 44 (July 24, 1990): section 2, 11–12.

Fuentes, Joe. "A touch of class: Office building offers something different." *Rocky Mountain News* September 1, 1985, 8.

Gersten, Alan. "Office tower to go up next to Denver church." *Rocky Mountain News* February 12, 1982, 4.

"Glass high-rise shares space with historical church." *Glass Digest* 65, no. 11 (October 15, 1986): 86–87.

Glasser, Lawrence R. "1999 Broadway becomes newest corporate icon." *City Edition* 4, no. 1 (November 13–20, 1985): 1.

"Government for the people, by the people." *Daily Journal* 94, no. 44 (July 24, 1990): section 2, 6–7.

"Grand Standing." *Denver Post* November 20, 1993, A18.

Griego, Diana. "Denver black heritage: Ceremony begins restoration of Dr. Justina Ford's house." *Denver Post* November 24, 1987, B1.

Hardenbaugh, Don, comp. *Retrospective of Courthouse Design 1980–1991*. Williamsburg, Va: National Center for State Courts, 1992, 64–65.

Hardy, Thomas. "Best of corporate art." *Rocky Mountain News* September 15, 1985, Sunday Magazine section, M7.

Harriman, Marc S. "Designing for daylight." *Architecture* 81, no. 10 (October 1992): 89.

Harrington, Maureen. "Defining Denver: C.W. Fentress." *Denver Post* February 23, 1990, Homestyle section, 8.

Hart, Rachel. "Sinai dream a reality."

Intermountain Jewish News 74, no. 37, September 11, 1987, 1.

Henderson, Justin. "Convening comfortably: C.W. Fentress J.H. Bradburn and Associates humanize the overscale in the new Colorado Convention Center." *Interiors* 150, no. 12 (July 1991): 44–49.

—. "For the People: Accessibility inspires the master plan for the Jefferson County Municipal Center by C.W. Fentress J. H. Bradburn and Associates." *Interiors* 150, no. 12 (July 1991): 50–51.

"How an unusual site influenced architecture." *Building Design and Construction* 21, no. 10 (October 1980): 56–57.

"Imagine a great convention center — then go and design it." *Daily Journal* 93, no. 230 (April 18, 1990): section 2, 8–10.

"Innovation in the Rockies." *Glass Digest* 66, no. 2 (February 15, 1987): 94–95.

"International design competition: The New Seoul Metropolitan Airport Passenger Terminal." *Architecture and Environment* no. 101, (January 1993): 123–71.

"Introducing One DTC." *Tech Center Squire* February 1986, 1–2.

"Jefferson County Administration and Courts facility is the pride of design participation." *Daily Journal* 93, no. 240 (May 2, 1990): 1.

"Jefferson County Government Center — in the spotlight." *On Site* 17, no. 5 (May 1992): 10–11.

"Jefferson County Human Services." *Progressive Architecture* 74, no. 3 (March 1993): 42–43.

Kania, Alan. "C.W. Fentress J.H. Bradburn and Associates celebrating ten-year anniversary." *Daily Journal* 94, no. 44, (July 24, 1990): section 2, 1–2.

"The Kittredge Building: 'Rewards outweigh the headaches.'" *Building Operating Management* 30, no. 9 (September 1983): 15–18.

Knox, B. J. "A contemporary saloon: Denver's historic Kittredge Building showcases a turn-of-the-century bar/restaurant." *Restaurant and Hotel Design* 6, no. 2 (March 1984): 76–77.

Landecker, Heidi. "Airport departures." *Architecture* 82, no. 8 (August 1993): 42–45.

"Landmarks get awards." Rocky Mountain News December 16, 1984, 127.

Levy, Howard Adam. "Upscale tower in Tucson: United Bank of Arizona, Tucson." *Designer Specifier* 31, no. 397 (June 1990): 42.

Loebelson, Andrew. "The 1985 second 100 interior design giants." *Corporate Design and Realty* 4, no. 3 (April 1985): 58.

—. "The second 100 interior design giants of 1991." *Interior Design* 62, no. 10 (July 1991): 49–64.

Luther, Carol. "Denver International Airport — Welcome to the future." *Corporate Connection* 6, no. 1 (Spring 1991): 14.

Maluga, Mark J. "Denver Permit Center: Fast-track facelift classically revitalizes a 1960's structure." *Building Design and Construction* 31, no. 11 (November 1990): 62–65.

"Mullionless look: Sealant is key to innovative glazing." *Daily Journal* 86, no. 162 (January 11, 1983): 1.

"Museums." *Today's Facility Manager* 5, no. 8 (October 1993): 44.

"The Navarre, Denver, Colorado: From girl's school, to bordello, to Museum of Western Art." *Building Operating Management* 31, no. 9 (September 1984): 22–26.

"The Navarre: School, brothel, eatery now restored, with dignity, as Museum of Western Art." *Daily Journal* 94, no. 44 (July 24, 1990): section 2, 4.

"New Airport to have a tent top?" *Denver Post* August 7, 1990, B1.

"New building designed for Temple Sinai." *Daily Journal* 89, no. 245 (May 9, 1986): 1.

"New center design looks like a winner." *Rocky Mountain News* June 29, 1988, 50.

"New downtown office has unique structural silicone curtain wall." *Daily Journal* 89, no. 52 (August 5, 1985): 30.

"A new financial center in Tucson draws on the mission style." *Interiors* 146, no. 4 (November 1986): 40.

"New Keystone hotel." *Intermountain Jewish News* 73, no. 24, June 13, 1986, 10.

"New Ramada announced at Republic Park." *Daily Journal* 87, no. 23 (June 23, 1983): 1.

"New Seoul Metropolitan Airport." *Progressive Architecture* 74, no. 3 (March 1993): 25.

"The new Temple Sinai." *Colorado Business Magazine* 13, no. 6 (June 1986): 48.

"New Temple Sinai building is designed by C.W. Fentress." *Intermountain Jewish News* 73, no. 20, May 16, 1986, 13.

"1985 PLI Awards." *Progressive Architecture* 66, no. 11 (November 1985): 27.

"1991 Denver design award winner: C.W. Fentress J.H. Bradburn Associates." *AIA Denver Newsletter* (April–June 1992): 1.

"1999 Broadway honored by AIA." *Denver Downtowner* 7, no. 23 (November 13, 1985): 24.

"1999 Broadway: Modern helps ancient." *Daily Journal* 96, no. 68 (August 27, 1986): Phelps section, 7.

"1999 Broadway: The new reflects the old." *Modern Steel Construction* 25, no. 2 (2nd Quarter 1985): 15–19.

"1999 Broadway wins design award." *Denver Post* November 10, 1985, E19.

Oliszewicz, B. Ann. "Young professionals competition." *Building Design and Construction* 21, no. 10 (October 1980): 54–55.

"Olympian design wins design/build competition." *Daily Journal* 94, no. 44 (July 24, 1990): 10.

"Olympia's Natural Resources Building." *Architectural Record* 178, no. 12 (November 1990): 15.

"On the boards: Natural Resources Building, Olympia, Washington. C.W. Fentress J.H. Bradburn and Associates." *Architecture* 80, no. 5 (May 1991): 48.

"On the horizon, Denver architects and their work: C.W. Fentress." *Colorado Homes and Lifestyles* 5, no. 2 (March–April 1985): 42–45.

"One DTC office tower." *Daily Journal* 89, no. 175 (January 30, 1986): section 2, 7.

"Passenger terminal takes form: Unique roof design becomes focus of terminal." *Engineering News-Record* 229, no. 10 (September 7, 1992): D5.

"Pencil Points: Shades of Saint Barts." *Progressive Architecture* 64, no. 10 (October 1983): 49.

Pierson, John. "Denver airport rises under gossamer roof." *Wall Street Journal* 127, no. 99 (November 17, 1992): Western Edition, B1.

"Preserving the best part for now and the future." *Daily Journal* 94, no. 44 (July 24, 1990): section 2, 4.

Price, Max. "1982 was momentous year on Denver's architectural scene." *Denver Post* January 2, 1983, G1.

—. "Fine arts." *Denver Post* November 8, 1985, H18.

—. "Restoration of Kittredge Building 'bonus' for mall." *Denver Post* June 14, 1981, G1.

—. "Young New York architect finding bright future in Colorado." *Denver Post* December 21, 1980, K1.

"Project Milestone Tower" *Daily Journal* 86. no. 144 (December 15, 1982): 26.

"Projects: Flights of fantasy." *Progressive Architecture* 73, no. 3 (March 1992): 105–6.

"Projects help shape Denver's image." *Denver Post* July 14, 1991, A12.

"Projects in progress." *Sun Coast Architect–Builder* 47, no. 8 (August 1982): 26.

"Projects in state win ten awards." *Rocky Mountain News* July 12, 1986, H5.

Raabe, Steve. "1999 Broadway among user-friendly designs." *Rocky Mountain Business Journal* 36, no. 8 (November 12, 1984): 11.

—. "Fentress team wins Seoul air terminal design contract." *Denver Post* November 21, 1992, C2.

— and J. Sebastian Sinisi. "Building a new Denver: Architect gets chance to reshape city image." *Denver Post* July 14, 1991, 1.

Rebeck, Gene. "Monumental potential." *Fabrics in Architecture* 4, no. 4 (July–August 1992): 16.

"Reflective glass on the Inverness Building." *Glass Digest* 63, no. 2 (February 15, 1984): 44.

"Restoration of Masonic Temple." *Historic Denver News* 12, no. 10 (October–November 1983): 4.

"Restoration revives architectural character yet permits modern styling." *Sun Coast Architect–Builder* 53, no. 5 (May 1988): 38–39.

Richardson, Glen. "Airport fever way out yonder." *Denver Business Journal* 12, no. 2 (November 1990): section 2, 24.

—. "Meetings come to order: The firm of Fentress Bradburn and Associates designs Denver a new convention center better, faster and cheaper." *Denver Business Journal* 12, no. 10 (June 1990): 21–24.

Roberts, Jeffrey A. "Ugly building turned into lovely home for state agency." *Denver Post* December 10, 1987, C6.

Ross, Joseph. "JCJA or Taj: Whatever it's name, it's quite a place." *Jefferson Sentinel* August 10, 1993, New Home section, 3.

Rothman, Howard. "Dynamic Denver." *Continental Profiles* 4, no. 8 (August 1991): 32–34.

Russell, James S. "Height + Water = Cool." *Architectural Record* 180, no. 8 (August 1992): 40–41.

"The saving grace of C.W. Fentress and Associates." *Designers West* 30, no. 10 (August 1983): 130–39.

"Saving grace: The survival of Holy Ghost Church in Denver, Colorado is secured by development." *Interiors* 141, no. 10 (May 1982): 22.

Schwed, Robert L. "Squeezing into the tight spots." *Engineered Systems* 4, no. 6 (November–December 1987): 30–33.

"Semi-circular structure necessitates custom fabrication of concrete framing system." *Daily Journal* 93, no. 206 (March 15, 1990): 12.

Shaman, Diane. "Seeking remedies for indoor air pollution problems." *New York Times*, April 12, 1992, section 10, 13.

"Silicone supports sealant." *Rocky Mountain News* January 16, 1983, 92.

Sinisi, J. Sebastian. "Box office architect." *Denver Post* April 5, 1992, Real Estate section, 10.

—. "Cityscape: Amazing space." *Denver Post* March 7, 1993, Sunday Magazine section, 15.

— and Steve Raabe. "Building a new Denver: Architects get chance to reshape city image." *Denver Post* July 14, 1991, A1.

Siuru, Andrea. "Opposites attract: When two magnetic forces meet, the result is dynamic design." *Colorado Homes and Lifestyles* 13, no. 1 (July–August 1993): 46–53.

"Six architecture firms take design awards." *Denver Post* December 8, 1985, E11.

"Six firms win architectural awards." *Daily Journal* 90, no. 109 (October 27, 1986): Wood section, 2.

"Skyscraper and sanctuary: Developer's 1999 Broadway building is a model of peaceful coexistence." *PPG Products Magazine* 94, no. 1 (Spring–Summer 1986): 16–19.

"Sloped terraces for an office building in Denver, Colorado." *L'Industria Italiana del Cemento* 651 (January 1991): 38–46.

"Soft light pitches tent at terminal." *Rocky Mountain News* October 21, 1993, 5.

"Solving the window problem of the Kittredge Building in Denver." *Glass Digest* 62, no. 6 (June 15, 1983): 80–81.

Stein, Karen D. "Snow-capped symbol." *Architectural Record* 181, no. 6 (June 1993): 106–107.

"'Sunday with the Architects' to feature downtown." *Denver Post* June 26, 1983, F2.

"Terminal roof look 'dramatic.'" *Daily Journal* 94, no. 58 (August 13, 1990): 1.

"Terrace Building honored as outstanding oncrete structure." *Denver Downtowner* 3, ᴐ. 47 (April 7, 1982): 2.

he Terrace Building was honored for outᴉnding use of concrete in an office builᴉng." *Rocky Mountain* News April 10, 1982, 44.

Terrace Building wins national honor." *ʔocky Mountain* News February 27, 1983, ;0.

'Terrace Building wins third award for 1982." *Intermountain Jewish News* 69, no. 47, November 19, 1982, 16.

"Thin sheets of air: Glazing has become stronger, more varied, and more selective in transmitting heat and light." *Progressive Architecture* 66, no. 6 (June 1985): 104–10.

"Three Tucson projects win 'Best in West'

awards." *Arizona Daily Star* July 28, 1987, K18.

"Top twenty architects." *Daily Journal* 95, no. 271 (June 17, 1992): Top 20 section 2, 2.

"Transit Center provides oasis of comfort for bus passengers." *Sun Coast Architect–Builder* 58, no. 5 (May 1993): W2–W3.

"Tucson bank tower suggests influence of Spanish missions." *Buildings Design Journal* 3, no. 9 (September 1985): 8.

Umlauf, Elyse. "Preventive action purges internal air quality (IAQ) problems." *Building Design and Construction* 34, no. 3 (March 1993): 38–40.

Walker, Diane N. ed. *American Architecture, the state of the art in the 80's.* Ashland, Ky: Hanover Publishing Company, 1985. 10–11, 132–33.

Weingardt, Richard. "Colorado architecture: The best buildings of the modern age." *Colorado Business Magazine* 17, no. 2 (February 1990): 38–43.

— and Jeff Rundles. "Magnificent Colorado structures never built." *Colorado Business Magazine* 19, no. 2 (February 1992): 41–44.

Weiss, Jean. "Tucson's tallest building takes on downtown." *Arizona Business Gazette* November 10, 1986, Real Estate section, 9.

—. "Building a new look: Old DU law school gets stylish lines." *Rocky Mountain News* October 10, 1988, 7.

"Young Jong Island: New international airport design competition." *Architectural Culture* 140 (January 1993): 204–13.

Zavodny, Steve. "The Colorado Convention Center: A pictorial essay." *Colorado Business Magazine* 17, no. 6 (June 1990): 98–103.

Illustration credits

Robert Ashe, 62

Patrick Barta, 166, 174

Jerry Butts, 81, 83

J. L. Curtis, 8, 282

Carl J. Dalio, 24, 44-45, 50, 76, 84, 92, 100, 158, 178, 208, 212, 220-222, 236, 260, 264, 272

Stan Doctor, 184-191, 254-255

Curtis W. Fentress, 25, 57, 69, 89, 129, 145, 179

Hedrich-Blessing: Nick Merrick, 34-36, 38-39, 42-43, 52-56, 59-60, 63-65, 67, 80, 82, 88, 93-99, 110, 112-114, 117-120, 122-128, 130-135, 144, 147-151, 154-155, 170-173, 175-176, 192, 194-205, 240-241, 244-251; Jon Miller, 75

Greg Hursley, 102-109

Timothy Hursley, 40-41, 66, 72-74, 91, 152-153, 156-157, 161-165, 206-207, 227-228, 230-235, 238, 242-243

Ron Johnson, 48-49, 68, 86-87, 136, 138-139, 142-143, 181, 182-183, 211, 216-219, 257-259, 262-263, 275-277

Andrew Kramer, 28-31

Thorney Lieberman, 168-169, 177

James Sobey, 278-281

Wayne Thom Associates, 71